OUR GAME

An All-Star Collection of Hockey Fiction

OUR GAME

An All-Star Collection of Hockey Fiction

EDITED BY

DOUG BEARDSLEY

POLESTAR

BOOK PUBLISHERS

Our Game is a revised and updated version of *The Rocket, The Flower, The
Hammer and Me*, edited by Doug Beardsley and published by Polestar Book
Publishers in 1988.

Polestar Book Publishers acknowledges the ongoing support of The Canada
Council, the British Columbia Ministry of Small Business, Tourism and Culture,
and the Department of Canadian Heritage.

Cover art: "Night Game" by Jennifer Ettinger, 1996. The painting is 17.5" x 24",
acrylics on canvas. The frame is metal wrapped in hockey tape, attached with
hockey skate laces through grommets.

Cover design by Jim Brennan.

Printed and bound in Canada.

Canadian Cataloguing in Publication Data
Our game
ISBN 1-896095-32-1
1. Hockey—Canada—Fiction. 2. Canadian fiction (English)—20th century I.
Beardsley, Doug, 1941-
PS88323.H62087 1997   C813'.0108355C97-910809-8
PR9197.35.H62087 1997

Library of Congress Card Catalog Number: 97-80431

Polestar Book Publishers
P.O. Box 5238, Station B
Victoria, British Columbia
Canada   V8R 6N4
http://mypage.direct.ca/p/polestar/

In the United States:
Polestar Book Publishers
P.O. Box 468
Custer, WA
USA   98240-0468

54321

To all shinny enthusiasts everywhere, and to all past, present and future hockey players in the Town of Mount Royal;

to John Atkinson, who, had he lived, would have loved this book;

and especially to my brother, David Beardsley, who on ice personified Hemingway's "grace under pressure."

CONTENTS

❖ Fans and Philosophers

Introduction

Our game? Our game?! With Russians travelling like Soyuz rockets over white spaces of ice, and Europeans avoiding the corners and bodychecks as if all Canadians were contagious, and American businesspeople buying our game away from Halifax, Quebec City, Hamilton and Winnipeg to exotic faraway places such as Tampa Bay, Florida, Phoenix, Carolina, San Jose and the mighty duckpond of California? What do people in these places know of Henderson's goal? What would it matter?

The stories in this anthology transport us back to a time when our game was still played in winter, in the cold, with freezing hands and feet. Our extremities were always in danger. Even the Original Six teams were ours then: Detroit, Chicago, New York and Boston were not far from the border. The first two were only water away — and that was frozen six months of the year. The Rangers and Bruins were always awful, so nobody in their Canuck mind bothered about them, and all the players in the world were Canadian so what did it matter anyway?

Now, it matters alot. It matters to those of us who grew up with our game. We still see hockey as metaphor, but the metaphor is no longer one of lost innocence or the dark side of the Canadian psyche. Now, it is a metaphor for selling out our game and our country to international business interests — mostly American at the moment. Read Don McKay's poetic nightmare about how the game today is promoted rather than appreciated, the unrelenting media hype a rap-like attack that pounds the spectator into commerical submission, everything designed to sell a product, everything designed to draw the fan away from the beauty and brilliance of the game. In another story collected here, Peter Pocklington's selling of Wayne Gretzky to Los Angeles is cited as "the first disaster of free trade," a deal made, "we were told, to improve American interest in our game." What did American interest matter to us? Johnny Canuck was forgotten in the rush of a few potential owners to enhance their positions on Millionaire's Row.

And yet, and yet … the stories collected in the original edition of this book (entitled *The Rocket, the Flower, the Hammer and Me*), and the ten new stories we've added to this edition, confirm that hockey is still our game, despite the score. It may be late in the third period, the puck a red halo, the game threatened by division into four quarters or two halves, but still the young Canadian hockey players who sweep over the blue line generation after generation carry with them something more than a puck and the desire to score. They carry the synthesis of spirit and skill that makes the game an extended metaphor for what it means to be Canadian. John Metcalfe once wrote, "A great hockey player emerges from a hockey world." Says Billy the Kid Semeniuk in Levi Dronyk's story, "any kid without an instinctive understanding of the game is genetically un-Canadian." Rudy Thauberger's "Goalie" echoes this thought: "What choice do I have? What else have I ever wanted to do?"

This new edition required a new ordering; in the end, we divided the stories into three parts. The first stories are about growing up with hockey, dreaming about hockey, even playing hockey and emulating the grown-up heroes of the game. The second section deals with adults (young and old) actually hitting the ice and playing the game. What does it mean to dream of playing as a child, and then to play as an adult? The third and final section of stories tells of hockey fans and philosophers — those who have taken one step back in order to see the metaphor of the game, to fit its grace and history and heroes into the way they see the world.

Even today, young hockey players bring to the game the mannerisms of their heroes, whether those heroes are immortals Rocket Richard and Gordie Howe or more recent knights in sweaty armour like Wayne Gretzky, Mark Messier, Eric Lindros and Mario "The Best" Lemieux. It is these imaginative poets on ice whom Michael McKinley evokes in his story "Next Year." And they are present in the distant ambience of a rink in Africa in the excerpt from Audrey Thomas' *Coming Down From Wa*. Puck magicians are followed by the enforcing winger or two, who employ their sticks as if they were swords or drop them at the slightest provocation to engage in fisticuffs. These are heroes of a different sort, and in the world of fiction they become Felix Batterinski in Roy MacGregor's novel *The Last Season*, Danulchuck in Don Gutteridge's *Bus Ride*, or Drinkwater in Mark Anthony Jarman's "Righteous Speedboat."

One way to play the game better is to play beyond yourself — to pretend that you are one of these hockey heroes when you are on the ice. In fiction, this impulse is what pairs author Hanford Woods "alongside Dallas Smith" on the Bruins blue line, or allows Batterinski to become Tim Horton. Your opponent is disadvantaged if he's no one but himself. It's not that he's limited in what he can do; it's simply that he's battling against two players — one a boy his age, and the "other" an NHL star. This fantasizing about stardom is common among those who've played the game since childhood. We all want to be Paul Quarrington's "King of the Ice"; all of us dream of being called to play like Brian Fawcett's character in "My Career with the Leafs." Does this give us our spirit and perseverance, the will to win that sets us apart?

Our game also serves Canadians as a metaphor for lost innocence. In this collection, such wistful nostalgia is best exemplified by Lionel Kearns' "Blue Moon," where Harvey Santini plays hockey with a self-confidence he is unable to emulate in the "teasing and ridicule" of real life. As Diane Schoemperlen writes in her story "Hockey Night in Canada": "Hockey, like stamp collecting, is a world apart ... " We may agree with Morley Callaghan's McAlpine, who says of the game: "It used to look wonderful"; and we may concur with the priest in the same excerpt who comments, "It's a different game today ... more of them can't hold on to the puck" — but however we think and feel, whatever our background and upbringing, as Canadians we are all involved and invisibly related to each other and our game. In the excerpt from Wayne Johnston's imaginative novel *The Divine Ryans*, Draper Doyle has "a theory that any team's fortune depended on the mood of their fans, the spirit in which they viewed the game." He goes on to muse, "I further believed that, on any particular night, this mood, this spirit, was the same among all their fans throughout the country." Who can claim that hockey is not one of the great unifying forces in Canadian life?

I'm delighted by the most recent additions to *Our Game*: classic hockey stories by Roch Carrier, Wayne Johnston, Michael McKinley, Richard Wright, Don McKay, Hugh Hood and Mark Jarman. Roch Carrier's "Hockey Sweater" is surely the best-known hockey story ever written. And I'm glad to have fellow Montrealer Hugh Hood under contract. I'm particularly pleased to welcome Audrey Thomas, Judith Fitzgerald and Marsha Mildon to the team — voices that add to women's writing about hockey. Much has happened for women and the game in the last decade or so. Not only do we have more women writing about the game, in Mildon we now have a woman writing about women playing the game.

In sum, I feel certain that the stories in this anthology, both old and new, capture the spirit, grace and beauty of our game. May it go on forever, like Aurel Joliat in David Gowdey's closing story, who skates in seemingly endless fashion up and down the Rideau Canal.

As editor, I'd like to thank Michelle Benjamin and Lynn Henry at Polestar Book Publishers for their encouragement, excellent ideas and enthusiasm for this new edition of hockey fiction. Special thanks to Lisa Power at the University of Victoria, who willingly spent many hours typing the manuscript. And special mention to Jerry McKenzie, the most underrated of Stan Kenton's drummers, who propelled me through this introduction.

Everlasting applause to my teammates Lin and Anna, lovely wingers who have supported me in mid-career. Finally, my greatest appreciation and admiration to all the writers included here, who have written about our game so well.

Doug Beardsley
Montreal, Victoria
November 1997

GROWING UP ON ICE

The Hockey Sweater

❖   ROCH CARRIER

The winters of my childhood were long, long seasons. We lived in three places — the school, the church and the skating-rink — but our real life was on the skating-rink. Real battles were won on the skating-rink. Real strength appeared on the skating-rink. The real leaders showed themselves on the skating-rink. School was a sort of punishment. Parents always want to punish children and school is their most natural way of punishing us. However, school was also a quiet place where we could prepare for the next hockey game, lay out our next strategies. As for church, we found there the tranquillity of God: There we forgot school and dreamed about the next hockey game. Through our daydreams it might happen that we would recite a prayer: We would ask God to help us play as well as Maurice Richard.

We all wore the same uniform as he, the red white and blue uniform of the Montreal Canadiens, the best hockey team in the world; we all combed our hair in the same style as Maurice Richard, and to keep it in place we used a sort of glue — a great deal of glue. We laced our skates like Maurice Richard, we taped our sticks like Maurice Richard. We cut all his pictures out of the papers. Truly, we knew everything about him.

On the ice, when the referee blew his whistle the two teams would rush at the puck; we were five Maurice Richard's taking it away from five other Maurice Richard's; we were ten players, all of us wearing with the same blazing enthusiasm the uniform of the Montreal Canadiens. On our backs, we all wore the famous number 9.

One day, my Montreal Canadiens sweater had become too small; then it got torn and had holes in it. My mother said: "If you wear that old sweater people are going to think we're poor!" Then she did what she did whenever we needed new clothes. She started to leaf through the catalogue the Eaton company sent us in the mail every year. My mother was proud. She didn't want to buy our clothes at the general store; the only things that were good enough for us were the latest styles from Eaton's catalogue. My mother didn't like the order forms included with the catalogue; they were written in English and she didn't understand a word of it. To order my hockey sweater, she did as she usually did; she took out her writing paper and wrote in her gentle schoolteacher's hand: "Cher Monsieur Eaton, Would you be kind enough to send me a Canadiens' sweater for my son who is ten years old and a little too tall for his age and Docteur Robitaille thinks he's a little too thin? I'm sending you three dollars and please send me what's left if there's anything left. I hope your wrapping will be better than last time."

Monsieur Eaton was quick to answer my mother's letter. Two weeks later we received the sweater. That day I had one of the greatest disappointments of my life! I would even say that on that day I experienced a very great sorrow. Instead of the red, white and blue Montreal Canadiens sweater, Monsieur Eaton had sent us a blue and white sweater with a maple leaf on the front — the sweater of the Toronto Maple Leafs. I'd always worn the red, white and blue Montreal Canadiens sweater; all my friends wore the red, white and blue sweater; never had anyone in my village ever worn the Toronto sweater, never had we even seen a Toronto Maple Leafs sweater. Besides, the Toronto team was regularly trounced by the triumphant Canadiens. With tears in my eyes, I found the strength to say:

"I'll never wear that uniform."

"My boy, first you're going to try it on! If you make up your mind about things before you try, my boy, you won't go very far in this life."

My mother had pulled the blue and white Toronto Maple Leafs sweater over my shoulders and already my arms were inside the sleeves. She pulled the sweater down and carefully smoothed all the creases in the abominable maple leaf on which, right in the middle of my chest, were written the words "Toronto Maple Leafs." I wept.

"I'll never wear it."

"Why not? This sweater fits you ... like a glove."

"Maurice Richard would never put it on his back."

"You aren't Maurice Richard. Anyway, it isn't what's on your back that counts, it's what you've got inside your head."

"You'll never put it in my head to wear a Toronto Maple Leafs sweater."

My mother sighed in despair and explained to me:

"If you don't keep this sweater which fits you perfectly I'll have to write to Monsieur Eaton and explain that you don't want to wear the Toronto sweater. Monsieur Eaton's an *Anglais*; he'll be insulted because he likes the Maple Leafs. And if he's insulted do you think he'll be in a hurry to answer us? Spring will be here and you won't have played a single game, just because you didn't want to wear that perfectly nice blue sweater."

So I was obliged to wear the Maple Leafs sweater. When I arrived on the rink, all the Maurice Richards in red, white and blue came up, one by one, to take a look. When the referee blew his whistle I went to take my usual position. The captain came and warned me I'd be better to stay on the forward line. A few minutes later the second line was called; I jumped onto the ice. The Maple Leafs sweater weighed on my shoulders like a mountain. The captain came and told me to wait; he'd need me later, on defence. By the third period I still hadn't played; one of the defencemen was hit in the nose with a stick and it was bleeding. I jumped on the ice: my moment had come! The referee blew his whistle; he gave me a penalty. He claimed I'd jumped on the ice when there were already five players. That was too much! It was unfair! It was persecution! It was because of my blue sweater! I struck my stick against the ice so hard it broke. Relieved, I bent down to pick up the debris. As I straightened up I saw the young vicar, on skates, before me.

"My child," he said, "just because you're wearing a new Toronto Maple Leafs sweater unlike the others, it doesn't mean you're going to make the laws around here. A proper young man doesn't lose his temper. Now take off your skates and go to the church and ask God to forgive you."

Wearing my Maple Leafs sweater I went to the church, where I prayed to God; I asked him to send, as quickly as possible, moths that would eat up my Toronto Maple Leafs sweater.

Saturday Evenings in the Church of Hockey Night in Canada

❖   JUDITH FITZGERALD

When you grow up with guys like Gordie Howe and Grandpa, you grow up street smart, turf tough and ever rough and ready. Long before you learn the alphabet, you learn the way things are, the way things went and the way they'll always be. And, if you get lucky, you never forget 'em.

Several decades after the facts, I vividly remember every detail of that catastrophic 1950 night when a case of bad timing nearly cost Howe his life. I remember the dribbly-grey day, the wind-blistery night, the violent smear of brilliant crimson clotting beneath my hero's skull as he lay obliterated amid pop-glittering flashes of photographers' bulbs. I shall never forget those faces frozen with fear, that premonitory hush, the collective howl of horror and heartbreak when Howe's buddies delicately removed my hero's lifeless form from that sea of blood and ice.

So even though I wasn't even *old* enough to go to Detroit's Olympia with Grandpa that fateful March night, I remember like yesterday the events he relished and embellished each and every time "ol' stinky Blinky" got into his famous fisticuffs and fights.

Grandpa, one scrappy Québécois named Gabby, migrated to Toronto in the latter half of the 1940s, right around the time "ol' stinky Blinky" joined the Red Wings. Looking back, I suspect the die-hard Leaf man secretly worshipped Gordie Howe, my one and only idol; however, his fever-pitched vocal eruptions will most likely remain imprinted on my brain forever: "Tsk-tsk and *tabernac*! My grand-daughter's gone off the deep end, for sure, for sure! Blinky? That stinky Detroit Red Wing nut case?"

Eyes glazing, arms flapping, fingers jabbing and colour rising high crimson in the gaunt hollows of his wrinkle-creased face, Grandpa glares and fumes with fulsome delight whenever I mention the player he loves to hate, belittle and endlessly berate. *Hell's bells and sacrifice!*

"*Merde, merde, merde,*" he moans in my direction, mock-maudlin features telegraphing deathly disgust, "wait 'till you grow up! *Then!* Then, you'll learn *the truth* about your precious darling Blinky!"

This morning — *the truth* uppermost in mind — various hockey books, bibles and microfilm copies of 1950s *Telegram* sports fronts collapse intervening decades and several living snapshots fan out on the floor of my brain: I taste sour metallic IPA bottle caps and smell the woody aroma of Black Cat tobacco, Grandpa meting out precise amounts of loose grains, delicate paper creased open by nicotine-stained fingers one moment, rolling off the tip of his tongue the next, measured *tamp, tamp, tamp* on the rose-flecked oilcloth covering the table completing the ritual.

Our kitchen resembles a poor man's Hockey Hall of Fame — huge team calendars, Leaf captain Ted Kennedy's autograph on a broken CCM stick, my younger brother Bobby's tabletop hockey game, programs, plus the usual paraphernalia fanatics inevitably accumulate.

Grandpa tacks sport-section fronts from the Toronto *Tely* on the wall above the kitchen table, strategically enshrining eye-level black-and-pink photographs of Teeder Kennedy sprawling into goalie Turk Broda, Detroit's Black Jack Stewart helping teammate Sid Abel carry an unconscious Howe on a stretcher and the Toronto captain's bewildered and sheepish mug (so I'd confront *the truth* at least three times a day).

The truth — always a murky issue when viewed through time's window — may never see the light. As both Grandpa and NHL president Clarence Campbell saw *the* incident that would eventually assume mythic importance in both the lore of the game and Howe's enduring fame, my idol's death-defying collision with the boards at the Olympia could not be pinned on Kennedy. No way. No how. Nosirree.

The truth? Four years after Howe broke into the major-league ranks with the Wings, he'd not only galvanized the game with his philosophy of "religious — *It is better to give than receive* — hockey," he'd also proved his prowess as a recklessly crazy maniac who could outshoot, outscore, outmanoeuvre and outsmart any player foolish enough to dally with the driving force of the Production Line.

As Maple Leafster Eddie Shack recalls (in *Squads and Demigods*), Howe regularly effected "pacts of non-aggression" with overzealous players; likewise, Howe himself points out he learned early such agreements helped avoid injury and ensured a long career. When a player did attack him, he would invariably get the last hit, even if it meant playing under "retributive-strike" conditions for five or six games.

By March 28, 1950, Howe's do-or-die reputation, well known among players unlucky enough to tangle with the titan, would certainly have figured in Kennedy's treatment of — and respect for — the agile ambidextrist.

"We were playing the Maple Leafs in Detroit," recalls Howe (in *Years of Glory*). "I was chasing Teeder Kennedy. He was coming down the left side of the rink, to my right, and I was going to run him into the boards. But my first thought was to intercept the pass I figured he'd make to Sid Smith, who was coming down the centre of the ice. I glanced back at Smith and put my stick down where I thought the pass might be going.

"What I didn't know as I turned back toward Kennedy was that, in the instant I'd turned away, he'd let the pass go, and now he was bringing up his stick to protect himself from my hitting him. I was still low, and the blade of the stick caught me in the face — tore my right eyeball, broke my nose and cheekbone. As if this wasn't bad enough, I then smashed into the boards, giving myself a whale of a concussion.

"They took me to the hospital in an ambulance, and within minutes I was on the operating table and they were drilling a hole in the side of my skull to relieve the pressure. I was awake through all this; I could hear the drill against the bone. But what was really on my mind was that they'd shaved part of my head. I was at an age when I needed my hair, and I was thinking, 'Oh, gosh, no, what am I going to look like?'"

When Red Wing officials flew in Howe's mother and sister from Saskatoon, Saskatchewan, Motown shut down. The hustle-bustle of the gritty industrial city ground to a halt, prepared for the jolt and prayed it wouldn't happen.

"For a couple of days, nobody let me sleep," says Howe, "They were afraid I'd go into a coma and never come out. They'd come along and scrape the bottoms of my feet every few minutes, and say, 'Don't go to sleep on us.'"

He didn't; instead, the resurrected Mr. Miracle attended the final game of the 1949-50 season and went weak in the knees when his Wings beat the New York Rangers 4-3 to claim the Stanley Cup: "My injury had been a big story in the papers and, as the Cup was being presented, the crowd started calling for me; I'd been watching from a seat near the bench. But as I went out on the ice, my worst fear came to pass. Someone grabbed my hat, and there I was in front of sixteen thousand fans with a big bald patch on my head. Oh, it was awful!"

As awful as Howe considered that crowning moment, less than a month after his near-death experience, his huge hands clasped hockey's Holy Grail for the first time while sixteen thousand fans simply went joyously berserk or, as Grandpa preferred, "Them Yankees flipped their lids."

The truth? I shall never forget Grandpa's version of Blinky and Teeder Bear's tête-à-tête, especially because his repeated retelling always included quasi-mythic tragicomic elements: Kennedy elicits near-tear histrionics complete with checkered hankie while Howe's "Blinky" nickname — freshly minted in the dawning era of eye-irritating television klieg lights and done to death by Grandpa — induces a string of damnatory epithets that leap from burning lips and run for cover in sheer sneer fear.

Now, according to Grandpa, Teeder truthfully told the *Tely* he saw Howe coming at him, stepped out of the way and stood powerless as he watched Number 9 crash into the boards. And, again according to Grandpa, Kennedy swore he'd take an oath to the effect his stick never touched Howe; further, Teeder Bear couldn't and wouldn't inflict that kind of injury on anyone, let alone Howe, a player already well known for his rough-and-rowdy attitude on ice.

"I was there! I saw the whole thing with my own two eyes! Here's Teeder minding his own beeswax skating with the puck ... Then, what? That crafty Blinky sneaks up on him and is gonna cram him but ... Teeder just puts on the brakes. Blinky takes a bite out of the boards! Slams them face first! That slinky Blinky, that Wing Nut! Look it! They didn't even call a penalty? What does *that* tell you?"

"*The truth*, right?"

"Right, Bobby, right. Teeder Bear innocent. Howe guilty. Case closed."

"But, Grandpa, Wings won the Cup, right?"

"*Câlisse*! They did so, *and* not a Blinky in sight! Oh, that Howe. He's one of the slickest, smoothest, smartest, sneakiest sons-of-bitches ever to lace up a pair of skates. Look it here! It says it all."

"Read it, Grandpa, what does it say?"

"It says, 'Teeder innocent, Howe guilty. Case closed.'"

"Where, Grandpa, where? Show me!"

"Right here, see? Right above the picture. 'Young Gordie Howe busts his head on the boards 'cause of his own stupid fault and Teeder didn't do nothing wrong.'"

Grandpa reads the headlines, captions and stories to us from the sports sections he religiously tacks to that wall. Usually, he reads them between periods, turning down the volume on the cream-coloured Bakelite radio so we don't miss his points: "Look it here," he jabs, "plain as the nose on your face: Howe intended to knock Teeder Bear's block off but the captain plain outsmarted the dumb right winger. See? Look at this picture! I was there! I saw it all with my own two eyes. Your guy made the big mistake and almost killed hisself! Blood, blood, buckets of blood and ol' Blinky in Cuckoo Land! *Stoo-oo-pid*!"

"But, he's okay now, Grandpa, and smart!"

"You think so? Look at this picture. Does this look like a smart guy, Bobby?"

"Nope."

"See? There you go. Look at this proof: 'Gordon Howe, the best right winger in the NHL *after* the Rocket, is just a dumb-dumb.' Now you believe me? It's right here in the *Tely*."

"Read it to me, Grandpa, read it!"

"See? Here? Right under the dumb-dumb's picture."

Of course, I couldn't read it.

Saturday nights, my mother — who considered hockey for the birds — would borrow two dollars for what Grandpa called "her stupid love-stuffy movie." He'd remind her to think of our good name when she traipsed down Yonge Street to the Rio.

After she'd depart, Grandpa always asked the same question: "She go?"

"She go."

"Good. Get the beer, eh, Doré?"

"Yes, Grandpa." I retrieve the case of IPA from the trunk of the battered blue Buick; Grandpa lines up his freshly rolled supply of cigs in the Black Cat tin; then, we get down to business.

"Doré, Blinky suits up for them Red Things. There'll be a hot time in the old town tonight. Now, who's the best team d'hockey?"

"*Wings*, Grandpa, not *Things*. Wings!"

"Bobby?"

"Leafs," he snickers, "right? Things! *Sacrifice*!"

Grandpa glares at Bobby.

Bobby studies the flowers on the linoleum, little pink roses adorning perfect crisscrossing rows of ivy.

"*Sacrifice*!" growls Grandpa, "you don't talk such words, Robert."

When Grandpa says Bobby's real name, Bobby sounds like a robber.

"I'm sorry, Grandpa. I just mean the Leafs are gooder than her team."

"Not gooder," I correct, "*better* … "

"Right," concurs Grandpa, "Leafs *is* better! Leafs is the best!"

"The berry best," adds Bobby, "and Doré's a dumb-dumb."

"And you're a boobie."

"By the jumpin'," scowls Grandpa, "enough! Just get your Grandpa a bottle o' beer, eh?"

Naturally, during our ritual pre-game wieners-and-beans confabs, we flank Grandpa who presides over the proceedings with all the pomposity and pontificating punch he can muster after working the janitorial beat at the bank downtown on Belinda Street.

Grandpa invariably begins our discussions with home-spun lessons about the evils lurking on Yonge Street: "*Bien*, guys, she's probably at some tavern by now ... "

"Mom went to the movies, Grandpa."

"*Phlitz*! She just says that for your benefit. She went to the nightclub for sure."

We don't know the difference between dayclubs and nightclubs, so we simply agree with Grandpa.

Neither Bobby nor I ever understood how anybody could skip our family congregations in the Church of Hockey Night in Canada, especially during *these* playoffs, particularly with Grandpa galumphing in his gloats ever since "ol' stinky Blinky" made his "stupidest move yet" and nearly met his Maker.

Grandpa does the incident to death each time Motown rumbles into the Gardens and inappropriately flattens his Leafs; however by March he turns his attention to more pressing matters, namely the Leafs' valiant struggle to topple my Cup-defending Wings during the down-to-the-wire race for the regular-season crown.

He whoops and hollers when Leafs set new win and point records; he dismisses Detroit's first-place record-setting finish by belittling the team's Rookie of the Year, freshly acquired goaltender Terry Sawchuk.

"Yeah," he scoffs, "the dumb Things trade Harry Lumley, the goalie who won them the Cup, and they trade away Stewart and Pete Babando for a bunch of babies. Smart cookies. They think Bob Goldham and Metro Prystai gonna win Stanley? Over my Leafs' dead bodies."

"They've got the best goalie in the whole NHL, Grandpa! They've got Marcel Pronovost, and don't forget Red Kelly and the Production Line ... "

"The *what*?"

"The Production Line: Gordie Howe, Ted Lindsay and Sid Abel!"

"Lemme see ... The Blinky Line? *Those* guys? Ain't they dead yet?"

"Grandpa! They set new records! Gordie scored forty-three goals and got forty-three assists! That's the best! You know it!"

"I don't know that. *Aujourd'hui roi, demain rien*. The team that wins the Cup's the best. I only know *that*. We'll see ... "

And see we did. We sat, we listened and we cast our eyes on page after humiliating page following each humiliating defeat, defeats made all the more humbling because Grandpa indubitably seized every available opportunity to reinforce his convictions concerning Howe's infelicitous mortal sin against the virtuous Kennedy.

"*Merde, merde, merde*," he'd splutter and spume, his abiding sense of rightness inevitably interfering with his almost insufferable self-righteousness: "Blinky just gots what he's always deserved! An eye for an eye! A tooth for a tooth! That's more like it, eh, Doré?"

During those semifinals, our trio arranges itself around the Bakelite box, scarcely daring to speak lest we interfere with the unfolding play-by-play action. Bobby and I miss the ending of the game opener between Wings and Habs because it goes into quadruple overtime and we must attend school the following day; however, when Rocket Richard finally puts the puck past Sawchuk, Grandpa's joyous outpouring wakes the dead: "*Hell's bells! Sacrifice*! Doré! Where's your Blinky now? Three full OTs! Then? Boom! Bye-bye Wing Nuts! Aw, Doré, don't worry. At least Blinky ain't bleedin' — yet — and they've got lots of games to go!"

Richard clinches Game Two with second OT win against Sawchuk, a fact providing Grandpa with further ammunition to prove his point about the departure of goalie Lumley, and although Detroit rallies for a pair at the Olympia, Montreal takes the series with back-to-back wins in Games Five and Six.

Predictably, Grandpa alternates between ecstatic *told ya sos*, clownish pirouettes complete with jitter-steppin' flourishes and equally annoying postmortems on "them Red Things" with Bobby. Although the stunning Canadien upset smarts, Grandpa takes great pains to delicately rub salt in wounds by gleefully reminding me, a bijillion times a day, *his* Leafs ousted *the* Habs, *the* team that ousted *my* team. *His* Leafs walked all over *my* Wings and returned Stanley to his rightful place as easy as taking candy from a baby.

Naturally, because *his* Leafs recaptured the Cup in 1951, Grandpa's bluster and braggadocio, almost unbearable at the worst of times, nearly drives yours truly to distraction but, like a million fans of a million teams, I counter with that tried and truest of retorts: "Wait until next year, Grandpa. Just wait and see."

The following year, Grandpa's hockey talks border on sermons from the chrome-chair pulpit. In full-flying language the colour of conviction, he holds forth on the pros and princes of his unbeatable Leafs with excruciating affection. He berates my allegiance to an American team, he denigrates Howe's ascending-star status and he ridicules "those stupid guys who don't know the difference between a hockey puck and makin' a buck," especially when one of his guys gets traded "for no good reason. *Sacrifice!*"

By the end of the 1951-52 regular season, Grandpa chalks up the fact Detroit finishes first — and, in the process, literally buries his Leafs — to luck and injuries. The Wings' one-hundred-point season wrap-up doesn't faze him; he simply counters with the team's one-hundred-and one-point failure the previous year.

"Well, Grandpa," I recounter. "Terry Sawchuk had twelve shutouts this year, you know? He'll get that Vézina Trophy, don't you think?"

"The Uke? Yeah, he could do that."

"And the Production Line scored ninety-four goals, Grandpa."

"Big deal! The Blinky Line? They don't stand a chance unless they do the Stanley dance," he beams, scoring a direct hit on Lindsay's arrogant over-the-head Cup hoist and victory skate following the Wings' impressive 1950 Stanley win (a practice Leaf captain Kennedy cemented as tradition the following year).

Household pandemonium rules prior to the playoffs. Grandpa hits his stride and regularly winds up to fever pitch bragging about his Leafs while bashing away at the competition.

"*Maudit tabernac!*" he hisses. "Montreal don't stand a prayer of a chance ... "

"'Course not, Grandpa, Gordie's going to win it for my Wings."

"Who? Blinky? *Sacrifice!* His days is numbered, Doré. 'Sides, ain't he going bald?"

"Wings, Schmings," Bobby pipes up. "Detroit's dead as a doornail on a hot-dog stand."

"Then how come they finished first in the league?"

"Okay, Miss Know-It-All," Grandpa taunts, "who's going to carry your Wings to glory when Blinky makes his next stupid move?"

"Grandpa, Gordie never made his *first* stupid move yet."

"*Pardon?* Go ask Teeder what *he* thinks."

"Grandpa, Teeder sticked Gordie. Gordie *never* made a mistake."

"By the jumpin'! What's this headline say? Listen up. It says, 'Teeder innocent. Blinky guilty. Case closed.'"

"No, it doesn't, Grandpa. It says, 'Some Good Hockey Between Brawls As Wings Tied It.'"

"Yeah? Then what does this one say?"

"'Never A Dull Moment In Leaf-Wing Stanley Cup Game.'"

"Okay. Try this here, then."

"'NHL Head Clears Kennedy.'"

"See! There you go! Teeder innocent. Blinky guilty. Case closed."

Of course, when I can read, I adopt Grandpa's practice of tacking key *Tely* stories outlining particularly stunning Howe feats (and Leaf defeats) to our wall. Stories with glorious Gordie photos Grandpa stands for two or three days before they invariably disappear; photos with rapturous stories Grandpa insists I read from start to finish each time I add a new one.

In between paragraphs, I take great pains to point out the obvious to Grandpa who, as far as I can see, never misses a trick; naturally, as I now see it, Grandpa merely feigns total lack of interest and busily dusts the knobs, dials, glass, top and cord of our radio with his multipurpose hankie to underscore his indifference.

Occasionally, his one and only act of housekeeping accelerates as those now-classic stories wrap up with yet another vindication of the innocence of one triumphant Mr. Howe. When this occurs, Grandpa extracts a dime from his change pouch, removes the screws from the particleboard back of the box and blows emphatically on its rows of pale orange tubes.

"Okay, Grandpa?" I'd ask after winding up for both flourish and finale.

"Yeah, okay," he'd laconically say, "but, know what? I don't care what they say. I know what I saw and I know what *I* say: Your Blinky never told Teeder he was sorry. *Quel toupet!*"

The Howe-Kennedy incident tops Grandpa's list of Wing transgressions and, as such, dominates our friendly feud until it assumes mythic importance as Grandpa's "ace-in-the-hole" card, especially when I single out Sawchuk, Kelly, Lindsay, Prystai, et al. for lavish (and deserved) praise.

"Yeah," he grudgingly admits, "they got a few good ones, but, then, they got Blinky! Blinky! He could kill hisself any minute. What kind of player they got there, eh? *Sacrebleu!*"

Whether Grandpa would or could ever openly acknowledge Howe's stunning five-decade contribution to the NHL (with Detroit and the Hartford Whalers), I do not know. I do know, with the luxury of hindsight, what kind of player he became by the time he retired at fifty-two: the finest all-round hockeyist in the history of the game.

So I shall never forget Grandpa's everlasting chagrin when unstoppable 1952 Red Wings roll past the Leafs in the semifinals and Habs in the finals to snag Stanley on a straight-eight (Octopus) ticket, a striking achievement made all the more spectacular by Sawchuk's unparalleled performance in goal that unforgettable season he breaks all standing records.

Those untarnished games of consummate perfection still shine in my mind; a watershed of civilization and supreme knowledge all proceeds apace with Howe, hockey, our little house on Church Street and one young Wingster enraptured with the stunning feats of a handful of truly extraordinary mortals.

From the opening frame, the sound of puck colliding with solid wood promising a singular series of outstanding achievements, Grandpa and I sit glued to our moods and track each remarkable accomplishment with reverence, respect and inexplicable awe. After all, my "Red Things" slay all contenders and outplay all pretenders with smarts, sass, savvy and a sheer burning love of the game, passion for perfection and will to win still unequalled in professional sports.

And although Howe doesn't score a goal in the Leaf semifinal, he scores five in the final against the Habs, a fact that nearly drives Grandpa to distraction. In Game Two of that series, Howe characteristically checks a Dollard St. Laurent charge by bestowing a lacerated eyeball on the up-start. (Equally characteristically, he helps the injured Canadien off the ice.)

Of course, Grandpa particularly relishes the fights, the fisticuffs, the down-and-dirty deviltry of a few dozen champions proving their prow-ess. In full-force conversation with disembodied voices, we simply sit, watch and listen to his inexhaustible running commentary punctuated by fists blasting imaginary jaws and hands clutching imaginary sticks only he can see in that Church Street kitchen. He swings his lefts, jabs his rights and hooks the air while engaging in some of the fastest chair-danc-ing footwork on the planet.

Each time Howe puts the puck past Jacques Plante or Gerry McNeil, Grandpa bangs his chair against the rag rug placed strategically beneath rubber-tipped feet and sends butts into orbit with a bright orange Canada Tavern ashtray, and valour drowns discretion in the outpouring: "*Sacrebleu!* Those Frenchies need a better guy! Those guys need Béliveau, the only player who can outshoot ol' stinky Blinky!"

"Grandpa," I insist, "Blinky isn't stinky."

He twitches his nose. "P-U! I can smell the guy from here."

Thus, when we take up our positions in the off-limits living room — Grandpa in his chair, Bobby sprawled on the floor and me on the has-sock near the chrome pedestal ashtray a foot or so from the new television — we stare at the green screen in anticipation of tiny tabletop hockey players coming to life on its other side and settle in for Game

One of the 1952-53 semifinal between Detroit and Boston.

In inimitable fashion, Grandpa tells me not to get my hopes up: first, he points out, Detroit lacks depth; second, Blinky's slipping after working so hard in the regular season (and *still* missing the fifty-goal mark by one); finally, Boston will shut the Production Line down *and* even though Delvecchio did score the league's shooter title *and* even though Red Kelly never looked better *and* even with Pronovost playing his heart out, *aujourd'hui roi, demain rien.*

Sometimes, when Grandpa shoots his mouth off, he scores; and sometimes, when Detroit doesn't live up to our expectations, he resorts to lessons about lesser players whom he believes will give Howe a run for his money.

That year, he favoured Max Bentley, "the farm boy from Saskatchewan who got good 'cause the little scrapper had the will to win."

"Gordie's got it too, Grandpa. Gordie comes from Saskatchewan, you know?"

"Yeah, the guy comes from *Floral!*"

"Yeah, but he moved to Saskatoon when he turned nine, Grandpa!"

"Yeah? Did he milk the cows, then?"

"Cows?"

"Yeah, Max milked cows in Saskatchewan."

"Naw, Grandpa, Gordie lived in skates and practised all the time, summer and winter, day in and day out."

"Yeah? Did you know his folks was poor? They couldn't even buy him a new pair of skates."

"Yeah, but his mom got him a used pair he stuffed with newspapers. He just wanted to play hockey so bad. And he got so good."

"Did not."

"Grandpa, Gordie just won the H ... "

"Hoogaw Trophy? That trophy they give to those guys that tell lies?"

"Grandpa!"

"Well? Did your Gordie tell *the truth?*"

"'Course, Grandpa. Did your Teddy?"

"*Pardon?*"

"Teddy ... Teddy *Kennedy.* Did *Teddy* tell the truth, Grandpa?"

"By the jumpin' ... "

To this day, I still gag when I see a bar of green Palmolive soap and recall his threat to wash my mouth out with same.

Two seasons later, with my Wings in stellar form and Grandpa's Leafs on the rebuild trail, he confidently predicts a shake-up showdown. In a way, he prognosticates correctly, except the showdown takes place between Habs and Wings (after Detroit destroys his Leafs in the semifinals).

"*Bien*," says Grandpa, "*très bien*. Now, watch what I mean. Those Frenchies finally got Béliveau."

"And Gordie just won his fourth straight scoring title, Grandpa."

"*Pas de problème*, Doré."

"Wanna bet?"

Back and forth goes the 1954-55 series. Wings win the first. Habs take the second. Wings nab the third. Habs tie it. Wings win the fifth. Again, Habs tie it. And so it goes right down to the wire: Wings and Habs face off for the seventh game before an overflow crowd at the Olympia, and, when Detroit's Tony Leswick drops the puck over McNeil's shoulder with the unexpected help of Canadien defenceman Doug Harvey in the fifth minute of overtime, Wings hoist the Cup and disheartened Habs leave the ice without the traditional handshakes, a gesture beyond Grandpa's comprehension.

"Doré, that's the meanest thing I ever saw. Didn't Wings just win that régular-season crown? Ain't Wings the best team d'hockey? Ain't they got Gordie?"

"Yup, Grandpa, Wings got Gordie."

Thus, when President Campbell suspends Richard for the three remaining games (and the playoffs) the following season, Grandpa's only comment, the one I shall never forget?

"The Rocket lost it."

After *the* riot and the anti-climactic playoffs, my Wings beat Montreal fair and square. Even Grandpa says so.

"*Sacrebleu!* Them Wings closed their case ..."

" ... and Gordie nailed it shut, eh, Grandpa?"

"Yup, ol' stinky Blinky couldn't have played better. He even shook hands with the Rocket!"

"Yup, Grandpa, Gordie played the best!"

"Yup, Doré, Gordie played the best."

Looking back, I recall Saturday evenings in the Church of Hockey Night in Canada with a mixture of bemusement and gratitude. I spent time with an extraordinary character who taught *the truth* in astonishingly simple terms: "*Aujourd'hui roi, demain rien*." Several decades later, my photograph of Grandpa standing in front of Betsy, his beautiful beat-up Buick, still hangs at eye level on my kitchen wall, right next to our favourite picture of Gordie, the one where the finest player in the history of the game first touches the cherished Cup, grinning deliriously, shorn skull and all.

I'm Dreaming of Rocket Richard

❖   CLARK BLAISE

We were never quite the poorest people on the block, simply because I was, inexplicably, an only child. So there was more to go around. It was a strange kind of poverty, streaked with gentility (the kind that chopped you down when you least expected it); my mother would spend too much for long-range goals — Christmas clubs, reference books, even a burial society — and my father would drink it up or gamble it away as soon as he got it. I grew up thinking that being an only child, like poverty, was a blight you talked about only in secret. "Too long in the convent," my father would shout — a charge that could explain my mother's way with money or her favours — "there's ice up your cunt." An only child was scarcer than twins, maybe triplets, in Montreal just after the War. And so because I was an only child, things happened to me more vividly, without those warnings that older brothers carry as scars. I always had the sense of being the first in my family — which was to say the first of my people — to think my thoughts, to explore the parts of Montreal that we called foreign, even to question in an innocent way the multitudes of immovable people and things.

When I went to the Forum to watch the Canadiens play hockey, I wore a Boston Bruins sweatshirt. That was way back, when poor people could get into the Forum, and when Rocket Richard scored fifty goals in fifty games. Despite the letters on the sweatshirt, I loved the Rocket. I loved the Canadiens fiercely. It had to do with the intimacy of old-time hockey, how close you were to the gods on the ice; you could read their lips and hear them grunt as they slammed the boards. So there I stood in my Boston Bruins shirt loving the Rocket. There was always that spot of perversity in the things I loved. In school the nuns called me "Curette" — "Little Priest."

I was always industrious. That's how it is with janitors' sons. I had to pull out the garbage sacks, put away tools, handle simple repairs, answer complaints about heat and water when my father was gone or too drunk to move. He used to sleep near the heating pipes on an inch-thick, rust-stained mattress under a Sally Ann blanket. He loved his tools; when he finally sold them I knew we'd hit the bottom.

Industriously, I built an ice surface, enclosed it with old doors from a demolished tenement. The goal mouth was a topless clothes-hamper I fished from the garbage. I battered it to splinters, playing. Luck of the only child: if I'd had an older brother, I'd have been put in goal. Luckily there was a younger kid on the third floor who knew his place and was given hockey pads one Christmas; his older brother and I would bruise him after school until darkness made it dangerous for him. I'd be in my Bruins jersey, dreaming of Rocket Richard.

Little priest that I was, I did more than build ice surfaces. In the mornings I would rise at a quarter to five and pick up a bundle of *Montreal Matin*s on the corner of Van Horne and Querbes. Seventy papers I had, and I could run with the last thirty-five, firing them up on second and third floor balconies, stuffing them into convenient grilles, and marking with hate all those buildings where the Greeks were moving in or the Jews had already settled and my papers weren't good enough to wrap their garbage in. There was another kid who delivered the morning *Gazette*s to part of my street — ten or twelve places that had no use for me. We were the only people yet awake, crisscrossing each other's paths, still in the dark and way below zero, me with a *Matin* sack and he with his *Gazette*. Once, we even talked. We were waiting for our bundles under a street lamp in front of the closed tobacco store on the corner. It was about ten below and the sidewalks were uncleared from an all-night snow. He smoked one of my cigarettes and I smoked one of his and we found we didn't have anything to say to each other except "*merci*." After half an hour I said "paper no come" and he agreed, so we walked away.

Later on more and more Greeks moved in; every time a vacancy popped up, some Greek would take it — they even made sure by putting only Greek signs in the windows — and my route was shrinking all the time. *Montreal Matin* fixed me up with a route much further east, off Rachel near St-Andre, and so I became the only ten-year-old in Montreal who'd wait at four-thirty in the morning for the first bus out of the garage to take him to his paper route. After a few days I didn't have to pay a fare. I'd take coffee from the driver's thermos, his cigarettes, and we'd discuss hockey from the night before. In return I'd give him a paper when he let me off. They didn't call me Curette for nothing.

The hockey, the hockey! I like all the major sports, and the setting of each one has its special beauty — even old De Lorimier Downs had something of Yankee Stadium about it, and old Rocky Nelson banging out home runs from his rocking chair stance made me think of Babe Ruth, and who could compare to Jackie Robinson and Roberto Clemente when they were playing for us? Sundays in August with the Red Wings in town, you could always get in free after a couple of innings and see two great games. But the ice of big-time hockey, the old Forum, that went beyond landscape! Something about the ghostly white of the ice under those powerful lights, something about the hiss of the skates if you were standing close enough, the solid *pock-pock* of the rubber on a stick, and the low menacing whiz of a Rocket slap shot hugging the ice — there was nothing in any other sport to compare with the *spell* of hockey. Inside the Forum in the early fifties, those games against Boston (with Rocket flying and a hated Boston goalie named Jack Gelineau in the nets) were evangelical, for truly we were *dans le cenacle* where everyone breathed as one.

The Bruins sweatshirt came from a cousin of mine in Manchester, New Hampshire, who brought it as a joke or maybe a present on one of his trips up to see us. I started wearing it in all my back yard practices and whenever I got standing room tickets at the Forum. Crazy, I think now; what was going on in me? Crying on all those few nights each winter when the Canadiens lost, quite literally throwing whatever I was holding high in the air whenever the Rocket scored — yet always wearing that hornet-coloured jersey? Anyone could see I was a good local kid; maybe I wanted someone to think I'd come all the way from Boston just to see the game, maybe I liked the good-natured kidding from my fellow standees ("ey, you, Boston," they'd shout, "oo's winning, eh?" and I'd snarl back after a period or two of silence, *"Mange la baton, sac de marde* … "). I even used to wear that jersey when I delivered papers and I remember the pain of watching it slowly unravel in the cuffs and shoulders, hoping the cousin would come again. They were Schmitzes, my mother's sister had met him just after the War. *Tante* Lise and Uncle Howie.

I started to pick up English by reading a *Gazette* on my paper route, and I remember vividly one spring morning — with the sun coming up — studying a name that I took to be typically English. It began *Sch*, an odd combination, like my uncle's; then I suddenly thought of my mother's name — not mine — Deschenes, and I wondered: could it be? Hidden in the middle of my mother's name were those same English letters, and I began to think that we (tempting horror) were English too, that I had a right, a *sch*, to that Bruins jersey, to the world in the *Gazette* and on the other side of Atwater from the Forum. How I fantasized!

Every now and then the Schmitzes would drive up in a new car (I think now they came up whenever they bought a new car; I don't remember ever sitting in one of their cars without noticing a shred of plastic around the window-cranks and a smell of newness), and I would marvel at my cousins who were younger than me and taller ("they don't smoke," my mother would point out), and who whined a lot because they always wanted things (I never understood what) they couldn't get with us. My mother could carry on with them in English. I wanted to like them — an only child feels that way about his relatives, not having seen his genetic speculations exhausted, and tends to see himself refracted even into second and third cousins several times removed. Now I saw a devious link with that American world in the strange clot of letters common to my name and theirs, and that pleased me.

We even enjoyed a bout of prosperity at about that time. I was thirteen or so, and we had moved from Hutchison (where a Greek janitor was finally hired) to a place off St-Denis where my father took charge of a sixteen-apartment building; they paid him well and gave us a three-room place out of the basement damps. That was *bonheur* in my father's mind — moving up to the ground floor where the front door buzzer kept waking you up. It was reasonably new; he didn't start to have trouble with bugs and paint for almost a year. He even saved a little money.

At just about the same time, in the more spacious way of the Schmitzes, they packed up everything in Manchester (where Uncle Howie owned three dry-cleaning shops) and moved to North Hollywood, Florida. That's a fair proportion: Hutchison is to St-Denis what Manchester is to Florida. He started with one dry-cleaning shop and had three others within a year. If he'd really been one of us, we'd have been suspicious of his tactics and motives, we would have called him lucky and undeserving. But he was American, he had his *sch* so whatever he did seemed blessed by a different branch of fate, and we wondered only how we could share.

It was the winter of 1952. It was a cold sunny time on St-Denis. I still delivered my papers (practically in the neighbourhood), my father wasn't drinking that much, and my mother was staying out of church except on Sunday — it was a bad sign when she started going on weekdays — and we had just bought a car. It was a used Plymouth, the first car we'd ever owned. The idea was that we should visit the Schmitzes this time in their Florida home for Christmas. It was even their idea, arranged through the sisters. My father packed his tools in the rear ("You never know, Mance; I'd like to show him what I can do ... "). He moved his brother Real and family into our place — Real was handy enough, more affable, but an even bigger drinker. We left Montreal on December 18 and took a cheap and slow drive down, the pace imposed by my father, who underestimated the strain of driving, and by my mother, who'd read of speedtraps and tourists languishing twenty years in Southern dungeons for running a stop sign. The drive was cheap because we were dependent on my mother for expense money as soon as we entered the States, since she was the one who could go into the motel office and find out the prices. It would be three or four in the afternoon and my father would be a nervous wreck; just as we were unloading the trunk and my father was checking the level of whisky in the glove compartment bottle, she'd come out announcing it was highway robbery, we couldn't stay here. My father would groan, curse and slam the trunk. Things would be dark by the time we found a vacancy in one of those rows of one-room cabins, arranged like stepping stones or in a semi-circle (the kind you still see nowadays out on the Gaspesie with boards on the windows and a faded billboard out front advertising "investment property"). My mother put a limit of three dollars a night on accommodations; we shopped in supermarkets for cold meat, bread, mustard and Pepsis. My father rejoiced in the cheaper gas; my mother reminded him it was a smaller gallon. Quietly, I calculated the difference. Remember, no drinking after Savannah, my mother said. It was clear: my father expected to become the manager of a Schmitz Dry Kleenery.

The Schmitzes had rented a spacious cottage about a mile from the beach in North Hollywood. The outside stucco was green, the roof tiles orange, and the flowers violently pink and purple. The shrubs looked decorated with little red Christmas bulbs; I picked one — gift of my cousin — bit, and screamed in surprise. Red chilies. The front windows were sprayed with Santa's sleigh and a snowy "Merry Christmas." Only in English, no "Joyeux Noel" like our greeting back home. That was what I'd noticed most all the way down, the incompleteness of the signs, the satisfaction that their version said it all. I'd kept looking on the other side of things — my side — and I'd kept twirling the radio dial, for an equivalence that never came.

It was Christmas week and the Schmitzes were wearing Bermuda shorts and T-shirts with sailfish on the front. *Tante* Lise wore coral earrings and a red halter and all her pale flesh had freckled. The night we arrived, my father got up on a stepladder, anxious to impress, and strung coloured lights along the gutter while my uncle shouted directions and watered the lawn. Christmas — and drinking Kool-Aid in the yard! We picked chili peppers and sold them to every West Indian cook who answered the back doorbell. At night I licked my fingers and hummed with the airconditioning. My tongue burned for hours. That was the extraordinary part for me: that things as hot as chilies could grow in your yard, that I could bake in December heat and that other natural laws remained the same. My father was still shorter than my mother, and his face turned red and blotchy here too (just as it did in August back home) instead of an even schmitzean brown, and when he took off his shirt, only a tattoo, scars and angry red welts were revealed. Small and sickly he seemed; worse, mutilated. My cousins rode their chrome-plated bicycles to the beach, but I'd never owned a two-wheeler and this didn't seem the time to reveal another weakness. Give me ice, I thought, my stick and a puck and an open net. Some men were never meant for vacations in shirtless countries: small hairy men with dirty winter boils and red swellings that never became anything lanceable, and tattoos of celebrities in their brief season of fame, now forgotten. My father's tattoo was as long as my twelve-year-old hand, done in a waterfront parlour in Montreal the day he'd thought of enlisting. My mother had been horrified, more at the tattoo than the thought of his shipping out. The tattoo pictured a front-faced Rocket, staring at an imaginary goalie and slapping a rising shot through a cloud of ice chips. Even though I loved the Canadiens and the Rocket mightily, I would have preferred my father to walk shirtless down the middle of the street with a naked woman on his back than for him to strip for the Schmitzes and my enormous cousins, who pointed and laughed, while I could almost understand what they were laughing about. They thought his tattoo was a kind of tribal marking, like kinky hair, thin mustaches and slanty eyes — that if I took off my shirt I'd have one too, only smaller. *Lacroix*, I said to myself: how could he and I have the same name? It was foreign. I was a Deschenes, a Schmitz in the making.

On Christmas Eve we trimmed a silvered little tree and my uncle played Bing Crosby records on the console hi-fi-shortwave-bookcase (the biggest thing going in Manchester, New Hampshire, before the days of television). It would have been longer than our living room in Montreal; even here it filled one wall. They tried to teach me to imitate Crosby's "White Christmas," but my English was hopeless. My mother and aunt sang in harmony; my father kept spilling his iced tea while trying to clap. It was painful. I waited impatiently to get to bed in order to cut the night as short as possible.

The murkiness of those memories! How intense, how foreign; it all happened like a dream in which everything follows logically from some incredible premise — that we should go to Florida, that it should be so hot in December, that my father should be on his best behaviour for nearly a month ... that we could hope that a little initiative and optimism would carry us anywhere but deeper into debt and darkest despair ...

I see myself as in a dream, walking the beach alone, watching the coarse brown sand fall over my soft white feet. I hear my mother and *Tante* Lise whispering together, yet they're five hundred feet ahead ("Yes," my mother is saying, "what life is there for him back there? You can see how this would suit him. To a T! To a T!" I'm wondering is it me, or my father, who has no future back there, and *Tante* Lise begins, "Of course, I'm only a wife. I don't know what his thinking is — "), but worse is the silent image of my father in his winter trousers rolled up to his skinny knees and gathered in folds by a borrowed belt (at home he'd always worn braces), shirtless, shrunken, almost running to keep up with my uncle who walks closer to the water, in Bermuda shorts. I can tell from the beaten smile on my father's lips and from the way Uncle Howie is talking (while looking over my father's head at the ships on the horizon), that what the women have arranged ("It would be good to have you so close, Mance ... I get these moods sometimes, you know? And five shops are too much for Howie ... ") the men have made impossible. I know that when my father was smiling and his head was bobbing in agreement and he was running to keep up with someone, he was being told off, turned down, laughed at. And the next stage was for him to go off alone, then come back to us with a story that embarrassed us all by its transparency, and that would be the last of him, sober, for three, four or five days ... I can see all this and hear it, though I am utterly alone near the crashing surf and it seems to be night and a forgotten short-wave receiver still blasts forth on a beach blanket somewhere; I go to it hoping to catch something I can understand, a hockey game, the scores, but all I get wrenching the dial until it snaps is Bing Crosby dreaming of a white Christmas and Cuban music and indecipherable commentary from Havana, the dog raced from Miami, *jai alai* ...

That drive back to Montreal lasted almost a month. Our money ran out in Georgia and we had to wait two weeks in a shack in the Negro part of Savannah, where a family like ours — with a mother who liked to talk, and a father who drank and showed up only to collect our rent, and a kid my age who spent his time caddying and getting up before the sun to hunt golf balls — found space for us in a large room behind the kitchen, recently vacated by a dead grandparent. There were irregularities, the used-car dealer kept saying, various legal expenses involved with international commerce between Canadian Plymouths and innocent Georgia dealers, and we knew not to act too anxious (or even give our address) for fear of losing whatever bit of money we stood to gain. Finally he gave us seventy-five dollars, and that was when my father took his tools out of the back and sold them at a gas station for fifty dollars. We went down to the bus station, bought three tickets to Montreal, and my father swept the change into my mother's pocketbook. We were dressed for the January weather we'd be having when we got off, and the boy from the house we'd been staying in, shaking his head as he watched us board, muttered, "Man, you sure is crazy." It became a phrase of my mother's for all the next hard years. "Man, you sure is crazy." I mastered it and wore it like a Bruins sweater, till it too wore out. I remember those nights on the bus, my mother counting the bills and coins in her purse, like beads on a rosary, the numbers a silent prayer.

Back on St-Denis we found Real and family very happily installed. The same egregious streak that sputtered in my father flowed broadly in his brother. He'd all but brought fresh fruit baskets to the sixteen residents, carried newspapers to their doors, repaired buzzers that had never worked, shoveled insanely wide swaths down the front steps, replaced lights in the basement lockers, oiled, painted, polished ... even laid off the booze for the whole month we were gone (which to my father was the unforgivable treachery); in short, while we'd sunk all our savings and hocked all our valuables to launch ourselves in the dry-cleaning business, Real had simply moved his family three blocks into lifelong comfort and security. My father took it all very quietly; we thought he'd blow sky-high. But he was finished. He'd put up the best, and the longest, show of his life and he'd seen himself squashed like a worm underfoot. Maybe he'd had one of those hellish moments when he'd seen himself in his brother-in-law's sunglasses, running at his side, knowing that those sunglasses were turned to the horizon and not to him.

an excerpt from the novel *The Divine Ryans*

❖ WAYNE JOHNSTON

I could think of only two things our family had done together on any-thing like a regular basis — one was watch the hockey game on Saturday night, and the other was go to early mass on Sunday morning. It had been Aunt Phil's practice to, as Uncle Reginald put it, "convene" a meet-ing of the Divine Ryans at her house whenever the Habs were playing the Leafs on TV. There had been no meetings since my father's death last March, not even during the playoffs in the spring when the Habs had won their second straight Stanley Cup. When, at dinner one night, Aunt Phil announced that the whole family was getting together for the Habs' first televised game of the season this coming Saturday, I screamed "hur-ray," causing Mary and my mother to roll their eyes.

"You're not normal, Draper Doyle," Mary said. "You're a fanatic."

"What's a fanatic?" I said.

"A fanatic," said Uncle Reginald, "is a fan who is so crazy you have to keep him in the attic."

"It's only a hockey game you know, Draper Doyle," Mary said.

"The Habs have won more Cups than any other team," I said. "Thirteen."

"Why do you like statistics so much, Draper Doyle?" Mary said. "They're only numbers, you know." Mary had a habit of reducing things to their basic elements to prove their worthlessness. "Why do you like all that candy?" she'd say. "Candy's only sugar, you know." Anything that could thus be broken down was worthless, as far as she was concerned.

"Hockey," she said, "all it is is people hitting a piece of rubber back and forth with sticks."

"Water," I said, "all it is is hydrogen and oxygen. Why drink it?"

"Just tell me one thing, Draper Doyle," Mary said. "Do you hate the other teams?"

"Yes," I said.

"They're human beings too, you know," she said.

"No, they're not," I said.

"Look," she said, "I'm not saying Montreal is not the best team. I know they are." The inevitable superiority of the Montreal Canadiens was something to which Mary was resigned, a concession she begrudgingly allowed me whenever we had these arguments, which was often. "I just want you to admit," she said, "that the Boston Bruins for instance are human beings too."

"They're not," I said. "Canadiens are human beings. But Bruins are bears. Black Hawks are birds. Red Wings are birds. Leafs are plants."

"What about the Rangers, Draper Doyle?" my mother said, looking triumphantly around the table. "Aren't they human? Aren't they?" I had forgotten about those damned Rangers. What were Rangers anyway — forest rangers? Were they human beings? I supposed they were. The New York Rangers hadn't won the Stanley Cup since 1947, but they were human beings, any way you looked at it. I thought about pointing out that Smokey the Bear was a Ranger, but decided against it.

"Shot down, Draper Doyle," Mary said, "shot down." Getting up from the table, she stretched out her arms and made the noise of an airplane, then did a sudden nosedive to the floor. "Boom," she said, so loudly that Aunt Phil was startled. "Shot down," she said, sitting down again.

"You never shot me down," I said. "Mom did."

My defeat at the dinner table notwithstanding, I could hardly sit still for excitement when Saturday arrived. Another season had begun. All week, I had been able to think of nothing else. The Habs had won the Cup the last two years, and had won their first five road games of the season. They seemed unbeatable. Now they were coming home to the Forum. I brought out my many hockey souvenirs from the closet, including a puck which my father had given me when I was seven. It had previously occurred to me that some sort of connection might exist between this puck and the one my father had lately been appearing with, though I couldn't imagine what that connection might be. On a piece of paper taped to one side of the puck, these words were written: "Deflected into the stands by Canadiens goalie Gerry MacNeil at 1:03 of overtime. Caught by Donald Ryan. Nineteen seconds later, Elmer Lach scored to win the Stanley Cup for Montreal. Montreal Forum, April 16, 1953." How I envied my father. I'd have given anything to be there when the Habs won the Cup.

Among my other hockey souvenirs, the most unlikely of the lot was a hardbound copy of the *Aeneid* which my father had given me for my birthday when I was five, an illustrated adaptation for children. *The Cartoon Vergil*, it was called. The full-page drawings were in the manner of the old *Classics Illustrated* comic books, full of lurid detail — I can still see the Frightful Forms, Death-dealing War and Mad Discord with "snaky, bloodstained hair." I knew *The Cartoon Vergil* by heart. Of all the adapted classics my father had had me read, I liked it best, particularly those parts which took place in the underworld. (There were also underworlds in *The Cartoon Homer* and *The Cartoon Dante*, but Vergil's was my favourite.) My father had shown me how the black, laminated cloth cover of *The Cartoon Vergil* could itself be a kind of underworld. On Saturday nights, I always had to go to bed after the first period of the hockey game, so my father, using a pen that had run out of ink, would "write" the score of the game on the cover of *The Cartoon Vergil*. At breakfast, after mass on Sunday mornings, I would put a sheet of paper over the book and shade it with a pencil until I found the score. "Here it comes," my father would say, "here it comes, emerging from the underworld."

And so it would. A kind of ghost of what he had written would appear. Montreal 5, New York 3. After a while, there were so many scores invisibly engraved in the cover of the book that my father had to start writing in the date to help me tell them apart. Montreal 3, Toronto 3, 02/12/65. A kind of memory slate is what the book became, for in the process of trying to find the score of last night's game, I would call up the scores of games played years ago, and we would stop at each one to see if we remembered it. Scattered haphazardly across the cover of *The Cartoon Vergil* in my father's handwriting were the scores of every televised Habs game from 1963 to 1966 when, because I was then allowed to stay up late, my father had stopped writing them. From then on, I had written the scores on the cover myself, with the used-out pen my father had given me.

Now, to remind me to write the score and date of tonight's game on the book, I laid the pen on the cover of *The Cartoon Vergil* and went downstairs just as Uncle Reginald was descending in the lift. We were both wearing Habs sweaters, his with number 9 and mine with number 4 on the back. "Good evening hockey fans from ghost to ghost," said Uncle Reginald. I grinned.

Aunt Phil, Sister Louise and Father Seymour were already in the living room when we got there. None of them had any real affection for hockey. As far as they were concerned, God had created hockey for the sole purpose of allowing Catholics to humiliate Protestants on nationwide TV. Most of Fleming Street was Catholic, but there were a few Protestant families. In fact, one of the city's staunchest Protestants and monarchists lived near the end of the street, her house just visible from Aunt Phil's. Millie

Barter was in every way Aunt Phil's opposite — a tiny, fragile woman who, according to Aunt Phil, considered work to be beneath not only her, but her entire family. The Barters were supposed to be distantly related to some obscure, umpteen-times-removed cousin of the Queen, prompting Aunt Phil to refer to Millie as Queen Millie and to her family as The Royal Family. The Barters had a fortune, said to be so old that even they could not remember how they came by it. The Barters, Aunt Phil said, had done nothing since coming to the New World but live off some Old World fortune. God only knew where their money came from, she said. They had lived on that side of the street for as long as the Ryans had lived on this side, and in all that time, no Barter had ever been seen to do a day's work. As far as Aunt Phil was concerned, all Millie Barter did was back such Protestant causes as the retention of the Union Jack and royal visits.

Despite the fact that the Ryans and the Barters had never spoken to each other, it had somehow become the custom that after each televised game between the Habs and the Leafs, the family whose team had won would phone the family whose team had lost, not to speak to them, of course, but only to let their phone ring three times — three rings, three gloating cheers. Just as the Americans and the Russians had the hotline, the Ryans and the Barters had what Uncle Reginald called "the knellephone," their only cold war communication.

Aunt Phil stood at her bedroom window just before the game, peeking out through the curtains, watching the Barter children arrive at what she derisively called Buckingham Palace. "Here they come," she said, "The Royal Family." Aunt Phil followed the comings and goings of the Barters as closely as other people did the real royal family. She began to announce their arrivals like some palace doorman. "Prince Pimple-puss," she said scornfully, "accompanied by his wife, Princess Pasty-face, and Child William, the Earl of Dirty Diapers." Laughing, Uncle Reginald wondered if Millie Barter referred to Aunt Phil's house as the Vatican, and watched it as closely as Aunt Phil watched hers. Perhaps she too had nicknames for all of us, he said.

"Like what?" I said.

"Well," he said, "what about His Mouldiness, Reg Ryan? What about The Infallible Philomena?"

"Don't be absurd," Aunt Phil shouted from her bedroom. "Don't be putting ideas in the boy's head."

Then she came out and, as she always did before a Habs/Leafs game, put the phone on top of the television set.

"We'll ring that woman's phone tonight, Draper Doyle," she said, "you just watch."

"Maybe she'll ring ours, Aunt Phil," Mary said, exchanging a smile with my mother.

When Montreal was playing Toronto at the Forum, as they were to-night, it was not a hockey game, but a holy war, a crusade carried on nationwide TV, Rome's Canadiens versus Canterbury's Maple Leafs, "the Heathen Leafs against the Holy Habs," as Uncle Reginald put it. Uncle Reginald said that the real coach of the Montreal Canadiens was the pope, who was sending Toe Blake instructions from the Vatican, where he and his cardinals were watching the game on closed-circuit television.

As it turned out, the pope and his cardinals had seen better days, be-cause to everyone's astonishment the Leafs took a 3-1 lead in the first period. Never mind the Leafs, Uncle Reginald said, assuring us that, be-tween periods, the pope and his cardinals would find a way of beating them. No one, he said, no one on the face of the earth knew more about hockey than Pope Paul VI. And no one knew less about it than Aunt Phil, I felt like saying. All Aunt Phil knew or wanted to know about the Leafs was that they were Protestant. Throughout the first period, because she was never entirely sure when something helpful to the Habs' cause was happening, she had me sit beside her and, in a low, confidential voice, asked me questions from time to time. When, near the end of the period, Montreal scored to make it 3-2 and the room erupted, she waited for the noise to die down, then said the score of the game as if she was keeping track for those who didn't know hockey as well as she did. "Three-two Toronto," Aunt Phil said.

It was a strange sight indeed, a roomful of people who otherwise never watched a hockey game, including Sister Louise and Father Seymour in their habits, acting as if their lives depended on the outcome. "C'mon Montreal," Sister Louise said, leaning forward in her chair, rocking back and forth. Father Seymour, standing up with arms tightly folded, would advance towards the television each time the Habs went up the ice, back-ing away when they failed to score.

The trouble was, Father Seymour knew almost as little about hockey as Aunt Phil and Sister Louise. "Yes," he said, when the puck bounced off Henri Richard's backside and somehow found its way into the net; "Yes," nodding his head, as if he had seen the goal shaping up, as if it was a classic example of the skill for which the Montreal Canadiens were fa-mous. "It was a fluke," I said scornfully, looking at Uncle Reginald who winked at me and shook his head slightly. It seemed to me that, as well as being a warning, the wink was also meant to tell me that he, too, was thinking of my father.

I remembered the way my father had acted the last few times we had gathered for a game. For someone who knew so much about hockey, he had been very subdued while watching it. He had sat there, in the corner armchair, staring at the television set, speaking only when someone spoke to him, smiling when the Habs scored, or rather when, by the cheer that went up, it was evident that the Habs had scored, for he hadn't seemed to notice until then.

Halfway through the second period, with the Habs down 4-3 but coming back, Aunt Phil started in with her very annoying habit of calling the Leafs "the Leaves."

"It's not the Leaves," I said. "It's the Leafs."

"The plural of leaf is leaves, is it not?" Aunt Phil said.

"Yes," I said, "but no one calls them that. They're called the Leafs."

"Why?"

"I don't know why, they just are."

"Well that's not good enough for me. I'll call them the Leaves until someone shows me why I shouldn't call them that."

"Didn't I just show you?" I said. I could just see her correcting this "mistake" in the next edition of the *Daily Chronicle*, the Leafs turning up as the Leaves all over the sports page.

Then Father Seymour joined in, joking about Protestants giving their team a name that contained a mistake in spelling, thereby leaving millions of people with no choice but to make the same mistake, over and over. "Well, I won't make it," Aunt Phil said.

"They score," screamed Danny Gallivan, and he didn't mean the Habs. I felt like telling Aunt Phil that it was her fault. I knew that because I had taken her up on it, she would say "Leaves" as often as possible throughout the evening and I knew that this would so irritate me that the Canadiens were bound to lose. I had a theory that any team's fortune depended on the mood of their fans, the spirit in which they viewed the game. I further believed that, on any particular night, this mood, this spirit, was the same among all their fans throughout the country. At this very moment, all across the country, I believed, Habs fans were becoming irritated, and this did not bode well for their team. It was still possible to turn the mood around, however. All we had to do was concentrate, focus on the game, try to ignore everything else.

At the start of the third period, I set about doing exactly that. I lay down on the floor in front of the television set and had soon regained my concentration to the point where the Habs scored to make it 5-4 when Father Seymour sat down on the floor beside me. I knew what was coming. It was his make-contact-with-the-boy routine. I could imagine how Aunt Phil and Sister Louise were smiling at each other, no doubt charmed by the sight of Father Seymour doing what they thought he did best. "Hello Draper Doyle," he said, sitting cross-legged beside me. He picked up my Pepsi and took a sip from it, and as if by this, some sort of bond had been established between us, laid his arm lightly on my shoulder.

"Do you know what the CH on Montreal's uniform stands for, Draper Doyle?" Father Seymour said.

"Yes," I said, "Canadiens/Habitants." Father Seymour said nothing, only looked around the room as if to see if anyone had heard us. Then he informed me that CH were the letters with which the word "church" began and ended. I nodded and went back to watching the game. I tried to think of a way to hurry his routine to its inevitable conclusion before the Leafs scored again.

"But you know," he said, "the word means nothing unless 'u r' in it." I must have looked mystified, for he laughed. "Do you get it, Draper Doyle?" he said, looking around the room. "U r in church. The word 'church' means nothing unless u r in it."

I rolled my eyes and, once again, rather nervously this time, Father Seymour looked around the room. I considered pointing out that UR stood for Uncle Reginald who hadn't been inside a church in twenty years, but thought better of it. Then he got up and went back to standing between Aunt Phil and Uncle Reginald, his arms folded, eyes intently focussed on the television set.

Once again, I set about concentrating on the game. By now, however, my mood was all wrong. There was no way the Canadiens would win with me feeling so anxious and irritated. "They score," screamed Danny Gallivan, and once again he didn't mean the Habs. The Leafs had put one into the empty net to make it 6-4, which was how it ended. When the siren sounded, to end the game I saw that Father Seymour was looking at me as if he was about to say something. The Leafs had won, Uncle Reginald said, despite Richard's fluky goal and despite the infallibility of our team's coach. It was obvious that Mary and my mother were delighted to have witnessed one of Montreal's rare defeats, though they didn't dare show it openly, what with everyone else looking the way they normally did at wakes. Mary gave me one of her "inside I'm celebrating" looks and my mother kept her head down to hide a smile that was pulling at the corners of her mouth.

"Toronto 6, Montreal 4," Mary said.

"That's nothing," said Father Seymour. "It's only one game."

"But it was the first game," I shouted at him, on the verge of tears. "The first game!" by which I meant not only the first of the season, but the first since my father had died, a fact which, though it had gone unmentioned, had obviously been on everyone's mind.

"Don't you speak to me like that, young man," said Father Seymour, advancing towards me, then looking at my mother in a kind of "I really think that was uncalled for" sort of way.

"Draper Doyle didn't mean anything by that, Father," my mother said, her voice strained with embarrassment. "He's just tired, that's all. Apologize to Father Seymour, Draper Doyle."

"I'm sorry," I said, feeling my face flush as Father Seymour, rising on his toes, looked down at me. My apology seemed to settle things. "The Habs will win the next one, Draper Doyle," he said. I nodded and gave him the smile I knew everyone was waiting for.

The prevailing opinion was that the game was a minor setback, the kind of defeat that would make victory that much sweeter when it came. Of course, there was still one thing left to do. We had to wait for the knellephone to ring, for Millie Barter to break the cold war silence for as long as it took the phone to ring three times. It had been ten minutes since the game ended, and the phone on top of the television set had yet to ring.

"She's making us wait," Aunt Phil said. "She always does."

We sat there for another ten minutes, in silence now that the TV had been turned off. We sat there, looking at that mournfully black phone until it rang at last, the first ring causing all of us to jump, then the second ring, then finally the third which trailed off into a kind of shrill silence.

"Ask not for whom the phone rings," said Uncle Reginald. "It rings for us."

Because I had always gone to bed right after the game and the next morning had gone to mass before breakfast, the hockey game and the mass, separated only by an interval of dreamless, timeless sleep, had seemed to run together. The Sunday after the Habs lost their home opener was no different. Weary from having stayed up late, I only half heard what the priest was saying, and the fact that the priest was Father Seymour, whose voice I had also heard throughout the game the night before, further added to my confusion. As I stood there in the pew, still half asleep, the dreams I had been too tired to have the night before began, snatches of Father Seymour's mass mixing with the play-by-play of both Danny Gallivan and Foster Hewitt, so that a kind of hockey liturgy went running through my mind, a strange game in which there were swirling litanies of saints and hockey players, and the Habs and the Leafs were being asked to pray for one another, a game in which St. Peter was "ad libbing his way to centre ice" and Toe Blake was saying "Upon this Rocket, I will build my Church."

I saw the referee and two opposing centremen line up for the face-off. But instead of dropping the puck, the referee broke it in half, held the pieces above his head for a moment, then gave one piece to each player. "Do this in memory of me," he said. Then, at the sound of the angelus bells, I thought our phone was ringing, ringing three times for someone or something that was lost. I turned and, looking out through the halo of one of the saints in the stained-glass window beside the pew, I saw my father, walking slowly up Fleming Street, his hands in his pockets, as if he was headed to work, headed to the *Daily Chronicle* perhaps, despite the fact that it was Sunday morning.

Through the yellow-tinted glass of the halo of St. Anthony I saw him stop suddenly and turn towards the church, then raise one arm as if to wave to me. Then I saw that there was a puck in his hand. He held it to one side of his head, between thumb and forefinger. He might have been a hockey player, posing with the puck he had used to reach some milestone in his career. But he kept glancing back and forth from me to the puck, a look of quizzical distress on his face.

I decided to wave to him, to tell him to come inside with the rest of us. I removed my hand from the pew in front of me, the hand which, as it turned out, was all that was keeping me up, for I had been asleep on my feet and now woke to find that I had fallen forward against the pew, and then to the floor. I sprawled out on the kneeler, my legs on either side of it, wrapping my arms around it and resting my head against the soft cushion. I would quite certainly have gone to sleep had my mother not reached down and, without so much as taking her eyes off her prayer book, grabbed hold of my blazer collar and pulled me to my feet.

Mary, in a vain attempt to hide this spectacle from the people in the pew behind her, began taking off her coat, shielding me with it. "Draper Doyle," she whispered, a threat through clenched teeth; then had me stand between her and the pew, pressing me against it, so that while I might still fall asleep, it was quite impossible for me to fall down.

I looked again through the halo to find that, now, Fleming Street was empty. It might have been some old photograph that I was looking at, some yellowed picture of Fleming Street that had appeared in the *Daily Chronicle* a hundred years ago. With the soft and surprisingly pleasant warmth of Mary's body pressed against me, I once again began to dream.

The Hockey Game

❖   WES FINEDAY

The knocking at my door woke me up. It was a Saturday morning, which meant that there was no school. I got out of bed, got dressed, then walked out of my bedroom and across the hallway to the bathroom. The door was closed. Someone was in there. I went back to the bedroom, made my bed, picked up my books and put them on the dresser. I had been doing my homework just before I fell asleep. There was still quite a bit to do.

Grade Nine sure wasn't easy, at least not as easy as Grade Eight. I had finished my Grade Eight at boarding school last year, had done quite well in fact. This year was different. The Department of Indian Affairs had sent me to live in Moose Jaw to do my Grade Nine. They had explained to me that they had found me a "good Christian boarding home" to live in. They also told me I should consider myself lucky to have this opportunity. At the time I wondered if it would be anything like the school I had left.

I went back to the bathroom. It was vacant. I had a good wash and went back to the bedroom.

They had driven me to Moose Jaw from the boarding school and with that move everything had changed. Now I was in a bedroom by myself instead of a dormitory with thirty other kids. The food eaten by these Christians was unlike anything I ever got at boarding school or at home. For breakfast they would eat dry cereal and pour milk over it to make it soggy. With this they ate toast that was also soggy with butter. For lunch and supper we would have meat and potatoes or rice. I'd eaten these before but not the way this woman cooked it. She used tomatoes and stuff that looked like powder that she kept in small jars over the stove. She must have had twenty different kinds of powder. It was awful. My stomach would hurt for hours after and sometimes I would get ill and bring it all up.

When I tried to tell her that I couldn't eat the food she called me ungrateful and told me my parents would be glad to have something like this to eat. I doubted that. My parents liked eating rabbit and bannock, berries and potatoes just fine. But I didn't tell her that. Arguing would just get me into more trouble.

Another knock at the door. "Come and eat your breakfast," called a voice from the other side of the door. I got up and followed my landlady to the kitchen. There on the table was my breakfast — cereal, toast and milk.

While I was eating breakfast, the woman who was my landlady explained to me that they were going on a family outing. "Not too many more nice weekends before the snow comes," she said. "We're going to take advantage of this one." I could hear their two little boys playing downstairs in the basement. They were playing with the electric train set their father had set up down there. I was not allowed to go near it. I was also not allowed to play with their two boys without permission. I wondered about that sometimes. I did not understand why they treated me so differently from the way they treated everyone else. I suspected they did not like me. The landlady's voice intruded on my thoughts.

"Drink up your milk now, and don't bother coming back until nine o'clock this evening. The house will be locked." These Christians sure don't trust Indians, I thought as I got up and took my dishes to the sink.

After breakfast, I wandered outside to the back yard. The landlord was already out there washing his car. I sat on the back steps and watched him. "Come over here and give me a hand with this," he called. So I did. When we were finished washing and waxing the car, he went back inside and soon they all came out. They seemed to be in a good mood, laughing and talking about the wild animal park. I got up and headed for the sidewalk and started walking down the street. I had nowhere to go, but I thought they would get mad if it looked like I was going to hang around the house all day. I was barely half a block from the house when they drove by. The parents were in front, looking straight ahead, the kids were sitting in the back, looking around. They waved as they went by. I waved back and smiled, trying to look happy.

I watched until the car turned the corner two blocks down the street, then I turned around and walked back to the house. I went into the back yard and stood on the backstep for awhile and finally sat down.

The back yard was separated by a tall picket fence from the yards on either side of it. There was also a garden at the back.

The neighbour's back door opened. A man and a woman followed by a little boy stepped outside. They did not see me. The man was dressed in shorts and a tee shirt, the woman in a bathing suit. They sat down on a couple of lawn chairs, which were placed around a small table. The little boy ran to the end of the yard, where there was a swing and slide and a sand box full of toys. I looked back at the parents. They had been joined by a small black dog with short curly hair. He was sprawled on the ground between the two people, soaking up the sun. I got up from the steps and went a little closer to the fence so I would be out of sight. They might get mad at me. From where I now sat, I could hear them talking about a new car they were planning to buy. The man talked about a contract for playing hockey. This meant they could get a new car. He also had another job. This would take care of their other bills.

I thought about my parents and family at home. My dad had more than two jobs. He had to catch horses before he could do anything. This was a job in itself. Our horses could run very fast and jump fences. Then he had to drive them out to the bush so he could chop wood and haul it home, where he sawed it into small pieces so it would fit into our cook-stove. He also had to haul water. And hunt. He usually did this when he was out in the bush chopping wood. I could see him standing on top of a load of wood on a sleigh, or maybe walking beside it if it was really cold. It was better to keep moving on very cold days. There would usu-ally be a rabbit or two and sometimes even three if he was lucky. We used to run outside to meet him and fight about who would carry the rabbits into the house to give to my mom. She was very good at cleaning and skinning rabbits. She had been doing it for years.

Too bad my dad couldn't get a job playing hockey, I thought. I was sure the folks back home who played hockey didn't get paid to do it. They just did it to be together and have fun. I had heard my dad telling a story to some people about a hockey game. They had cleared the ice on a section of the creek that runs through our reserve. A group of young fellows had got together to have a game. There were just about enough of them for two teams, but one of the teams was minus a goaltender. They managed to talk Leo, who didn't know how to skate, into putting on a pair of skates and being their goalie. Leo shoved some newspapers up each pantleg and wrapped them around his ankles and tied them up with twine. Two of his teammates supported him on either side and pulled him out to his goal. He managed, barely, to stay on his feet by propping himself up with the crude goalie stick someone had hastily nailed to-gether for him. For a puck, they were using a freshly frozen piece of horse dropping they had picked up in someone's barn. Dad said these really smarted if they hit an unprotected spot. The other boys had chopped down suitably curved willow trees for hockey sticks.

Leo's team won the game. Ecstatic over their victory, they all rushed off to the fire, which was roaring beside the creek. They didn't notice Leo until someone started laughing and pointing at the rink. There was Leo, crawling across the ice on his hands and knees toward the fire, dragging his stick behind him.

I smiled remembering the story. Suddenly, I heard a car starting. I had forgotten about the people next door. While I had been thinking, or daydreaming as my teachers called it, the neighbours had moved back inside. Now they had come back out and were about to drive off in their car. I looked up at the sun and realized I had been sitting there daydreaming all morning. And now I was hungry.

Back home if you were hungry you just went somewhere to visit at mealtime and you would be sure to get fed. I decided to give it a try. I tried to think of someone I could go and visit. There was Allen, who lived across the street and was in my class at school. But he hadn't been very friendly to me. I decided not to go over there. A few houses down lived another kid who was in my class. His name was Robert. He had asked me if I wanted to come to the field beside their place and play football. I had wanted to but I didn't know how to play football, so I had declined the invitation.

I got up and walked down the street. When I reached their house I almost turned around but I was hungry. I thought it was a funny thing no one ever used their front door since it was closer to the street. They all used the back door. Our house at home only had one door so we had no choice.

I stood there trying to muster the courage to knock on the door. The screen door was the only obstacle between me and the food I could smell cooking inside. That spurred me on. I knocked and waited. I could hear voices and finally a very tall lady came to the door.

"Is Robert home?" I asked, hoping she would invite me in.

"Yes, he's in," she replied. "But he's having his dinner. Why don't you come back in half an hour or so? He should be finished by then." With that she closed the door and walked away. I felt embarrassed, thinking she must have known why I was there. Well I wouldn't try that again. I turned around and retraced my steps to the back yard of the house where I lived. It was then I noticed the carrots in the garden. Too dangerous, I decided; my landlady would notice if I took even one. I sat down by the fence and immediately fell asleep. I must have slept most of the afternoon, because when I awoke the neighbours were back. I could hear them talking on the other side of the fence. I got up and went over to the fence. There was an outside tap sticking out of the wall of the house. The landlady ran a hose from it to the garden to water those carrots. I thought of them again. My hunger had returned. It was more urgent now. I turned on the tap and let the water run over my arms and hands. It felt cool and refreshing. I cupped my hands and filled them up, stuck my face in the water and felt a tingle go all the way down to my toes. I was awake again. I dried myself off with my shirt sleeves. Then I went and sat back down in my spot. There I felt safe.

"Make mine kind of rare, I like it like that," said the woman. Suddenly I was blasted by the aroma of meat cooking over a fire. I knew the smell, having often eaten meat cooked over a fire. I was just drifting off on memories of home when the man next door yelled. "That damn dog!" Just then the dog came bounding around the corner of the fence and into the yard I was in. It was carrying a steak in its mouth. The man was not far behind. He came running around the fence, still carrying the huge fork he must have been using to turn the meat. So preoccupied with what was behind it that it totally ignored anything in front of it, the dog ran right into me. The dog and the man came to a dead stop.

"Well, hello there. I didn't think there was anyone home here," the man said to me.

"There isn't," I answered. "They went somewhere for the day. They're not going to be home until around nine o'clock."

"Do you live here?" he asked, seeming to have forgotten about the steak.

"Yes," I answered.

"Have you eaten yet?"

"No," I replied, not daring to look at the man.

"We were just going to eat. You could join us if you wanted to. Come on," he urged. I did not need much urging. He speared the steak the dog had dropped, turned around and started to walk back into his yard, his dog and me close behind.

I did not leave any of the huge steak they served me. I could barely move, but I somehow managed to put away a large helping of ice cream for dessert. It was the best meal I had eaten in a long time.

The man's name was Jake. It turned out that he played hockey for the Moose Jaw Canucks. He gave me a couple of tickets to the next game against the Regina Pats. I didn't go to the game but I hope they won.

Next Year

❖   MICHAEL McKINLEY

"This isn't really Canada."

To punctuate this bit of treason, my cousin Dermot horked a green whopper sideways into the balmy December breeze. The backspray hit my toque.

"And you don't need one of those either. Nothing but a bunch of fems in this town. I mean, lookit, it, man. Useless."

It was useless. We were three weeks into December in Vancouver, British Columbia, and it could have just as easily been March. The temperature at a recalcitrant fifty-six degrees; no hope of snow or ice now, or before Dermot headed back east, or probably ever again.

"It can rain pretty bad," I volunteered, looking for a sign of rough winter in the flawless sky above the playground of Sir Wilfrid Laurier Elementary School Annex — an arena ringed not with boards, but chain link fencing, and whose asphalt surface was decorated with red lines and blue lines for hopscotch, not hockey. Still, it was here that almost every afternoon we cinched our roller skates tight with our fathers' frayed neckties, and with SuperBlades and tennis ball, tilted at the windmill that we too were Cournoyer, or Esposito, or Mahovlich, until darkness or hunger dropped us back into reality.

I had been forced to take my cousin here when he demanded to see my "new rink," even though no game was scheduled today because half the squad was celebrating Hannukah and the other half, like me, spent the first part of this Saturday afternoon in the last catechism class before Christmas, praying for ice to pave the streets by the time Sister Jospehine released us into the heathen world. It never did, and we resolved that God's hockey loyalties lay elsewhere.

My mother, Cecilia, in her usual carefree way, had endorsed Dermot's and my mission with two edicts: "Ignatius don't take off your toque because you can't trust the weather, and Dermot, don't use any bad words or Ignatius will tell me — won't you dear? — and I'll tell your father — if he's still conscious." Not words to endear a fellow to an older, violence-prone blood relative, especially if you'd seen Uncle Fergus flooded with Crown Royal, the jaws of anger on him.

With the warning of a snake, Dermot shot his hand out and snatched my toque off my head. Though the association pained me, my cousin's toque-grabbing style was not unlike Gump Worsley's glove hand, a blessed union of intuition and physics through which The Gumper would snatch the puck from some perfidious Leaf trying to rob the Montreal Canadiens from their rightful place as the best hockey team in the known world.

The fact Worsley played for Minnesota now was something I chose to overlook, for in my heart — and in his, I liked to think — he was still a Hab.

Dermot, should he have a heart, was just an ignorant lout, a trait my mother said was common to all but one member of my father Liam's side of the family, my lucky escape engineered by the civilizing influence of my mother's genetic code. Or as she put it, "an intimacy with sobriety."

Dermot, a prophylactically large thirteen year old, was currently on intimate terms with my toque, an item consigned to my head by my mother in fear her first-born male child might fall prey to a sudden blizzard, the odds of which were as good as the Los Angeles Kings winning the Stanley Cup. Should the Americans and the Russians fail to work things out and kill us all with nuclear war any time between the beginning of December and the end of January, I would go to my reward in my white toque.

Or perhaps even sooner, after Dermot recovered from his mute and horrified stare at something I had tried my damnedest to hide: a red and blue Montreal Canadiens' crest sewn at the inside base of the white — and now slightly speckled green — wool hat.

"What. Do. You. Think. You're. Doing?" Dermot's brown eyes were aswirl with the blasphemy of it all.

And the simple response "worshipping at an altar at which you're unworthy, Dimrot (my unspoken name for him)" was unavailable to my eight-year-old brain, and one to which I would not come until much later, when I had learned the glories of single malt whiskey and late night *esprit de l'escalier*. So what I said then, was:

"Trying not to catch a cold."

Dermot blinked as if in underwater time, just in case I didn't fathom the mortal consequences of what he had just seen. "You are a spaz. I can't believe we're related."

The same thought had occurred to me, and I wished Christmas would just have the good grace to cancel itself this year, and Dermot and Fergus could go back to Toronto right about now, which was half an hour after they'd arrived.

Dermot dropped the offending toque on the ground, then stood on it with his filthy Adidas just in case it tried to escape. "Let me put it in a way that a kid without a brain can understand." Dermot ran a hand over the strawberry fuzz on his chin colouring his passage into puberty. "You have this piece of shhh ... garbage ... on your little femmy hat, but you have it hidden. Why is this?"

So I don't get hung out the living room window by my ankles, as Dermot essayed the last time he was here, when I dared to venture that I like the Habs and he tried to drip some sense into my head.

"I don't hear you, Ignatius." Dermot said my name as if it were a by-product of leprosy.

"I didn't say anything."

"Exactly." Dermot grabbed me by the white woolly lapels of my tartan bomber jacket and hoisted me into vapour-range of his gob-breath.

At the time, I thought it unfortunate that Madeleine Montmorency chose to pass by this patch of school-ground at the exact moment when my bad day increased its angle of decline: Dermot adjusted his grip and shifted around so that I could now look my adored Madeleine straight in her alarmed green eyes.

"Hello Ignatius. Do you want me to get your mother?"

I shook my head tersely "No," as if I were at the crucial moment of some sort of impenetrable male ritual in which I was in complete control.

Dermot craned his neck nearly a half turn at the sound of this female voice. "Oooh, it's a girlie. This your girlfriend Ignatius?"

No, no, a thousand times no, Madeleine Montmorency from the City of Montreal in the Province of Quebec is not my girlfriend because I am a mortal and she is a year older, which, in the hierarchy of childhood crushes, makes her divine. She is, however, my great and true love, though I had not yet occupied the perfect moment to inform her thus. And this was not it.

"I think she is, aren't you little girl?" Dermot put me down and turned to Madeleine, who wisely started to move on. "Hold it. I asked you a question."

Madeleine stopped and thought about it. "Do you have a girlfriend?"

Dermot blushed. "Hey, that's not a Canadian accent. Where are you from?"

"Here." Madeleine smiled at me, then turned to continue on her way. The panache of the older woman made my heart beat even faster.

"Whoa, whoa, whoa." He grabbed me around the waist and spun me upside down. "You stay put, girlie, and answer my questions or Ignatius here is going to be dropped on his head."

Though he made it sound as if my imminent hard landing had nothing to do with him, I was firmly of the opinion she should stick around.

Madeleine fixed Dermot with her emerald eyes, then shrugged in that devastatingly Gallic way of her forbears. "Who are you?" Then she walked on.

"Madeleine, please." My voice was unusually husky, given my inexperience at speaking upside-down, and the manly timbre of it made her stop and turn. Dermot cackled.

"Madeleine, eh? Little Frenchie, eh? So that's why Ignatius loves the ..." he spat again "... Montreal Canadiens." The expression on his face was akin to that I'd see on my mother's, after she had walked into our bathroom without any warning that my father had just exited after lengthy deliberations.

Madeleine walked up to my cousin, folded her arms, and tossed her ebony ringlets in dudgeon.

"Ignatius, do you know this person?"

"Heez my cuzzin." My voice was getting deeper.

"Ignatius's cousin, I will tell you two things. Firstly, you do not treat your cousin like that, so put him down and then I will talk to you."

I felt his grip loosen in shock, and I managed to splay my arms out before hitting the school-yard asphalt in a belly flop.

"That wasn't what I meant." Madeleine was annoyed.

"Hey, he did it." Dermot's metaphysics were again clearly a genetic legacy.

"Ignatius, are you all right?"

I rolled over, sat up, and surveyed myself. There was no blood, but the front of my jacket would need reupholstering. "I think so."

Madeleine nodded, then turned back to her dragon-slaying. "Now, for the second thing, Ignatius's cousin: Ignatius likes the Montreal Canadiens because if he didn't, he would have to like the Toronto Maple Leafs. It's obvious."

Ah, that's my heroine, the blood of Descartes flowing through her magnificent heart. Dermot's curiously elfin face swelled in a sneer.

"That's the dumbest thing I've ever heard. Ignatius is *supposed* to be Canadian. The Leafs are *Canada's* team. He's *supposed* to like them. But I guess you wouldn't understand that, you people, causing trouble."

I stood up, and Madeleine frowned at me. "What does he mean?"

"I don't know." And I didn't, except that in the last two years that

Dermot and his father came to our house for Christmas, my father would say to me "Be nice to him old pal, he hasn't got a mother, like you do" and my mother would say "Help me turn the labels," which meant spending the hour before Dermot and Fergus arrived in energetic spinning of all labeled foodstuffs in the refrigerator and pantry so that the French side faced outwards. For the relations' easy reading.

"I mean that Montreal isn't really Canada because of all those Frenchies, and Vancouver isn't really Canada because you can't skate outside, and there's no NHL team here anyway, so anyone with a brain can figure out that this leaves Toronto as your only real choice." Dermot spat again, this time missing my collar.

"We'll have one next year. The Canucks."

"What?" Dermot fixed me with a suspicious eye.

"It's true." Madeleine nodded. "The Canucks. Until then, we'll cheer for the Canadiens."

Dermot stared at the two of us as his mind scrambled to counter news which had clearly not reached his command module in civilization. I felt sorry for him.

"Really, Dermot, next October we'll be able to cheer for Vancouver. You can too, if you like."

This invitation made out of friendly fear restored his malevolence. "Jeezuz-k ... Can you be any more of a farmer? Why would I do that?"

I didn't think he'd understand the complex reasons, but thankfully, Madeleine stepped in.

"Because the Leafs are getting too old. And anyway, Montreal won the Stanley Cup last year."

Dermot nearly gagged on the next bit of hork cued up in his gullet. "What kind of shhh ... garbage ... is that?"

"That's what my Dad says."

"Mine too." It wasn't true, as my Irish-immigrant father sacreligiously preferred football to ice hockey, but I felt that loyalty to my future spouse demanded it. Dermot grabbed me and spun me upside down again, this time holding me by my ankles. I was a breath away from painful union with the asphalt.

"No he fuuuhhh ... doesn't. And Ignatius, consider yourself dead."

He began to shake me up and down in a fairly sincere fashion, the only good thing of which was that my lips brushed Madeleine's bare leg when she kicked Dermot in the shins with her Buster Brown's. She tasted like cinnamon.

"Gawdddammit to hell!"

Dermot dropped me again and I rolled, knocking Madeleine over on top of me so that we were now entwined in a parody of *al fresco* rutting, while Dermot hopped about, exhausting his cussing lexicon, my mother's warning cancelled by pain.

It was in this state that The Elderly Gentleman decided we were worth speaking to.

"Is everything all right, there?"

Despite my cousin's caterwauling jig, I was not unhappy to be tangled up with Madeleine's warm cinnamon self, so I smiled and nodded at the old man, dapper in his tweed suit. He smiled back.

"That fellow seems to be in some difficulty."

"He's used to it."

Madeleine giggled at this, and I felt my cheeks redden. The Elderly Gentleman smiled again and moved nearer with a careful, noble step.

I had seen him before, strolling the neighborhood on the arm of his walking stick, a gnarled beast which must have been as old as him, which I pegged at around two hundred years. When we encountered him on the street, my mother would say "Good day, sir" as if addressing the Pope, and he would tip his hat to her, and to me.

Afterward she would remind me that "The Elderly Gentleman" had once been the glory of the Empire for what he could do with a puck on ice. "In the days of gentlemen." To which my father Liam would add — for the sake of domestic balance — "A game for hooligans, and played by them too."

Dermot had now becalmed to the point where he'd noticed The Elderly Gentleman leaning on his walking stick and talking to me and Madeleine about what we hoped to receive from Santa in a week's time.

"There's no Santa Claus." Dermot, I might say here, did not end up in the diplomatic service.

The Elderly Gentleman widened his eyes, as if this was the first time he'd heard this news. Madeleine's eyes were already moist.

"It's okay," I volunteered. "He told me the same thing last year, and Santa still came."

Both the old man and Madeleine looked relieved, while Dermot snickered.

"That was your parents who came, Ignatius. Boy, are you ever a retard."

At the sound of my name, The Elderly Gentleman gave me the smile of an accomplice. "It's been a long time since I heard that name 'Ignatius.'" He pronounced it with the Latin music my mother Cecilia said it deserved. "We used to have a trainer named Ignatius. Marvelous. Ignatius Martin, a great boxer as well as a hockey man. *He* knew how to put an edge on my skates."

At this possessive mention of trainers and skates from a man who needed help walking, Dermot narrowed his eyes.

"What are you talking about?"

"A long time ago, my boy. A long time ago." His eyes took him back, and it seemed advantageous to use his departure to help my cousin out.

"He used to play hockey in the days of gentlemen."

The old man wasn't as far away as I thought, chortling now as he took me in. "Tell me, how did a young fellow like you know that, Ignatius?"

Both Dermot and Madeleine clearly wanted to know the same thing, though Madeleine was smiling at me in what I hoped was admiration. I was flustered.

"My mother told me because I like hockey. She said you were famous all across the world."

The Elderly Gentleman dipped his head in a courtly bow. "Tell your mother I thank her. You might also tell her that some of my gentlemen colleagues would thank her too, especially the one who liked to resolve battles for the puck by hitting the fellow *with* the puck over the head with his stick. And I was only famous for a little while, and not every-where. But while I was, it was glorious."

While Madeleine and I let this vast biography seep in, Dermot found his skating legs.

"I know what you're talking about. You played for the Leafs in the olden days!"

The Elderly Gentleman feigned surprise. "No, young fellow, I did not. Whatever makes you think that?"

Dermot rolled his eyes at the fact there was not a working brain within fifty paces of him. "Because the Leafs are the best."

The Elderly Gentleman arched his eyebrows to me and Madeleine. "I think whoever owns that toque lying on the ground knows who is the best. This year."

As Dermot threaded the logic of the old man's speech, the warmth from the little triumph spread from my heart to my hand. Which was odd. When I looked down, Madeleine was holding it.

"Montreal is the best. That's what my Dad says." She was beaming.

"They are very good indeed. But what do you yourself say, young lady?"

"Ignatius and I both like Montreal. But next year we'll cheer for Van-couver."

Dermot flapped his arms, as if we were benighted foreigners, without shoes or hope. "Vancouver will *stink*! It will take them *years* just to play in the same rink with the Leafs! He rattled his mucous, pre-launch. "Van-couver has no tradition." Then he spat.

It was his words, not his spit, that splashed hot into my face. And The Elderly Gentleman, his expression grave, reached into his waistcoat pocket, not for a Kleenex, but for a gold medallion on a chain.

"I must say, sir, you're wrong there. Very wrong. Take a look at this."

We all moved closer. The medallion featured two crossed hockey sticks, framed by filigreed arches above and below inscribed "World's Champions, 1915, Vancouver."

Dermot narrowed his eyes at me, as if I had somehow set this encounter up. "World's Champions, eh. Well, in Toronto, we've had the Stanley Cup."

"This 'World's Champions' refers to the Stanley Cup, young fellow. I won it with the Vancouver Millionaires in 1915, when we beat the Ottawa Senators, who claimed the sea air here fatigued their legs." He smiled at the memory. "The one thing that seems constant in hockey is an excuse for losing."

Dermot was now completely off balance, staggering as if he'd been body-checked into our chain-link boards by one of The Big Guys in high school who often kicked us off our patch asphalt to play for real. Madeleine and I were too pleased to speak.

"Vancouver won the Stanley Cup?"

"Yes indeed."

"Well ... well ... why don't they have a team here now?"

"As Ignatius and his friend I believe mentioned, we will have one next year. It's been a long time between Stanley Cups, I must say. We Millionaires thought we'd win another one in 1916, but 'next year', as you will discover, can be a long time in coming."

He smiled with a wisdom I could only guess at, then checked his watch. "Goodness me, my grandchildren will think I've gone west. It has indeed been a pleasure. And make sure to leave something out for the reindeer. Something sweet — they get weary of carrots." He tipped his hat, adjusted his walking stick, and ambled off.

Dermot's peasanty suspicion suddenly jolted him into a shout. "Hey Mister! What's your name? I'm gonna look you up in my hockey book."

The Elderly Gentleman returned, and handed us a small white card. On it was the name "F.W. Taylor."

"If you get no satisfaction, you might check under my nickname, which seems a jest of nature now. They called me 'Cyclone.'" And then he stepped into the warm blue shadows of that December day.

Dermot fingered the card, then looked at me. "The Stanley Cup, eh. We'll see." But he spoke with the voice of a man who knew he had lost, and Madeleine winked at me.

"I think he was Santa Claus."

"Shhh ... ure he was. Kids." Dermot shook his head at us both. Then he grunted what I'm sure was the most forbidden of the profanities, from which he gained strength to pick up my soiled toque and pull it down over my eyes for a dark moment, before rolling the base back up so my Montreal Canadiens crest now proclaimed to the world my tribe. But it was a loyalty whose fabled torch had just been passed, backward to *that* year, and forward, forever, to the next.

The Puck Artist

❖   LEVI DRONYK

At the age of nine I discovered that I needed more than food and shelter. Yet I knew nothing of purpose, of what was important to me. There were friends, but they meant very little. Then I saw television. *Hockey Night in Canada*.

It was at my uncle's, during the regular whiskey ritual he performed with the Oldman, while my aunt and mother sat apart from the men, knitting, chatting and shaking their heads over each drink poured.

Over the noise of the women's gossip and my cousins' shrieking, I saw the first goal, scored by Jean Béliveau. Or was it "the Rocket"? It was beautiful, and at that moment, not knowing that all I wanted was a sense of originality, I found something inside my uncle's TV set.

My imagination surpassed television technology in that I had slow-motion instant replay. For the record, I invented it that Saturday night: the Canadiens split two checks at centre ice, left an embarrassed defenceman at the blue line, held the other away with a strong arm as he cut for the net, keeping the puck on his backhand, leaning forward, already manipulating the goalie, a head fake, a dipped shoulder. Clear of the second defenceman, the Canadien convinced the goalie the shot was coming from the forehand; he flopped in that direction just as the Canadien whistled a backhander.

The puck was swallowed by the roar. The Canadien raised his arms, and I looked at my own, skinny, covered with goosebumps. I heard one of my cousins scream, and mistakenly thought she was also thrilled over the goal. But she was only in a panic about her date arriving in twenty minutes. Apparently, it was a big deal to be going out with Billy Semeniuk.

Back home that night from my uncle's while listening to the Oldlady bitch at the Oldman for drinking too much, I drew the number 4 on the back of my pyjamas, and replayed the telecast yet again. Then Sunday, listening to Danny Gallivan call the play-by-play, I scored a thousand times. Béliveau got two. "Rocket" Richard, one. I dreamt of stickhandling across Montreal Forum ice. A puck was all I had. I needed a stick, and a pair of skates.

The stick came from the lumber yard and hardware store where the Oldman worked. I hounded him relentlessly. He threw in a roll of tape just to get rid of me; all he wanted was to get back to "the boys' in the back room, sitting on nail kegs, sipping whiskey, "shooting the shit." A puck and a stick, but still no skates. There was no money for skates. The priorities were bread, meat and whiskey, then poker and used cars. I remember the cars, as many as five lined up outside the house. The Oldman turned them over regularly, for little or no profit.

I stickhandled on the icy roads of Blackwater, to school and back, at noon, at recess, always stickhandling, head up, hands up high on the shaft of the stick. Down the road, sometimes having to dodge traffic. Once, Billy Semeniuk almost ran me over. He swerved to avoid me and the truck went into a "doughnut," a complete three-sixty. I was scared when he got out of the truck. He just laughed and told me to keep my head up. But the Oldlady, who saw everything through the kitchen window, said it was "too much goddamn sticks all the time." She wanted me to go to church on Sunday, and catechism classes on Saturday. No way. She threatened to "throw those sons a bitchin hockey cards into the stove." Fortunately the stove was natural gas, not wood burning.

I didn't blame her. It was the school principal. At a Home and School meeting, he'd told her that if I spent as much time on my spelling and arithmetic as I did memorizing the backs of hockey cards, I'd be an honours student. I stuck with the cards — goals, assists, total points and penalty minutes. The principal was an asshole. He took our class to the Rink once, and I remember watching him skate, arms flailing, legs jerking, the ass of his pants all wet from falling so much and I lost all respect for him. I was the only kid there without skates, and he couldn't have cared less.

At night, when I should've been doing homework, I was out in the back yard packing down the snow with my boots and a snow shovel. I'd line up three pucks and rattle shots off the garage wall. The Oldlady would flick the porch light off and on when she wanted me in. Sometimes I'd ignore her, and she'd scream, "break that goddamn stick across your back." I'd send her to the penalty box. A five minute penalty for intent to injure. Then I'd go inside and complain I was the only kid in the world without skates and a back yard skating rink.

I couldn't believe it. The middle of December, and the Oldlady was outside clearing snow, down to the frozen earth so she could flood me a rink. And me with no skates telling her that wasn't the way to do it. She called me an "ungrateful little bastard" and said I'd be happier when she was "dead and buried in a grave." My point was that a successful back yard rink had to be started in October. After the garden was harvested, it had to be dug up, raked and packed down with a roller. Then the boards could be placed, and the flooding would start around Hallowe'en, and with any luck there'd be skating by Remembrance Sunday. I figured the Oldlady was flooding me a rink of bumps and hills in December because I was getting skates for Christmas.

I was wrong. The Canadiens sweater, toque and leggings helped soften the disappointment. The Oldlady cut the number 4 out of an old white rag and showed me how to sew it on the back of my new sweater. I didn't spend much time sulking over the skates situation; talked the Oldman out of some two-by-four scraps, and stole some nails while he visited the back room.

I built a goal. The two-by-four frame wasn't quite regulation size, and for netting I used old burlap potato sacks, but to me it was the opponent's goal at the Forum. Toe Blake tapped my shoulder. I hopped the boards. I was a rookie, and in the Canadien tradition, I saw little ice time, except for the power play. I waited in the slot, gun loaded. Trigger impatient. *Bang*. Red light flashing behind the potato sacks.

My break came when one of my fat friends, Larry Vietch, showed me his new skates. I was jealous, but showed him nothing but nonchalance. He said Santa brought them. "Yeah, sure." It was mid-January and I was only sorry I hadn't known sooner. Larry hated the skates. His preferences were food and television, particularly doughnuts, potato chips, the Lone Ranger, Wild Bill Hickok, the Cisco Kid and all those sidekicks like Pancho, Jingles and Tonto. We used to play "guns" in the summer, first thing in the morning, having something to do with "cowboys" and "sunrise." By breakfast time, the fat boy was pooped and sweaty. I'd killed him forty or fifty times while remaining unscathed.

How he hated those skates. His obese mother withheld doughnuts to get him on the ice. She scared me: it was the fear of being fallen on. I usually waited outside for him, shoveling or sweeping his ice to kill time, waiting for his mother to throw him out. Then he'd skate on his thick ankles for twenty minutes, go back inside and whine that his feet hurt, that he was tired and hungry. She would shout that he wasn't trying. But in the end, he got his doughnuts. I'd tiptoe in, watching from a safe distance, and once Larry was lost in sugar and Roy Rogers, I'd ask Mrs. Vietch if I could try out the skates. More goosebumps the first time she said yes. Soon I was skating like a beloved Canadien, head up, puck attached to the stick blade like it was in love.

The back door slammed. Virgin Mary shook in her frame above my bed. But she was safe. I had her surrounded with hockey stars cut out of *Weekend Magazine*. Memorizing hockey cards and listening to the radio. The deejay mourned Buddy Holly, playing "That'll Be The Day" yet again. It was Saturday, February 7th, 1959.

The Oldman, on his way to the lumber yard to finish the books before opening at eight-thirty, left without lighting the heater. I got up. Remember, "light the match first, then turn up the gas." I also lit the stove, put milk on, then got dressed: long underwear with trapdoor; les Canadiens leggings over jeans, with old "sale" catalogues between them, all secured with rubber rings; the sweater over a parka; and of course, the ridiculous red, white and blue toque.

My back yard rink, more like the Company's really because Imperial Lumber owned the property, was covered with fresh snow, which I cleared before running down the alley to Veitch's. I shoveled their ice, and the sidewalks too. The shovel scraping against cement woke Larry's older brother. He stuck his head out the door. I wanted to throw something at him. He looked meaner than usual — his eyes narrowed, and fat, liver lips hooked in a sneer.

"Goddammit Krapko, it's seven fuckin' thirty!"

"Oh."

"Whata ya want?"

"Nothing."

I could see he was looking for something to throw, so I ran around to the back of the house. He thought I was gone. I tried the back door. It opened. The skates. I pulled them out, slowly. It took me thirty seconds to close the door. Larry said it was okay to take the skates, as long as I didn't keep them overnight. A dumb rule, but I respected it.

Back on home ice, I glided through some figure eights, first without, then with the puck. I practised skating backwards, head up, ass out. After firing a hundred wrist shots at my makeshift net, I was ready for a game.

Sammy Martinyuk was a drinking buddy of the Oldman's. He built a classy back yard rink every winter for his kids, Kenneth, a sickly boy who kept skipping grades in school, and Sharon, a tough girl who was built like a linebacker and hit twice as hard. She actually played middle linebacker on our Southside, under-twelve football team. All three were out on the ice. Sammy was painting a faded blue line while the kids skated around and over him, jumping as close to his brush as they could without hitting it. Sammy laughed when he saw me.

"Baniak, yak tam kolo vas?"

I answered in English. I'd lost my first language. To compete with "the

English" was to learn their language. According to the Oldlady, "the English" included everyone who didn't speak Ukrainian. She was also big on "modern education," whatever that was, and constantly reminded me that if I talked like a "d.p.," I'd end up with a "d.p. job shoveling shit for some English bastard with two cadillacs."

Baniak, eh?

Literally, a *baniak* is a pot; in the vernacular, it becomes a "dummy." Among Ukrainians, it's used in a self-deprecating context, or, as with Sammy, an endearment. If "the English" used the word, or the malicious "bohunk," which amounted to calling a Ukrainian "nigger," to address us, a fistfight usually resulted. Two weeks earlier, I'd popped Doug Atwood in the mouth for calling me "bohunk." He'd thought to yell and run. He wasn't fast enough.

"Gonna have a game?"

I hit the ice, did a quick turn and stopped hard. The ice spray messed with Sammy's paint job.

"*Tchikaj, tchikaj*, the paint's not dry," Sammy shouted.

Sharon, never impressed by anything I did, skated by, dipped her shoulder and knocked me over the boards. A *baniak* in the snowbank is how Sammy described me. Sharon laughed. Kenny had a coughing fit and Sammy yelled at him to get in the house. Sharon waited for me to retaliate, but I didn't.

"Hey Sharon, wanna get a game going at Lambert's?" I said. "We could get Fatty and Raymond and Dash."

Fatty Johnson lived next door, so I yelled for him.

"Hey FATTY!"

He was probably listening to his sister's forty-fives. Once, he played "Splish Splash" fifteen times in a row.

"Hey, Fateee."

"*Baniak*, quiet, sshh," Sammy frowned. "Why you have to be so noisy? How come?"

"I dunno."

"You old man, he don't teach you like that."

Raymond Krasnik's father glared at me. He was the neighbour on the other side. Old Krasnik never said anything. Sammy said he wouldn't say shit if he had a mouthful. Colonel Nick, Sammy called him. "Colonel Nick the D.P." "Colonel Nick, that dumb prick" was how Sammy began stories about him in the back room at the lumber yard. Colonel Nick was wearing his military overcoat and fur hat. Apparently, he'd been an officer in the Polish army during the war. "Probably the first one to surrender to that *baniak* Hitler."

"Is Raymond home?" I asked.

He only glared at me.

"The bugger don't speak English," Sammy said.

Sharon and I left for the Lambert rink, one of the truly great back yard rinks. It was approximately two-thirds regulation size. There were boards all around it, and behind the goals chicken wire had been installed to the height of eight feet. Talk about classy, the goals were of welded steel with nylon cord for the net. There were three strings of lights across the ice and floods at either end for night hockey. Blackjack Lambert, who played defence for the Blackwater Pontiacs, built it all. That winter he'd added a shack, complete with benches and a potbelly stove. It was a courtesy to visitors like me, but I usually walked over in Larry's skates. Besides, Blackjack never lit the stove, and the shack was always full of snow. It just drifted in.

Wayne Dashenko, "Dash" because he was a fast skater in the winter and runner in the summer, and the Dwerninsky brothers, Donnie and Pinka, were warming up. Pinka had the pads on. A cigarette hung out of his mouth. At twelve, he was already a chainsmoker. I picked up a stray puck and snapped it high. It screamed past Pinka's ear and tested the chicken wire.

"Fuckin' Crapper," he mumbled, "keep 'em down, ya punk."

Crapper. I hated that nickname, but when your name's Metro Krapko, it's a natural. Fully, it was "Meatball Crapper," and first used by Blackjack's nephew Robby. I hated "Crapper." Robby was okay.

We were honoured that day. Blackjack himself came out to play. I'll never forget it, because he tossed me an old pair of gloves, the palms worn thin from stickhandling, and said I could keep them. Better still, I was on his team. Me, Sharon and Blackjack against Dash and the Dwerninsky brothers.

"Stick to Dash," Blackjack told me. "Smack him into the boards, knock him on his ass."

I took it all very seriously. Blackjack asked me if I was constipated. Then he laughed and slapped me on the ass with his stick. I played my heart out. Dash got his goals, but none came easy. I was on him like ugly on ape. I hit him, slashed him, bumped, hooked and tripped him. I suckered him, out-hustled, elbowed and muscled him in the corners. We had a great time. Blackjack egged us on. We never stopped skating. Like the oil wells across the road, we kept pumping, and like them, believed we'd go on forever.

And old Pinka was sprawling and cursing. I deked him so sweetly, he almost swallowed his butt. He whacked me with his goalie stick and called me a "fuckin' punk bohunk," which was okay, I said, because he was one too. Blackjack fed me breakaway passes. Sharon hit Dash so hard against the boards that he had to sit out for a while. Coming back, he was feeling just a little mean, and gave me a two-hander across the neck that made me forget it was Saturday. Sharon hit Pinka in the head with a backhander. We all laughed, even Pinka. It was a soft shot. The only harm done was Pinka lost his cigarette, one he'd just lit. Blackjack told him to get his greasy head off the ice. Pinka grinned and dug another smoke out of the pack before getting up.

"Here, smoke this," Blackjack ripped a shot into the upper corner. PING, it sang, grazing the post on the way.

By noon, my fun was over, stolen from me by the arrival of five of Blackjack's friends. Then Robby showed up. There was a game in the works. They were short of four a side. One short. Me. I wished. Then Billy the Kid Semeniuk showed up.

"Aha," he shouted, "it's that time again gentlemen, the great hockey challenge, where the puck artist rises above the scorn of the masses, men against men, boys will be boys, wot, where the weak shall merely fade and the one great puck artist shall inherit the frozen earth to skate upon as yet he dares to skate into the icedream heaven where cold arms embrace ..."

"Fuck off Semeniuk," was the most popular reply.

"Blow it out your ass Kid."

"Fuckin' everyone wants to be a preacher!"

"Yeah, save it for Sunday school."

"Gentlemen," he answered, "I hope your blades are sharper than your wits."

"Ah come on, jam it Kid!"

The collective voice.

"You realize of course, that the wit and the blade are inseparable."

"So's yer head from yer ass," Pinka mumbled.

Only I heard him.

We were chased off the ice. Pinka said he knew where there was a bottle of beer. He left blowing smoke rings and whistling "Be Bop a Lula." His brother went the other way, uptown, to the pool hall. Donnie was an ace shooter, the best in town until Pinka learned the cue and became unbeatable. He became famous in Edmonton a few years later. His victory over Benny the jockey is considered a classic.

"A magic pirouette" is what Billy the Kid called it, the two revolution spin he did after scoring a goal.

"Hey hotdog where's the mustard?" Blackjack invariably said.

"I am ze puck artiste, mmmm wah!"

Sharon and I watched them play. I believe she identified with Blackjack, with his bulk and physical strength. I was with Billy the Kid all the way. He was the greatest. The Oil Kings were interested in him, but Billy didn't care. He was fifteen, nearly sixteen. He called the Oil Kings "sanctimonious puck busters."

"Yeah you got a problem, Kid."

Blackjack had dubbed him the Kid, after seeing the Audie Murphy movie, the one with Fats Domino singing "I found my thrill on Blueberry Hill."

Billy the Kid scored again, fashioned another whirl.

"Yeah, you still got a problem, Kid."

Billy blew Blackjack a kiss.

"That punk mouth is going to be your downfall."

"This mouth is going to suck the tits of angels."

Yeah. Billy the Kid was something. He walked around Blackjack again, and the puck being quicker than the eye, it was in the net before I'd finished marveling at the first move.

"Child's play, for kids, like me. But what say you Blackjack? What, a man's game? Nay, not for the roughnecks or the toolpush, neither for the whiskey drinkers nor lusty fornicators, right Blackjack? Speak to me, my sage."

Blackjack laughed. One of his friends cursed. Then Blackjack caught Billy the Kid with his head down and knocked him ass over tea kettle. The Kid was dazed. Blackjack looked worried.

"Nice check Blackjack," Billy grinned.

"You okay Kid?"

"Blackjack, ass black, big and mean, biggest *putka* I ever seen."

I could've watched all afternoon, but the desire to play was greater. Sharon didn't feel like going to the Rink, so I went alone. I stopped at the lumber yard to bum some money. The Oldman was weighing nails for a customer. His pals were in the back room.

"Hello *baniak*."

Sammy Martinyuk was there. And Dash's old man. He had the Pacific Petroleum dealership and owned a yellow Bluebird bus to haul farmers' kids to school and back. Louis Lagrande was there. While his wife and children lived off welfare, he travelled from town to town looking for card games. He was the best dressed bum around. They were drinking coffee. No whiskey yet. They'd start later, or sooner, soon as one of them rose from his nail keg to go to the liquor store.

"Can I have two bits, Dad?"

"What for?"

"I'm going to the Rink."

"That don't cost anything."

"Wanna get a hot dog."

"Where'd you get the skates?"

"Larry's."

"Where's your boots?"

"At home."

"You walking?"

"Yea."

"In skates?"

"Sure."

He flipped me a quarter. I crossed the tracks to the Northside. Walked through town. I stopped at the theatre to check out the movies. Playing: *Pillow Talk*. I made a face. The road by the library wasn't sanded, so I stickhandled the length of it. I turned right after the school, stopped at the Curling Rink. I bought a hot dog and watched curling, the most boring game in the world, worse than bowling, or golf. I punished the dog in record time, and left. The Rink was a block away.

It was the facility for all Blackwater hockey teams, from pee wee to senior, that played teams from other small towns, like Gibbons, Thorhild, Newbrook, Fort Saskatchewan, Radway, Bon Accord, Half Moon Lake and Bruederheim. There was adjacent ice for figure skating, and public skating, where Sousa marches played over the public address. Kids played crack-the-whip. Adults drank coffee and whiskey from thermos bottles. Teenagers skated hip to hip, stealing quick kisses.

There was lots of action on the hockey ice. A veritable free-for-all. Twenty of us chasing one puck. The more prominent stickhandlers included Moon Myroon, Jimmy Donald, Bobby Walker, Nicky "the Stick" Toronchuck, Harvey Court, Randy Hnatiuk and Les Tarapatsky. Among the others was my only enemy, Clark Bonk. I don't know why, but he chose me as his rival. He was at best, when playing over his head, an average athlete. I was considered excellent in the big three — hockey, football and baseball — and was routinely chosen first or second in pickup games. Hockey was my newest sport, but I was getting better every day.

Clark Bonk always covered me in the Northside/Southside football games. I must've burned him for a million touchdowns. Our quarterback, Raymond Krasnik, was always looking at me in the huddle, telling me to go deep. And in baseball, Bonk always had to pitch. He was lousy. I hit more homeruns off him in one summer than the Babe hit off American League pitching his whole career. I should've felt sorry for Clark Bonk. I wanted to, but my contempt always won.

That Saturday, he was more determined than usual. Maybe the pirouette I'd adopted from Billy the Kid rubbed him the wrong way. He kept hitting me with his stick. I took it, and gave it back. He high-sticked me.

I gave him the butt end. He swung his stick, missed my head, and I dropped my new gloves, and he dropped his, just like we'd see on *Hockey Night in Canada*. I smacked him in the head three or four times, not one a serious blow, pulled the sweater over his head, and gave him a couple more. Bobby Walker pulled us apart. Moon Myroon escorted me to the penalty box. Everyone laughed over that, except Clark, who left the ice, after promising to kill me. I thought nothing of it. I should have.

When I came off the ice, the rink shack fell silent. I loosened my skates to give my feet some air before the walk home. I looked up. He was standing over me. Mike Bonk was a year older and maybe fifteen pounds heavier than me, but at that moment he looked like the giant from *Jack and the Beanstalk. I* thought I heard "fe fi fo ... "

"Bohunk son of a bitch," was all he said before beating the living shit out of me.

Someone pulled him away, or he would've beaten me unconscious. The room was a red blur. All I knew was how much it hurt. I managed to transfer the pain to Clark Bonk's impending death. Bobby Walker wiped my mouth with a wet paper towel. The pain returned. Tears burned. Randy Hnatiuk walked with me as far as the tracks. I remember being grateful that I hadn't lost any teeth. My chest burned, and I felt like throwing up.

"Lord Jesus Christ what in the hell happened."

The Oldlady was surprised, but far too solid for hysteria.

"Got beat up," I said, as best I could.

"Who did it?"

"Nobody."

"Who's nobody. You tell me."

I knew what she'd do. She'd phone, offering to go over and put Mike Bonk across her knee. She'd curse out the whole Bonk ancestry, and later, hound the Oldman. "Those goddamned Bonks, not one of them worth a shit," and remind him, over and over, "if one of those little sons of bitches lays a hand on him, I'll throw him in reform school by myself, you tell them that, if you don't I sure as hell will." I also knew she'd find out. One or two phone calls and she'd know. I told her.

"Mike Bonk."

"Mike Bonk?"

"Yeah."

"Goddamn English bastards."

"Mom don't phone."

"Go lay down."

"Please don't phone."

"I said go."

"Don't phone." I started crying.

"Now go."

She cranked the phone.

"Julia? Give me the Bonks. No, not Bill Bonk! Frank Bonk! Yes, Goddammit, connect me and get off the goddamn line!"

I fled to my room, hitting the bed hard. I turned the radio up to obscure her voice. It blared "Sea Cruise." While I sniffed and slobbered, Frankie Ford sang "oo-wee, oo-wee baby," and the Oldlady shouted obscenities, promises and threats, the power of the words left to my imagination.

Asked to kill Clark Bonk, my imagination gave me a screenplay:

On the football field, after school, with the entire student body circling us, Clark Bonk on his knees before me. Beaten body, he snivels for mercy. The circle closes. "Death," it shouts. I bow, sweeping my right arm before me. Three quick steps. I hoist my right leg, connecting perfectly under Bonk's chin. His head flies. Straight. True. Between the uprights, three points. And still flies, into the blue until lost in the clouds. The cheering circle tightens.

That was my movie. I saw it many times, frame by frame, in slow motion and speeded up. Nothing could distract me from it, not the hockey broadcast on the radio, neither the music nor the arguing of my parents. I fell asleep to Clark Bonk's head turning end over end, floating through a nimbostratus cloud shaped like a rat, disappearing into the mouth, whipped by the tail as it came out the cloud's ass.

My revenge came that spring, vicariously, through Randy Hnatiuk. It was after Little League practice. Randy was showing Clark how to throw a curveball, one of those fat, roundhouse curves that need the element of surprise to work. Clark couldn't snap his wrist right, and Randy said that teaching him to throw a curve was like teaching a steer to read. Bonk threw a bat at him. Randy ducked. Then, in a most peculiar move, Randy tore off one of his spikes and charged. He swung the shoe, ripping Clark's cheek with the cleats. He further kicked Bonk in the nuts. Seeing him on his knees, doubled over, blood and tears mixed with insults, I wanted to kick him in the head, to fulfill the fantasy, but I couldn't. Randy screamed at him to get up, but Clark Bonk wisely stayed down. Randy walked away, to piss in the dugout. We pissed in the dugout all the time, but only after the coach was gone, and only in the visitors'. Two years later, when Randy and I were best friends, we took Sonja Bankow and Cheryl Poderski into the home dugout and kissed them.

It was the same every Sunday, the Oldlady screaming that it was time for church. The Oldman, hungover, yelling for peace and quiet.

"Get your ass out of bed. Drive me to church."

"Shut up already, I'm up I'm up, Jesus ... "

"Metro, get up, go to church for once."

As usual, I feigned sleep. She could shake me but not move me. "Okay, you wanna go to hell, you'll go to hell." But mine was a good fake, an honourable one. I could always wait her out. That Sunday, she was easier on my ears. I guess the beat-up face helped. The Oldman looked in on me.

"You okay?"

I stuck with the sleep act. They left. I got up. The Oldman wouldn't be back. He'd sit at Elsie's until church was over, drinking black coffee, smoking Export A and playing birdie-in-the-bush with his friends, all of them waiting to pick up wives after church. Then he'd go to the lumber yard, maybe to unload a trailer of cement, all by himself, with no help from his friends.

In the mirror, I saw a fat face with black rings, with gaps of yellow and purple, the left eye worse than the right. It hurt to open them. Nose hurt too. "It's broken." "Nah, it's just crooked." My mouth wasn't swollen enough to keep me from eating. I warmed up some leftovers, *perohy* fried in butter, then simmered in heavy cream, fresh from my uncle's farm. I cracked a quart of plums, and drank the juice straight from the jar. Setting the garbage pail in the middle of the kitchen, I spat plum pits into it. When I missed, it was Clark Bonk's fault.

Getting beat up was no excuse for not returning Larry's skates. All I needed was his fat brother wailing on me. But I had a plan, a doughnut bribe. Larry was the only one up when I got there. He was pouting over the skates, but brightened when I showed him the bag of home-made doughnuts, six of them, three sugared and three others jellied. He forgave me and said I could have the skates again, for the day. I'd been counting on it. So I left him scattering crumbs over a pile of *Archie* comics, soiling the escapades of Betty, Veronica and Jughead. I hated all of them. Bunch of dorks; Veronica the bitch, Reggie the asshole, Moose the dolt, Archie the freckled fag, and poor Betty who only wanted to get into Archie's pants. They were so much smaller than life, each the antithesis of what a comic book hero should be. I preferred the irony of "Spy vs. Spy," the bullet holes in Fearless Fosdick's chest, Alfred E.'s stoned grin, and the mercurial grace of the Flash.

I arrived at the Lambert rink before anyone else. The beauty of the ice, swept clean and flooded during the night, and the brightness of the day, overwhelmed me. I could see my reflection. Something caught in my

throat. Then those stupid tears. I quickly turned whatever it was off. I cut
the fresh ice with figure eights. I shot bullets at the net.

"Hey Crapper, who fell on your face?"

"She kissed him just once, but oh what a kiss!"

Robby and Billy the Kid. As they laced their skates and taped new
sticks, I told them the story of my poor face. Robby laughed at first, then
got serious.

"Want me to get him?"

"No, it's okay."

"Never liked him much anyway."

"Yeah," Billy the Kid said, "but he loves you, madly, the unspoken
passion driving him to ... "

"Fuck off Semeniuk. I don't like him 'cause the son of a bitch bit my
leg in a pile up. If you want me to, Crapper, I'll fuckin' kill him."

"I'm going to get Clark," I said, "all by myself."

"Thata boy Crapper," Robby approved. "You whip his ass real good."

"Forget it," Billy the Kid said.

Robby gave him a nasty look.

"Really, forget it. It's no great tragedy. Leave it alone. You get him. His
brother gets you. Robby gets him. Somebody gets Robby. Blackjack man-
gles that somebody and so on and so on. Forget it."

"That's chickenshit Semeniuk, that's bullshit." Robby was almost angry.

"Listen numbnuts, there's enough trouble in a lifetime without looking
for extra. Skip the grief. All I'm saying is 'be cool, don't get all shook
up.'"

Billy the Kid whipped his arm across his hockey stick like it was a
guitar and he was Elvis. He dropped to his knees.

"I'm in love," he sang, "I'm all shook up."

Robby fired a puck at Billy the Kid, who, after ducking, transformed
his stick into a machine gun. Robby hit the ice laughing.

"So Mr. Krapko." Billy the Kid looked at me. "Leave it alone. Let him
come to you. Don't ever go looking for it. If he comes after you, it no
longer has anything to do with his big brother, right?"

His logic was lost on me, but not his eyes, or his voice, or the way he
carried the puck as he spoke. I believed what he said but I also had to
believe in revenge for a while yet, at least until my face healed.

"Wanna put on the pads?" Robby asked. "You're ugly enough to be a
goalie."

"Nope."

Before he could insist, Pinka arrived. I was off the hook, but had to
explain my face again. Pinka figured all the Bonks were "a bunch of

peckers." I was getting nothing but sympathy. Pinka even offered me a cigarette, a wonderful gesture, considering they were like gold coins in his pocket. He looked relieved when I said no.

We passed the puck around. Picked the corners. Thumped Pinka's pads. We needed more bodies for a game. Billy the Kid Semeniuk directed the conversation. No one pretended to understand what he was talking about. No one cared, but we all listened.

"So you see," he completed the first dissertation, "any kid without an instinctive understanding of the game is genetically un-Canadian."

"Eat my shorts, professor," Pinka mumbled.

"Hockey's in our blood," Billy the Kid added.

"So how come all of us ain't in the NHL," Robby wanted to know.

"What I said, butternuts, is that we all have an understanding. Not everyone has the skills."

"Big fuckin' deal." Pinka wasn't impressed.

"But the game's losing its purity."

"What!" Robby demanded.

"Too much money. It's taking over."

"Fuck off Semeniuk, it's a job, they gotta get paid."

"I know. So it's no longer a game. And all of us have to grow up." Billy the Kid laughed, but it wasn't a real laugh.

"You're nuts, Semeniuk."

"Sure," Billy the Kid agreed, then changed the subject. "Howe got three last night."

"Frogs win?" Pinka asked.

"Yeah."

"Nobody'll touch 'em," Pinka said.

"You're right."

"Fuckin' French punks!"

"Not punks; puck," Billy the Kid said. "Puck artists, those Canadiens, like yours truly," and took a bow.

Pinka did the splits, kicking out Billy the Kid's low shot. Billy picked up the rebound, and without looking put the puck on my stick. I was amazed.

"Did ya hear about Zenny?" Robby said.

"What?"

"Got new seat covers, white ones."

"Everybody knows that," Billy the Kid said.

"Yeah? What about Friday night?"

"What about it?"

"Carol's on the rag, right? All over his new seat covers."

Robby and Pinka howled over that. Billy the Kid only smiled.

"Hope he got plugged in," Pinka choked.

"That's terrible." Robby stuck his finger down his throat. "On the rag? Ugh! Blah!"

"Actually," Billy the Kid was looking studious again, "they get very hot during that time, particularly at the end of the period."

"Yeah," Pinka chortled, "'specially if they're on the power play."

That broke Robby up all over again.

"You're nuts Semeniuk," he spat.

"I know, I know." Billy the Kid was getting touchy. "So I'm nuts, but what I say is t.r.u.e."

"They're different, man, they really are. We get a hard on, bang! Let's go. It takes them more time. You wanna know something? They get a kind of hard on too. They do."

"Fuck off."

"You're nuts."

I'd followed the conversation through "the rag" and "getting plugged in." I understood all that, but this new angle confused me. Again, I wanted to believe Billy the Kid; Pinka and Robby insisted he was making it all up. I thought of mean old Sharon Martinyuk with a hard on, and it seemed possible.

"No, listen you guys." Billy the Kid appeared very serious, his voice edgy. "There's this thing they have, a little organ, right! sort of a bud, and it's like a miniature cock. Like a magic button. Rub it, drives them crazy!"

That was too much. Pinka and Robby cracked up. Billy the Kid split a gut; holding his sides, he swore what he said was the truth, and nothing but. The laughter, of course, was contagious. I caught it. Dash arrived, and fell into it.

"Better than a punch in the face, huh Kid?" Billy the Kid winked at me.

I believed it was. Billy the Kid continued, giving us terms for the exotic things he described. I believed everything the puck artist said. His words inspired my bedtime movie that night. I lined up the girls at school, my cousins, and even more bold, I pictured grown women and tried to find their hidden little organs. I forgot about hockey. The songs on the radio seemed closer, blending easier with what I was thinking, fitting better now than they had with the Forum fantasies. For the first time, the songs became the soundtrack. The hockey passion was suddenly tempered. I had to know about Buddy Holly. I had to know about the wetness Billy the Kid so eloquently described. The new ideal, to be like him, required three things: skates, more sweet music and the warmth of a strange new escape.

an excerpt from the novel *The Saxophone Winter*

❖   ROBERT HARLOW

The town had grown up so that it had two centres. Up-town there were the school grounds and the residential streets. Downtown clustered around the civic hall, which stood in a little park, and the streets — all named after British cities — connected downtown with uptown. The river came in from the west and curved south so that it held the whole community in the crook of its arm. At the southwest was a range of a half-dozen hills called the Castles because they stood as if separate from each other, although they weren't. The smaller five hills were good for downhill skiing; the central and tallest hill had a ninety-foot trestle on top of it, used by the men who jumped on Sundays for a ten dollar prize, winner take all. Halfway down the hill's left-hand side there was another jump built into the slope which was called the boy's jump, and at the bottom of the hill, was a meadow that ran all the way into town and stopped at the skating rink. Long River was very compact, miniature. Its population was maybe four thousand, and without the highway, railroad, cement plant and the lumber mills further west along the river, where it seldom flooded, there would be no reason for its existence. The plant and the mills worked short shifts now, when they worked at all.

Christopher's father was General Foreman under Harrison Dodd, the Municipal Engineer, whose department looked after the powerhouse, the water system, the roads, the streetlights and the sidewalks. It wasn't the job he should have had, but it was a good one in 1938. Fielder's father had a two-ton truck, only it was owned by the Royal Bank.

When he walked from his house on York Street to downtown, Christopher had to pass first the half-burned high school and the two-storey elementary school. When he and Fielder headed down from Field-er's place over on Sheffield to go skating, they often wanted to go into the school and look around, but they didn't dare. Evil-eye Grandison came by every hour, as if it were his duty to guard the place from vandals.

He and Fielder walked on past the school with their skates slung over their shoulders. The outdoor rink opened during the holidays at two-thirty and closed down at five-thirty and then opened again from seven o'clock to ten o'clock. Howard Streeter, who was old enough to have grey hair, ran it with the help of some rink rats who got free skate time and sometimes a little money for scraping the ice and shovelling snow off it after a storm. Howard seldom left his ticket booth and candy shop, which was between the women's and the men's dressing rooms, except to kick someone out. He wore laced rubber hightop boots with his pants tucked down into them. He didn't just point the way when he told some-one to leave, he kicked them and kept on kicking them until they were out the door. His rubber boots did double duty. They weren't so hard-toed that they did any real damage to those they came in contact with, and they kept his feet dry when he was out on the rink with the hose making ice.

Fielder never did anything unless he could do it well. He could shoot marbles, play basketball, play lacrosse and skate. He didn't have skis and his mother sent him by bus to his grandparents at the coast in the sum-mers, so Christopher had never seen him swim or dive. The rink was crowded. Fielder never just entered a room, he plunged in, especially into a room full of people bigger than he was. The rink was a place where those who had quit school and didn't have a job hung out. All of them were over sixteen; some were over twenty. It was a long day for them. They had to come early to sweep the ice, shovel snow, sweep the floors, build fires and then reserve a place on the benches that were nailed to the walls on both sides of the dressing room.

It was important to follow Fielder's natural example at the rink. The rats sat around looking as if they were just going to go to sleep, but if someone came in hesitant and alone, one of them would ask, "What d'you think you're doing? Hey look what's here. Didn't you hear? No York Street snots allowed in today, especially you." Everything stopped then — no skates were laced or tightened, people heading out the door onto the rink turned to watch, everybody on the benches sat up, and Howard Streeter pretended not to notice.

The rat couldn't throw you out. Your nickel was already paid. But you didn't say that and spoil his fun. You sat down near the door and took your boots off and stuffed them under the bench where ten other pairs were. There was silence, which was part of it.

"Going to take a hint, kid?"

One word in reply was an excuse to get worse than you were already going to get. And there was no appeal. Howard's reply was always, "Go tell you mommy." And there was no hurry; it kept on happening whether something was done or not. The worst thing they could do was shove you down the hole in the outhouse attached to the far end of the dressing room. Not all the way down, but close enough to make you think you were going to wind up in ten feet of shit at the bottom.

The idea was to take it. Say you did do something in retaliation and somehow won — only a fantasy, because no one ever did win — say you called the police or your parents, you'd be decked after that every time you came around a corner, or worse. Stories in *Chums Annual*, or *Triumph*, or *The American Boy* where the little guy stood up to the bully and won were stupid. In real life there wasn't an end to the story; it kept right on happening. There were two ways out: one was to put your head the down and wait until they were through with you, and the other was to grow big enough to join them. Or not.

Fielder sat down and began to put on his skates. No one picked on him. It was a kind of class thing, or maybe it had to do with being powerful in a certain way. The Police Chief's kid got it the worst. The Magistrate had four boys and they travelled together.

Christopher sat beside Fielder and unlaced his boots. John Purvis was there on the bench down at the back of the room. He coughed and got up and came over. He was nearly eighteen now. He'd quit school when he was still fifteen, but not because he was dull. He never gave a reason.

"I got four from Paraguay." He reached into his jacket pocket. "I ordered a bunch on approval. Look. Twenty-five cents."

The stamps had yellows and purples and bright blues and reds on them. "You gonna get them?"

"The old man's away again."

Christopher nodded. John's father's second wife looked like a hen with glasses on and didn't want to fix meals for him, let alone give him money for his stamp collection. She had married John's widowed father, who was a commercial traveller, and had her own children since. Sometimes she locked the doors on John, and Howard let him stay and keep the fire going all night so he could sleep on the bench nearest it.

Purvis had a face like a rising moon. It was big — big eyes, mouth, teeth — and its skin was yellow with a tinge of orange. Somewhere in the Purvis family there was Indian blood.

Now he said to Purvis, "I've never bought a Paraguay."

"Do you like these? Four for two-bits is a bargain."

"We could buy two each?"

"I'm broke."

"I could lend you. I've been saving."

Purvis got up. "No thanks. They don't have to go back until December 27th." He coughed and laughed at the same time. "Maybe I'll get a dollar out of the old man when he goes on his Christmas drunk."

"Hope so. Those are good ones. Are you skating?"

"No. I'm making ice for Howard at the supper break."

Fielder got up. "Going to skate or collect stamps?"

"Both."

"The joint closes at five-thirty."

"Go then, go."

He stood up and looked out onto the ice. There were maybe a hundred people there, going around and around to the waltz music Howard played through a loudspeaker connected to his gramophone. Outside, a fence surrounded the rink. The boards were grey, weathered, twelve feet tall. Fielder was already warmed up and flying. Backward, forward, quick loops and on to full speed again, dodging between people and bouncing off the boards. It was good exercise for hockey, and it was a game: seeing how fast he could go before Flynn, Howard's rat on the ice, whistled him off.

Christopher left the gate and began to skate stiffly down the boards, and then out into the middle where the ice was nearly clear of people. He rode his skates hard and got them comfortable on his feet. Fielder went by. He chased him, caught him, gave him a hip and sent him into the boards. Fielder came back, grabbed him, and they tripped and fell. People swerved and skated around them. They lay dead on the ice. Callaghan jumped them, and then Christopher looked up and saw Emily swerve away, unsteady on her skates, and hold onto the boards. Flynn's whistle sounded. Christopher jumped up and stood beside Emily. Flynn ushered Fielder off the ice and signalled for Christopher to follow. He took Emily's arm and held her up. "Come on," he said. "Flynn won't touch me if I'm helping you."

She laughed. "I'm not very good at skating." Her face was red. He held her left hand in his left and put his arm around her, because that was the thing to do, and they moved off, not quite in time with the music. He hadn't skated with a girl before, let alone put his arm around one, except when Miss Garrett was invited by Blenkin to come to P.E. to teach them ballroom dancing. Last time, he'd got Monica Lewis to waltz with.

Every now and then she tripped, but he managed to hold her up until she was able to skate again. They were beginning to laugh, and Emily was more relaxed. Flynn appeared in front of them, skating backward. "I told you to get off."

"Come on, I'm not bothering anybody."

"I put Fielder off." He looked righteous. "Got to be fair." He was the oldest of the rats, and on the ice he sounded like a schoolteacher.

Emily pulled away and stopped at the gate to the women's dressing room. "Thanks," she said.

"I'll be back," he told her.

"Not until the next change," Flynn said.

Christopher went inside and saw that Fielder was pitching pennies with Smith. Obviously, he was winning, because Smith wanted to go double or nothing. Fielder nodded and pitched to within an inch of the wall. "Emily Gordon?" he said, while Smith was getting set to pitch.

"We're friends," Christopher said, not sure where the words or the easy tone of voice came from.

"Since when?"

He decided on the truth. "Since the fire."

"I was at the fire."

"Afterward."

Smith pitched. His one-cent piece hit the wall and then it spun in a circle and fell closer than Fielder's.

"Does that count?" Fielder said, too loud.

"Tricky," Smith said. "Come on, gimme."

Fielder gave him four cents and sat down on the bench.

The music stopped, the whistle sounded out on the ice, the people reversed and skated the other way to a new waltz. Christopher got up and went outside. The sun was far gone. In a few minutes the lights would be turned on. He looked up. The clouds over the river were thickening. It might snow. He hoped so. The hills out at the Castles needed another foot or two to make for really good jumping.

He wanted to see Emily again. Saying they were friends in front of Fielder and Smith had released a new feeling in him. He skated hard to hold the emotion down until he saw her in the crowd with Dody Wentworth. They were skating slow and easy. Emily's ankles were strong; her skates stood straight on the ice. He cut in front and faced them while he skated backwards. "You just never tried very hard before," he said to Emily. She looked pleased, and he watched her eyes watch him as she skated to the music.

"Were you skating with him?" Dody asked.

"Until he got kicked off."

"Kicked off?" She made it sound as if he'd won a prize. Emily wanted to skate with him. He could see it in her eyes. She glanced at Dody, and Dody's face grinned. "What is this, huh? Who do I get to skate with?"

"Be on the other side," Emily said.

He turned and skated forward again. Emily was on his right and Dody, laughing so hard she was sliding around instead of skating, held onto his left arm. It was hard going, awkward. Dody never got in step and kept giving him the hip as if they were playing hockey. Emily stood straight on her skates and went stiffly forward. In the middle, he was off balance. People were beginning to look. The lights came on and their shadows flickered around them as they moved along the ice. Dody got control of herself, and then she saw Trudy Olson skating alone. "Bye, you two," she said in a loud voice, pronouncing them gossip, and left to tell Trudy about it. He didn't mind. Fielder and Smith knew. Dody and now Trudy knew.

He looked at Emily, and she said, "Dody's a nut."

He skated with her, his gut-muscles tight and his breath short. It began to snow. The flakes were dry and powdery. By the time they'd gone around twice more the rink was white; there was snow in her hair and, when she looked up at him, he could see it sparkling on her eyelashes. He put his arm around her and said, "Let's see how fast you can skate."

She nodded. "And then I have to go."

He sped up gradually, and she skated with him until the first corner, then she coasted around it. On the next straightaway she couldn't keep up; she collapsed and hung on so that he stopped skating and they coasted until they came to a halt at the women's dressing room.

"Thanks," she said.

"This is the third time — " he stopped, awkward.

"For what?"

"Parting," he said, and had to laugh. "I mean, you never say goodbye. Just thanks."

She frowned.

"Are you going home alone?"

"With Dody."

He did a perfect circle on his skates and wound up in front of her again. "Well, see you."

"Walk with us," she said. Her voice had a low note that made it soft at the edges.

He did the circle again. People had to get out of his way and, as he went past her going into the loop, he told her Yes, and he didn't see her going into the dressing room because he was hit and knocked down by a pair who were waltzing. Flynn blew his whistle. "That's it for you. Off, get the hell off."

"Quit picking on me," he shouted.

Flynn looked at him, surprised. "Kid, do what I say or I'll break your damned arm." But there was a small smile on his face.

Christopher laughed, and ran on the points of his skates at Flynn, dodged him and headed for the gate. It felt as if suddenly everyone was saying "Yes."

Half the rink was getting ready to leave. He got down on his knees and felt under the bench where he'd left his boots. Smith and Callaghan were sitting there. "Move," he said, and found them. "Where's Fielder?" Smith pointed. He looked around; Fielder was eating a chocolate bar. "You win?"

Fielder nodded, and Smith said, "There's something stupid about double or nothing. Ineluctably, aromatically stupid." His act was big words. He found them in his dictionary and used them any which way.

"It's okay when you win," Fielder told him.

"Punch him out," Callaghan said.

Fielder began to move. Callaghan and Smith stood up, and Smith grabbed at the chocolate bar before Fielder could get to the door.

Christopher wedged himself between them and put an elbow in Smith's chest. Fielder shoved Callaghan out of the way.

"Outside," Howard shouted from the candy counter. "And watch that hot stove." He sounded like everybody's parents.

They stopped shoving, and Fielder escaped through the door to the rink. Christopher went after him. When they were on the ice, he said, "I'm going with Emily."

Flynn was there. "What did I tell you, Waterton?"

"I'm going. I'm going." He still had his boots in his hands to show him. To Fielder, he said, "Want to come? Dody Wentworth's with her."

Fielder looked at him. "What's going on?"

"Nothing. She invited me."

"Emily did?"

"And Dody's with her. Come on."

Fielder skated in a circle. "I can't figure you, Waterton. They're in Grade Eight, eh? Bloody cradle-snatcher."

"Are you coming?"

"No."

"All you have to do is walk with her."

Fielder skated away. It was snowing hard. Howard would close the rink soon. He had a cowbell he rang that meant time was up. Christopher skated back to the door and went in. Smith and Callaghan were gone. He knew what was going to happen now, and it made him wish he hadn't asked Fielder to come. He'd go with them all right, but it would be in his own time and they'd be kept waiting. He changed into his boots and dunked his skates in the tin tub of hot water on top of the stove to get them clean. The door opened a dozen times, and then finally Fielder came in.

"Too late," Christopher told him.

"Don't give me that, Waterton."

"Are you coming?"

"Maybe."

"They're waiting." He could see Dody standing near the entrance of the women's dressing room.

"Where's my boots?"

"How am I supposed to know?"

"We came in together."

"They're beside where mine were." Christopher pointed, then bent over and fished them out.

Fielder sat down and took his skates off. Now Emily was at the women's entrance too.

"Dody Wentworth," Fielder said. "The things you do for a friend."

"Hurry up. They'll leave."

"Why don't I walk with Emily and you go with Dody?"

"Come on, Fielder."

"Keep you out of mischief."

Christopher tied the laces of his skates together and hung them over his shoulder.

He waved at Emily and held up one finger to show they'd be right there.

They moved together to the main exit door. Dody's eyes were big and she was quiet, as if that were protection — like a rabbit in the snow. Emily stood solid as she always did. "Fielder's coming too," he said. He opened the door, and Fielder went out first.

"You open doors real good," he said.

Dody laughed and caught up with him. She was no more than an inch taller than Emily, but she was loose at the hips and the shoulders. Gangly. She stood beside Fielder, looked up at him and then turned to Emily with her eyes wide open and her hand over her mouth. Emily didn't react. She looked away from her and up into Christopher's face. Then she smiled, confused a little by Dody and Fielder. It was a serious thing she'd done and the smile trusted that he wasn't just funny like Fielder was being. They began to walk, and her mitt, wedged between his elbow and his ribs, was a sensation he'd not felt before.

Hockey Night in Canada

❖   DIANE SCHOEMPERLEN

We settled ourselves in our usual places, my father and I, while the singer made his way out onto the ice and the organist cranked up for "O Canada" and "The Star Spangled Banner." Saturday night and we were ready for anything, my father half-sitting, half-lying on the chesterfield with his first dark rum and Pepsi, and me in the swivel chair beside the picture window with a box of barbecue chips and a glass of 7Up.

My mother was ripping apart with relish a red-and-white polka dot dress she hadn't worn for years. There were matching red shoes, purse and a hat once too, but they'd already been packed or given away. Trying to interest someone in her project and her practicality, she said, "Why, this fabric is just as good as new," pulling first one sleeve, then the other, away from the body of the dress.

But the game was starting and we were already intent on the screen and each other.

"They don't stand a chance tonight," I said, shaking my head sadly but with confidence as the players skated out.

My father grinned calmly and took a drink of rum.

"Not a chance," I prodded.

"We'll see, we'll just see about that." Even when they played poorly for weeks on end, my father remained cheerfully loyal to the Chicago Black Hawks, for no particular reason I could see, except that he always had been. He must have suffered secret doubts about the team now and then — anyone would — but he never let on. I, having no similar special allegiance and wanting to keep the evening interesting, always hoped for the other team.

We were not violent fans, either one of us. We never hollered, leaped out of our chairs, or pounded ourselves in alternating fits of frustration

84

and ecstasy. We did not jump up and down yelling, "Kill him, kill him!" Instead, we were teasing fans, pretend fans almost, feigning hostility and heartbreak, smirking and groaning gruesomely by turns, exaggerating our reactions mainly for the benefit of the other and sometimes just to get a rise out of my mother, who was by this time humming with pins in her mouth, smoothing pattern pieces onto the remains of the dress, and snipping merrily away with the pinking shears, while scraps of cloth and tissue paper drifted to the floor all around her.

The dress, I discovered, was to be reincarnated as a blouse for me, a blouse which, by the time it was finished (perfectly, seams all basted and bound, hem hand-done), I would probably hate. Between periods, she took me into the bathroom for a fitting session in front of the full-length mirror. I did not breathe, complain or look as she pinned the blouse together around me, a piece at a time, one sleeve, the other, half the front, the other half, back, collar, the cold silver pins scratching my bare skin just lightly.

By the time we got to the three-star selection after the game, my mother was off to the back bedroom with the blouse, whirring away on the Singer.

When her friend Rita was there, my mother at least played at watching the game. Whenever the crowd roared, my father groaned and Rita began to shriek, my mother would look up from her stamp collection, which she was endlessly sorting and sticking and spreading all over the card table, and smile encouragement at the TV.

"Who scored?" she asked innocently, as she put another page in her album and arranged another row of stamps across it. Russia was her favourite country for collecting, the best because their stamps were bigger and grander than any, especially ours, which looked stingy and common by comparison. The Russians had hockey players, cosmonauts, fruits and vegetables, wild animals, trucks and ballerinas, in red, blue, green, yellow, and even shiny silver and gold. We had mainly the Queen in pastels. My mother's everyday fear and loathing of Communists did not enter into the matter.

"Just guess, Violet, just you guess who scored!" Rita crowed.

"Don't ask," my father muttered.

"Most goals, one team, one game," Rita recited. "Twenty-one, Montreal Canadians, March 3, 1920, at Montreal, defeated the Quebec Bulldogs 16 to 3."

"Ancient history," said my father. "Besides, who ever heard of the Quebec Bulldogs anyway? You're making it all up, Rita. Tell me another one."

"Fewest points, one season," Rita chanted. "Thirty-one, Chicago Black Hawks, 1953-54, won twelve, lost thirty-six, tied four."

"Not quite what I had in mind." My father rolled his big eyes and went into the kitchen to fix more drinks, one for himself and one for Rita, who took her rum with orange juice, no ice. I said nothing, not being sure yet whether I wanted to stick up for my father or fall in love with the Canadiens too.

Rita had followed the Montreal team for years. Unlike my father and me, she was a *real* fan, a serious fan who shrieked and howled and paced around the living room, calling the players by their first names, begging them to score, willing them to win with clenched fists and teeth. She did not consider her everyday dislike of those Frenchmen (as in, "I've got no use for those Frenchmen, no use at all") to be contradictory. Hockey, like stamp collecting, it seemed, was a world apart, immune to the regular prejudices of race, province and country — although she did sometimes berate my father for siding with a Yankee team.

When the Black Hawks lost another one, Rita and I (for I'd been won over after all by her braying) took all the credit for knowing the better team right off the bat, and heaped all the blame upon my father who was now in disgrace along with his team — a position he took rather well. When they did win, as far as he was concerned, it was all or mainly because he'd never given up on them.

After the game my father and I usually played a few hands of poker, a penny a game, with the cards spread out on the chesterfield between us. My mother and Rita were in the kitchen having coffee and maybe a cream puff. The hum of their voices came to me just vaguely, like perfume. I wanted to hear what they were saying but my father was analyzing the last power play and dealing me another hand. I won more often than not, piling up my pennies. For years after this I would think of myself as lucky at cards. In certain difficult situations which showed a disturbing tendency to repeat themselves, I would often be reminded of Rita's teasing warning: "Lucky at cards, unlucky at love."

Later, after Rita had gone home, I would find the ashtray full of lipstick-tipped butts which I pored over, looking for clues.

My mother had met Rita that summer at Eaton's where Rita was working at the Cosmetics counter. Rita still worked at Eaton's, but she was in Ladies Dresses now, having passed briefly through Lingerie and Swimwear in between.

To hear Rita tell it, you'd think their whole friendship was rooted in my mother's hair.

"I just couldn't help myself," Rita said, telling me that story. "There I was trying to convince this fat lady that all she really needed was a bottle of Cover Girl and some Midnight Blue mascara and up walked your mother with her hair."

Patting her hair fondly, my mother said, "I couldn't figure out what she was staring at."

I already knew that before Rita had come to live in Hastings, she was a hairdresser in Toronto. She'd been to hairdressing school for two years and still took the occasional special course in cold waves or colouring. She was about to open her own beauty parlour just when her husband Geoffrey killed himself and everything was changed. It was not long afterwards that Rita gave up hairdressing and moved to Hastings to stay with her younger sister, Jeanette. Six months after that Jeanette married a doctor and moved back to Toronto. But Rita stayed on in Hastings anyway, bought herself a second-hand car and rented an apartment downtown in the Barclay Block above an Italian bakery (which was the very same building my parents had lived in when they were first married, a fact that I found significant and somehow too good to be true).

My mother always did her own hair, putting it up in pincurls every Sunday night so that it lay in lustrous black waves all round her face and rolled thickly down past her shoulders in the back. But what Rita meant was the streak, a pure white streak in the front from the time she'd had ringworm when she was small. Even I had to admit it looked splendid and daring, although there were times when we were fighting and I wanted to hurt her and tell her she looked like a skunk. Rita's own hair was straggly and thin, half-dead from too many washings, a strange salmon colour, growing out blonde, from too many experiments. Her bangs hung down almost to her eyebrows. Sometimes she wore them swept back with coloured barrettes, revealing the delicate blue veins in her temples.

"Anyway," Rita said, pausing to light another cigarette with her Zippo, "I finally got rid of the fat lady and your mother and I got talking. Just seeing her hair gave me the itch again — I could just picture all the things I could do with that hair. We went up to the cafeteria for coffee — "

"And we've been friends ever since," my mother said in a pleased and final-sounding voice, the way you might say, And they all lived happily ever after.

My mother had never really had a friend of her own before. Oh, there was a neighbour lady, Mrs. Kent three doors down, who would come over once in a while to borrow things that she never returned — the angel food cake pan, the egg beater, the four-side cheese grater. And so my mother would go over to Mrs. Kent's house occasionally too, to get the things back. But it was never what you would call a friendship, so much as a case of proximity and Mrs. Kent's kitchen being sadly ill-equipped.

I had never seriously thought of my mother as wanting or needing a friend anyway. Friends, particularly best friends, I gathered, were something you grew out of soon after you got married and had children. After that, the husband and the children became your best friends, or were supposed to.

But then she met Rita and it was as though Rita were someone she had been just waiting for, saving herself up for all those years. They told each other old stories and secrets, made plans, remembered times before when they might have met, had just missed each other, almost met, but didn't. Rita was at least ten years younger than my mother. I suppose I thought of her as doing my mother a favour by being her friend. In the way of young girls, I just naturally imagined my mother to be the needy one of the two.

When Rita was in Cosmetics, she would bring my mother make-up samples that the salesmen had left: mascara, blusher, eyebrow pencils and sometimes half-empty perfume testers for me. And her pale face was perfect. Once she moved to Ladies Dresses, she hardly ever wore slacks anymore, except when the weather turned cold. She was always trying out bold new accessories, big belts, coloured stockings, high-heeled boots. I could only imagine what she'd bought while she worked in Lingerie — the most elegant underwear, I supposed, and coloured girdles (I didn't know if there were such things for sure, but if there were, Rita would have several), and marvellous gauzy nightgowns.

On her day off during the week Rita was usually there in the kitchen when I came home from school for lunch. While my mother fixed me a can of soup and a grilled cheese sandwich, Rita sipped black coffee and nibbled on fresh fruit and cottage cheese. This was the first I knew of dieting as a permanent condition, for although Rita was quite slim and long-legged, she was always watching her weight. My mother, who was much rounder than Rita anyway, had taken up dieting too, like a new hobby which required supplies of lettuce, pink grapefruit and detailed diet books listing menus, recipes and calories. She'd begun to compliment me on my extreme thinness, when not so many years before she'd made me wear two crinolines to school so the teachers wouldn't think she didn't feed me. How was it that, without changing size or shape, I had graduated from grotesque to slender?

"How's school going this week?" Rita would ask, offering me a tiny cube of pineapple, which I hated.

She listened patiently, nodding and frowning mildly, while I told her about Miss Morton, the gym teacher who hated me because I was no good at basketball; and about my best friend Mary Yurick who was madly in love with Lorne Puhalski, captain of the hockey team and unattainable; and about everybody's enemy, Bonnie Ettinger, who'd beat up Della

White on Monday in the alley behind the school.

It was easy to get carried away with such confidences in the hope that Rita would reciprocate, and I almost told her that I was in love with Lorne Puhalski too, and that Bonnie Ettinger was going around saying she'd knock my block off if she ever got the chance. But I talked myself out of it at the last minute. I wanted so much to have Rita all to myself but somehow it never was arranged.

With Rita there, my mother could listen to my problems without worrying too much or wanting to do something about them. She and I probably learned more about each other from those kitchen conversations with Rita than we ever could have any other way.

Sometimes it was as though they'd forgotten all about me. One day when I came home for lunch my mother was sitting wrapped in a sheet on the high stool in the middle of the kitchen while Rita gave her a cold wave, something she'd been threatening to do for weeks. I made my own sandwich.

My mother was saying, "I was so young then, and everybody said I was pretty. We were in love but when they found out, they shipped him off to agricultural school in Winnipeg. I still think Sonny was my own true love."

"What about Ted?" Rita asked, wrapping pieces of hair in what looked like cigarette rolling papers and then winding them nimbly onto pink plastic rods.

"Oh, Ted."

Ted was my father of course, but it was strange to hear my mother call him by his name when usually she called him "Dad" or "your Dad."

"Yes, well, Ted. That was different. I was older. I'm even older now. I didn't tell Ted about Sonny until long after we were married."

I went back to school that afternoon with a picture of my mother as another person altogether, someone I had never met and never would now. This woman, mysterious, incomplete and broken-hearted, pestered me all day long. The stink of the cold wave chemicals lingered too, bitter but promising.

At other times it was as though my mother could tell me things through Rita that she could never have expressed if we were alone.

One Saturday night after the hockey game I left my father dozing on the chesterfield and went into the kitchen.

Rita was saying, "When Geoffrey hung himself, his whole family blamed me. They said I'd driven him to do it. They kept bringing up the baby who died and then Geoffrey too, as if I'd murdered them both with my bare hands. I had a nervous breakdown and they said it served me right. It was then that I realized I would have to leave town." She spoke calmly, looking down at her lap, not moving, and a sense of young tragic death wound around her like scented bandages, permanent and disfiguring, the way Japanese women used to bind their feet to keep them dainty. She was doomed somehow, I could see that now, even though I'd never noticed it before.

"You have to be strong, we all have to be strong," my mother said without looking at me. "We're the women, we have to be stronger than they think we are."

I could hear my father snoring lightly in the other room, no longer harmless. The kitchen was snug with yellow light. The window was patterned with frost like feathers or ferns and it was just starting to snow. My mother pulled the blind down so no one could see in. We could have been anywhere, just the three of us, bending in together around the kitchen table, knowing things, these sad things, that no one else knew yet.

That night Rita slept over. An odd thing for grown-ups to do, I thought, but I liked it.

After I'd gone to bed, it reminded me of Christmas: something special waiting all night long in the living room: the tree, the unopened presents, Rita in my mothers new nightie wrapped up in an old car blanket on the chesterfield.

Around the middle of December, Rita flew to Toronto to have Christmas with her sister Jeanette and her doctor husband. My mother had somehow not considered exchanging presents with Rita and was horrified when she appeared the morning she left with three gaily-wrapped boxes, one for each of us. Even more surprising was my father, who handed Rita a little package tied up with curly red ribbons. She opened it on the spot, still standing in the doorway, and produced a silver charm of the Montreal Canadiens' crest.

On Christmas morning we opened her presents first. She'd given my mother a white silk scarf handpainted with an ocean scene in vivid blues and greens. My father held up a red Chicago Black Hawks jersey with the Indian head on the front and the number 21 on the back. I got a leather-covered date book for the new year in which I immediately noted the birthdays of everyone I could think of. Rita's presents were the best ones that year.

After dinner, we called all our relatives in Manitoba and then my mother took some pictures of the tree, of my father in his new hockey sweater and of me eating my dessert behind the chicken carcass. My friend Mary called and we told each other everything we got. I thought Rita might call later but she didn't.

Between Christmas and New Year's my mother went out and bought a braided gold necklace to give to Rita when she got back. The silver charm was never discussed in front of me.

Not long after Rita returned from her holidays, she was moved from Ladies Dresses into Ladies Coats. Now when she came over she wore a knee-length black coat trimmed with grey Persian lamb at the collar and cuffs. She always hesitated before taking it off, caressing the curly lapels, picking invisible lint off the back, giving my mother and I just enough time to notice and admire it again. She knew a lot about mink and ermine now, how the little things were bred and raised on special farms, how vicious they were, how many tiny pelts it took to make just one coat. She lusted uncontrollably, as she put it, after one particular mink coat in her department but had resigned herself to never being able to afford it and seemed both relieved and disappointed the day it was bought by some doctor's wife.

"Just between you and I," my mother said right after Rita phoned to say she'd sold the fabulous coat, "I think mink is a waste of money. It's only for snobs. I wouldn't wear one if you gave it to me." Ten years later, my father bought her a mink jacket trimmed with ermine and she said, hugging him, "Oh Ted, I've always wanted one."

It was an extravagant winter, with new records set for both snow and all-time low temperatures. My father seemed to be always outside shovelling snow in the dark, piling up huge icy banks all around the house. He would come in from the cold red-cheeked and handsome, trying to put his icy hands around my neck. Rita came over less and less often. She said it was because her car wouldn't start half the time, even when she kept it plugged in.

On warmer days when Rita wasn't working, my mother often took the bus downtown to her apartment. When I came home from school at three-thirty, the house would be luxuriously empty. I curled up on the chesterfield with the record player on and wrote in the date book Rita had given me or worked on the optimistic list my friend Mary and I had started: "One Thousand Things We Like." Well into its second spiral notebook, the list had passed seven hundred and was coming up quickly on eight with:

cuckoo clocks
Canada
lace
my mother's hair
comfortable underwear and
having a bath without interruptions

being the most recent additions.

My mother returned just in time to start supper before my father got home from work. She was distracted in a pleasant sort of way, all jazzed up and jingling from to much coffee or something, gabbing away gaily as she peeled the potatoes. Rita had given her some old clothes which could be made over into any number of new outfits for me. There was a reversible plaid skirt I'd always admired and wanted to wear right away but my mother said it was too old for me.

One Saturday afternoon when we had been out shopping together, my mother suggested we drop in on Rita before catching the bus home. I had never been to her apartment before and as we waked up Northern Avenue to the Barclay Block, I tried to imagine what it would be like. Small, I supposed, since Rita lived alone — and was, in fact, the only person I'd ever known who did. Such an arrangement was new to me then, a future possibility that became more and more attractive the more I thought about it. The apartment would be quite small, yes, and half-dark all the time, with huge exotic plants dangling in all the windows, shedding a humid green light everywhere. The rooms smelled of coffee and black earth. The furniture was probably old, cleverly draped with throws in vivid geometrics. The hardwood floors gleamed and in one room (which one?) the ceiling was painted a throbbing bloody red. I thought that Rita and I could have coffee there just the two of us (my mother having conveniently disappeared) and she would tell me everything I needed to know. Why did Geoffrey hang himself, what happened to the baby, do you go out with men sometimes, do you think I'm pretty, do you think I'm smart? She could tell my future like a fortune.

We climbed a steep flight of stairs up to the second floor. The smell of baking bread rose up cheesy and moist from the Italian bakery below. I'd forgotten that my parents had lived here once too, until my mother said, "I always hated that smell, we lived in 3B," and pointed to a door on the left. I could not imagine anything at all about their apartment.

My mother knocked loudly on Rita's door. Further down another door opened and a woman in her housecoat leaned out into the hall, expecting somebody, I guess, or maybe just spying. "Oh, it' s you. Hi," she said and ducked back inside.

My mother knocked again, and then once more.

"Maybe she's working," I offered.

"No, she's not. She definitely told me she was off today."

"Where can she be then?" I was pretty sure I could hear a radio going inside.

"How would I know?" my mother said angrily and sailed back down the hall.

Only once did I find my father and Rita alone in the house. I came home from Mary's late one Saturday afternoon and they were drinking rum at the kitchen table, with the record player turned up loud in the living room. They seemed neither surprised nor sorry to see me. There was something funny about Rita's eyes when she looked up at me though, a lazy softness, a shining, which I just naturally assumed to be an effect of the rum. She poured me a glass of 7Up and we sat around laying bets on the playoffs which were just starting, Montreal and St. Louis, until my mother came home from shopping. As it turned out, the Canadiens took the series four games straight that year and skated back to Montreal with the Stanley Cup.

Rita stayed for supper and then for the game. I went back over to Mary's and then her father drove us downtown to the Junior A game at the arena. Rita was gone by the time I got home and I went straight to bed because I'd had one shot of rye in Lorne Puhalski's father's car in the arena parking lot and I was afraid my mother, who still liked to kiss me goodnight, would smell it.

They were arguing as they got ready for bed.

"She lost her son, Violet, and then her husband too," my father said, meaning Rita, making her sound innocent but careless, always losing things, people too. But he was defending her, and himself too, protecting her from some accusation, himself from some threat that I'd missed, something unfair.

"Well, I *know* that, Ted."

"Don't forget it then."

"That's no excuse for anything, you fool."

"I didn't say it was."

"Be quiet, she'll hear you," my mother said, meaning me.

an excerpt from the novel *The Age of Longing*

❖   RICHARD B. WRIGHT

When I was three or four years old, I used to look for the Stanley Cup in my mother's china cabinet. This search arose from perhaps my earliest memory: my father is holding me under one arm while I grip the basin of a drinking fountain in Little Lake Park. With his free hand, my father presses the lever, and looking down I am both astonished and delighted by the cold water gushing from the white mica ball. Around me are the cries and laughter of the bathers and my mother's voice, insistent and hectoring, the voice of the schoolteacher who is used to issuing instruction or admonition.

"Be careful, Ross! Don't let his mouth touch that!"

For my mother, polio germs lurked everywhere, but especially in places touched by the lips of strangers. Drinking thirstily, I hear too the voices of children nearby.

"That's Buddy Wheeler. He played for Montreal and he won the Stanley Cup."

They are talking about the man who is holding me, my father. And where then was this cup he had won? Why was it not with the other cups in the kitchen cupboard or the china cabinet? Of course, those children got it slightly wrong as most of us do when we hear stories. My father did play four games in the National Hockey League with Montreal. But it was the year *after* they won the Stanley Cup. And I am referring to a Montreal team that is now only a glimmering memory for a few old people. They were called the Maroons.

This summer I returned to my mother's house to begin the sober task of tidying up after death. Even the frugal gather around them a remarkable array of possessions over a lifetime, and after sixty years a house is bound to be filled with things. Before others can move in and begin a life here, there must be a general clearing out. So much has to be retrieved from drawers and closets and then discarded. The lamps and beds, the chairs and tables can be sold to the second-hand furniture people, but no one wants an old woman's shoes or camisoles. They must be cast away, along with the blouses and cardigans, the cough syrup and hand cream, the scarves and winter coats, the jars of pickles in the cellar, the box of baking soda in the refrigerator; it all must go into garbage bags which I carry out to the street each Thursday. It is an arduous and depressing business for a middle-aged man who is trying to recover his health.

Improbable as it may sound, my mother and I both had heart attacks in the same week; as a matter of fact, they occurred within a day of each other, and Mother's, of course, was fatal. That was to be expected perhaps, for she was in her eighty-third year. The circumstances surrounding her death were rather gruesome; apparently she collapsed while preparing her breakfast and lay undetected on the kitchen floor for three days. It was June and unusually warm for early summer. Normally a neighbour looked in on her every day, but during that particular week she was out of town. It was just one of those bits of bad luck where a vicious irony seems to prevail over a sense of decency and order that against all evidence many still imagine to exist. By that I mean that it was not a fitting end to Mother's life. One could justifiably say, I suppose, that decomposing on a kitchen floor in the heat of early summer is scarcely an appropriate conclusion to anyone's life. But for Mother it was especially savage in its irony, for above all other virtues, her Presbyterian soul yearned most after order and tidiness. She was the sort of person who, after her evening bowl of bran flakes, washed and dried the spoon and dish before retiring. Her cheque-book on the top shelf of the secretary in the front hallway was accurate to the day she died. Her corpse was eventually discovered by a fellow from the gas company who had come in to clean the furnace.

I knew nothing of this for several days because I was confined to intensive care in the Toronto Hospital. My "coronary incident," as Dr. Khan insists on calling it, happened about nine in the morning, just before our sales conference for the fall list. I was alone in the washroom drying my hands, probably rehearsing (I can't remember) what I was going to say to the sales staff about my three books. I have done this sort of thing hundreds of times in my thirty years in publishing, though never without that surge of anxiety that always accompanies performance. So, I was drying my hands on the stiff white cloth of the roller towel when I felt suddenly burdened by a terrible fatigue. It seemed as though a great weight were pressing against me from within and my skin felt greasy.

When I looked in the mirror, I was appalled at my pale sweating face. Stepping carefully into one of the cubicles, I sat on a toilet seat cover, where I was found by a colleague and rushed to the hospital. I am enormously grateful for not being able to recall the melodrama of that trip in the ambulance with its siren and revolving light.

My illness then prevented me from going to the funeral which was sparsely attended. No surprise there. Mother made few friends in her life, and most of them had preceded her to the grave. She was one (I am another) who seemed to need few people around. Her last years in particular were almost completely solitary and she was not unhappy. I received a letter from the minister who buried her. A few months earlier Mother had told me that Knox Church now had a new man. He was, she said, "a little too evangelical to suit me." He would be the ninth man in the pulpit since she set foot in Knox Presbyterian Church as a child during the First World War.

June 20, 1994

Mr. Howard Wheeler
The Toronto Hospital
200 Elizabeth Street
Toronto, Ontario
M5G 2C4

Dear Mr. Wheeler:

It is with great sadness that I write to tell you of your mother's passing. A Mrs. Collins gave me your home and business numbers, and when I could not reach you at your residence, I phoned your place of business and spoke to a Ms. Macklin. She informed me of your sudden and unfortunate illness, and I send you my very best wishes for a speedy recovery, and the hope that God will bless you at this trying time in your life. Your mother's funeral was Monday. It was a beautiful summer day here in Georgian Bay. Although the service was not greatly attended, it was, I venture to suggest, moving. I chose 1 Corinthians, Chapter 15, where Paul speaks of God's gift of everlasting life.

For since by man came death, by man came also the resurrection of the dead. For as in Adam all die, even so in Christ shall all be made alive.

Between you and I, Mr. Wheeler, I did not have the opportunity to know your mother very well. I have only been serving now at Huron Falls for three months. But I did greet your mother each

Sunday after worship and fully intended to get around to seeing her on my home visits. Unfortunately time did not permit this. I had the impression, however, that your mother was a very independent person who provided leadership and learning to generations of schoolchildren in Huron Falls.

I am sure that she was a kind and caring person, and I imagine that hundreds of young people now grown to adulthood remember her with great affection.

I am sorry to learn of your double misfortune and I certainly hope that you are feeling better soon. When you have recovered and find yourself in Huron Falls, I hope you will drop by and say hello. Karen and I would be delighted to meet you.

Yours faithfully.

Barry Lawson, B.A., D.M.

I have inherited, no doubt from my mother, a critical disposition; over the years it has been useful in my vocation as book editor, though it has caused some distress in my life and certainly in the lives of those who have had to share time and space with me. Still, *between you and I?* You would think that a man of the cloth with a university education would have a better grasp of fundamental grammar. Mr. Lawson is also wrong about Mother. I am referring to that part of his letter in which he imagines her to have been a kind and caring person. Those are not exactly the words that come to mind when I attempt to describe her. Responsible and diligent are perhaps closer to the mark. Sober and critical and unsparing might do just as well. Certainly she did not inspire affection in her pupils, and I grew up under the shadow of their resentment over her forbidding manner in the classroom. I had few friends. As a child, Halloween was a night of watchful and humiliating anxiety. What would some of my schoolmates do to our property? Soap the windows? Scatter our garbage cans? Paint an obscenity on the garage door? Someone once left a human turd on a piece of newspaper on our veranda.

Only the other day I was thinking of the perpetrator of that vile act. It was during one of my walks along the streets of this town where I spent the first eighteen years of my life. Dr. Khan insists that I walk a brisk two miles a day as part of my recovery program. I was thinking during my walk that the person who deposited the excrement on our doorstep fifty or so years ago may very likely still be around. He would be my own age or slightly older, perhaps even the son or younger brother of the man who stopped me outside the legion. He was gruff and elderly, dressed in tan pants, work shirt and a Blue Jays cap. One of those quarrelsome old men whose age now protects him from the blows that he doubtless provokes and deserves each day in the beer hall. We stood talking under the sunlight of an August afternoon.

"You're Buddy Wheeler's boy, aren't you?" he asked, his fierce blue eyes fixing me in a glare.

In 1935 you could buy a Chevrolet Master Six for eight-hundred and fifty-four dollars and a cord of hardwood for twelve dollars. Someone named Ed would clean your chimney for seventy-five cents: Call Ed. Job guaranteed. The headline on the sports page for a Thursday in March of 1935 reads: "Wheeler Scores Three as Flyers Nip Port Edward 5-4 to Win Series." There is a picture of my father standing in his hockey gear beside the team owner and manager George W. Fowler who has his arm around my father's shoulders.

This man Fowler changed my father's life. He came to Huron Falls the summer my parents were married ... Fowler was then somewhere in his early fifties I would guess: a stocky man of medium height, an eater of steak and eggs, a teller of blue stories, a man among men in smoke-filled rooms. There is something a little proprietary and disdainful in the manner in which he embraces my father. This is a man who is used to having his way with his fellow creatures. In the meaty Rotarian face, you can still see the boarding-school bully who played left guard for the football team and flicked a towel at the backsides of rookies in the locker room. But whatever his failings as a human being, George Fowler had an eye for hockey talent, and in Buddy Wheeler he saw a player who may have reminded him of other swift light men on skates like Boucher and Joliat. Watching Buddy Wheeler dip and swirl among his teammates during those Sunday morning practices in October, Fowler may even have considered phoning Tommy Gorman. But Fowler wanted a championship team in his first year, and for that he needed Buddy Wheeler. He also had to bring in a player or two from beyond the league to strengthen what was already a fairly solid local team. By the end of October, a big defenceman named Red Hanna had joined the Flyers along with George Doucette, a speedy centre who had once played in the Can-Am League with Philadelphia and Providence.

That winter, while George Fowler sat behind the players' bench in his fur-collared coat and homburg, watching Red Hanna knock down opposing forwards, and the line of George Doucette, Cully Crawford and Buddy Wheeler score goals, my mother carried me within her and taught grade three pupils how to read and write and do their sums at Dufferin Street Public School. Although physically strong, she was often tired after a day in the classroom, walking along the snowy streets with a briefcase full of scribblers, arriving home to find her young husband still sleep. It was irksome. Supper was prepared and eaten in silence, the beginning of those festering silences that over the years would poison the air of our house.

My father still had no job, though there had been an offer from old Jim Stewart who was now reconciled to his daughter's choice of husband and lived alone, waiting for a grandchild, in a big house on Park Street. But my father was not keen on foundry labour. He worried about an accident: an iron pig dropping on his foot, or an injury to one of his hands. His season would be finished. There was no telling what could happen to a man in a foundry. He had talked to Mr. Fowler about it, and the owner had agreed that foundry work was not for Buddy Wheeler. Besides, there would probably be something for him at the car lot in the spring when things picked up, as they surely would. In the midst of the Depression, men like George Fowler always spoke about "things picking up" in the manner of those who are not particularly affected by hard times. "Things aren't so bad now, Bud, and they will get even better. You mark my words." When Buddy spoke to Grace about this, she studied his face and thought about George Fowler and the kind of man he was.

Meantime there were other disappointments. When my parents moved into this house, there was a great deal of work that needed doing. Rooms had to be stripped of wallpaper and redone, a cumbersome job demanding teamwork and patience. They couldn't afford to hire tradesmen and so they had to manage themselves. But Grace soon discovered that Buddy was hopeless at these things. She could drive a nail with more accuracy than he could. And like a child, he soon wearied of the simplest task; he couldn't scrape old paint from a baseboard without growing sulky. His normal good spirits would sour before her eyes, and at supper there would be excuses.

Several nights a week he was playing hockey, and so she was alone, managing somehow to fit the large unwieldy sheets of wallpaper into place. When he crawled in beside her late at night, she could smell the alcohol and tobacco smoke on him. Now and then he wanted her and she endured his quick frantic thrusts. But mostly he lay there talking about George Fowler.

"Mr. Fowler is going to do this for me." "Mr. Fowler is going to do that for me." "Mr. Fowler thinks I can play in a professional league next year."

Listening to this, Grace grew sick of the man's name. She had seen him going into the Huron House, a self-important figure and mildly sinister in her opinion. A crony of Leo Kennedy's who defends every scapegrace in town and sells Irish Sweepstake tickets on the side. They belong to a fast crowd, a demimonde, that Grace has little use for and doesn't trust. Yet lying beside her unemployed young husband, she realizes that she might need George Fowler's goodwill if Buddy is to find a job. And then one night, shortly before Christmas, an opportunity arises. She and Buddy are invited to a party in Fowler's rooms at the Huron House.

Grace is now three and a half months pregnant, her tall form filling out, though she can still wear her dove grey wedding suit. Buddy too wears the suit he was married in. After pulling on galoshes and overcoats, they walk downtown in silence through a cold still night to the Huron House. Earlier that afternoon they quarrelled over a bottle of whisky on the kitchen table. When Grace arrived home from school, she found Buddy sitting in the kitchen with a big red-headed man. In front of them on the table were tumblers and a bottle of Canadian Club. There it was! A bottle of whisky on her kitchen table! It is probably difficult for most of us to comprehend the kind of outrage that such a sight would have stirred in the hearts of certain people who were raised in this province in a particular way and at a particular time. Grace had grown up in a house where alcohol was not only forbidden, but was also condemned as the very fountainhead of ruin and disgrace. Her mother had been a member of the Women's Christian Temperance Union, obdurate lifelong enemies of booze. Grace's view of the scene before her on that December afternoon probably went something like this: it is one thing to have your husband drink in arenas and hotel rooms; it is quite another to have liquor available in your own house. That this probably makes no sense to most of us nowadays is neither here nor there. These were convictions held close to the heart of women like my Mother. Grace watched the big man's freckled hand clasp the bottle and pour some whisky into a glass.

"Gracie?" said Buddy. "This is Red Hanna. He plays with me. Red once played for the Senators."

Red Hanna wagged a large forefinger at Buddy.

"A try-out, chum. Training camp. Exhibition games. Do not mislead your good lady wife."

"You played with Clancy. You told me that."

"So I did, Bud. So I did. For two exhibition games. In the year of our Lord, nineteen and twenty-eight."

Red Hanna turned to Grace and raised his glass. He had startling blue eyes.

"Ma'am," he said.

"How do you do?" she said coldly, reminding herself to be careful. Like many others, Buddy doubtless saw the Christmas season as an excuse for licence. A chance to get drunk. But this was the first time he had brought drink into the house.

"We have to go out tonight, Ross," she said.

Buddy nodded. "I know that, old girl. Red, here, is going too. We're all going. It's going to be a time."

The big red-headed man was now going through an extraordinary routine, a pantomime of someone engaged in a futile search: he looked under the table and into his armpit; he peered beyond Buddy's shoulder at the doorway to the dining room; he even arose and opened a cupboard door. He was an excellent actor, his face a study in contrived wonder. Buddy found this performance hilarious.

"What are you doing, Red?" he laughed.

"I'm looking for some guy named Ross. Have you seen him, Bud?"

This convulsed Buddy. "That's me, dope. That's my name."

Red Hanna leaned back, his hands spread across his chest, eyes wide in disbelief.

"You are Ross? You are the actual owner of that name? Oh, Ross! I am so sorry. Let me shake your hand."

He got up at once and went around the table to pump Buddy's hand. Buddy was now beside himself with laughter. Grace had seen about enough of this foolishness and turned to leave. But not before Red Hanna made an elaborate bow and added, "Nice to have met you, ma'am. Maybe sometime soon, me and my missus will have you and Ross here over for tea."

He gave Buddy a broad wink. Grace briefly regarded the man's brutal grinning face with its nicks and scars, the immense head of stiff coppery hair, itself a kind of weapon. A born bully, she decided. One of those touchy brutes who know they can get away with sarcasm and scorn. Worse for Grace, however, was the realization that this awful man was in fact more intelligent that her own husband who was still laughing at all these antics. And at that moment, a terrible sentence passed swiftly through her mind: *I married a child.*

This was her introduction to my father's world, and as he helped her out of her coat in the lobby of the Huron House on that evening in late December of 1934, she must have considered it both alien and fantastical. It was a world in which men gathered to recall games and monkeyshines played yesterday or long ago; where mythic figures, renowned for body checks or organ size, were paraded forth in the telling. It was a rough, gregarious male world of gags and practical jokes where women were mostly decorative. It was a world of play and irresponsibility. Years later my mother told me how astonished she was to overhear the conversations of hockey players in which were discussed the latest adventures of comic-strip figures like the Gumps and Moon Mullins.

Some of them ate glass and others put their hands under their arms and made farting noises. Everything was for laughs, and the object of life, or so it seemed to my mother, was never to grow up. She used to claim that many of her pupils had more sense than my father's friends. As in most of her assessments of human conduct, I think her judgement was too harsh. Many of these men had families and responsibilities, and they took care of that part of their lives. But when they got together, a kind of collective mania surfaced. I can remember big men with bellies visiting my father in the summers when I was a young child. After a few drinks, they would start in on the jokes or ask me to guess which hand held the monkey. Mother, as usual, had no patience with the frivolous side of life.

On this December evening in 1934, there is a large Christmas tree in George Fowler's apartment which is crowded with guests: the players, of course, with their wives or girlfriends, but also local businessmen and lawyers like Leo Kennedy. The sports editor of the Huron Falls Times, Chip McNeil, a thin lugubrious alcoholic who bears a remarkable likeness to the comedian Buster Keaton, is there. Included among the young women is Buddy's sister Mildred. Grace is surprised by the sight of her. She remembers Mildred as a timid little creature in high school; now she is a pretty woman with soft blonde curls and a bosom. She is smoking a cigarette and laughing with two young men. There is something guileless and vulnerable, an attractive humanity, about Mildred. She is a female version of her brother and not at all like Martha or Muriel who are tougher, shrewder types.

There is beer and whisky and gin and a phonograph playing Christmas carols and pop tunes. Someone is especially fond of a novelty hit called "Who's Afraid of the Big Bad Wolf?" The song is played over and over until the big man Hanna removes the record from the player and holding the disc in both hands, breaks it apart like a biscuit. No one sees fit to argue with him. The room is hot and smoky and Grace is tired; she longs to be away from here. In her own house lying in bed under blankets, looking out through the window at the branches of the bare trees and the winter sky beyond. Thinking of the life that is growing within her. Everyone in the room talks so loudly and laughs so much that she feels the onset of a headache.

She can see George Fowler making his way through the various knots of people, grasping an elbow here, trading a joke there. The squire from the manor house mingling among the tenants at Christmastide. When Fowler sees Grace, he smiles and squeezes past several people to the chesterfield where she is seated holding a glass of ginger ale. He stands in front of her, smoking a cigar and jingling the change in his wide pants, offering her a view of himself, a plane of blue pin-striped cloth. His flies, a foot long, are inches from her face.

"Mrs. Wheeler?" he asks, smiling down at her.

Grace looks up at him. "Mr. Fowler?"

He takes a hand out of his pocket and for an instant she thinks that he is going to offer it in greeting. She nearly brings forth her own, but sees in time that he is merely using the hand to take the cigar from his mouth. It is a practiced piece of business meant to convey authority.

"Haven't seen you with some of the other ladies up at the rink. What's the matter? Don't you like watching your husband play hockey?"

Grace sips her ginger ale and wishes he would move. It is infuriating to have him standing above her like this. Crowding her. A clumsy attempt at intimidation. She knows her face is flushed.

"I'm not very interested in sports."

"Is that so?" says Fowler, rocking on his heels. Through the choking cigar smoke he appears to be studying her and she believes that she can read his thoughts. What does Buddy Wheeler see in this long plain drink of water?

"You should come and watch your husband play sometime," Fowler says. "He's a helluva hockey player. Excuse my language."

Grace says nothing to this.

"I think," Fowler continues, "I can get him a professional contract next year. What do you think of that?"

"I would be happier if you could get him a job, Mr. Fowler," says Grace.

"A job?" Fowler says. "You mean a job around town?"

"Why yes. Where else?"

"You shouldn't hold this boy back. It's Grace, isn't it?"

"Yes."

She notices that he doesn't offer his first name. But he does finally settle in beside her. She can feel the pressure of his stout thigh against her. For a few moments they both watch the party in silence. Then Fowler turns toward her, placing his arm across the back of the chesterfield.

"Buddy tells me you teach school. He's very proud to have a school-teacher for a wife. He tells me you read books together. That's really nice."

The mockery in his voice is deliberately casual, perfected after years of treating most people with contempt. She thinks that by now he may not even be aware of this cruelty in his voice. But she is furious with Buddy for revealing intimacies of their marriage to a man like this.

"And I understand," Fowler adds, "that a little Wheeler is on the way."

Grace ignores his coyness and stares ahead. Fowler leans forward.

"When, may I ask, is the blessed event?"

The blessed event. She turns to look at Fowler's smirking face: the meaty cheeks and thick neck; his eyes are narrow through the cigar smoke. Looking at him, it occurs to her that nothing is sacred to this man. Even the birth of a child can be made to seem ridiculous and trivial. And looking at him she knows that she will never ask George Fowler for anything. She will tolerate him for her husband's sake, but she will never seek a favour from him.

"Our child is due next summer," she says.

Fowler nods. "Well, you two certainly didn't waste any time, did you?"

Her look is so corrosive that Fowler is taken aback. It's as though he realizes that he has finally gone past an acceptable boundary with this woman.

"Exactly what are you implying by that, Mr. Fowler?" Grace asks.

Implying! It wasn't a word he was used to hearing from hockey players' wives in places like Huron falls. In any case, George Fowler has had enough of Grace Wheeler and her snotty, schoolteacher ways. He smiles at her with amused dislike.

"Oh, I wasn't implying anything, Grace," he says. "I never imply anything. I just come right out and say it."

He taps her empty glass.

"Have another toddy and enjoy yourself! And come up to the arena sometime and watch your husband play. He's a crackerjack. I'll bet you he is playing professionally this time next year." He pauses to examine the end of his cigar. "Be a shame to hold a talented boy like that back."

Grace watches the chunky figure disappear among the couples now dancing in the middle of the room. She has made an important enemy tonight; she can feel it in her bones. Buddy is now dancing with Mildred, brother and sister executing a smart little fox-trot to the tune of "Isle of Capri." They are graceful and lithesome together, a pleasure to watch, and Grace feels a surge of tenderness for her young husband. Now and again Red Hanna interrupts Mildred and Buddy and introduces him to others. "This is Ross. Have you fellows met Ross?"

In a corner of the room a big, dark-haired young man named Leo Fournier is about to perform a trick. A crowd has gathered to watch. Fournier is lying on the floor with a glass of beer on his forehead. He has wagered with several people that he can get to his feet without spilling a drop. Soon everyone is around him, a thick circle of people cheering him on. Only Grace is left alone, sitting on the green leather chesterfield, waiting to be taken home.

PLAYING THE GAME

an excerpt from the novel *Bus Ride*

❖   DON GUTTERIDGE

The snow came down upon the village that night as it had for the last seven days. Not continuously of course. At unexpected moments it would cease and there would be sun again, blinding and new, or sudden stars, startling in the brilliant dark. Then mysteriously, snow again, coming out of nowhere, and everywhere: humped over window-sills; drifted against walls, fences, doors; rings around trees and hydro poles; filling up the ruts, paths, roadways, even footsteps made only an hour before.

And like the night in question, there was no wind driving it in from the frozen Lake. It fell, unaided, with the soft profusion of its own weight, straight down, in perfect verticals, as if it would not bend even with the urgent turning of the earth under it. And so thick that night the Bridge was only a broken shadow through it, and you could not see the Lake standing on the shoreline, or the dark ridge of the forests to the north and the east, or the bright lights of the country across the River, or the City which lay to the south. Its falling was almost imperceptible — that kind of snowfall which seems, looking up at it, as if it's moving up and down at the same time, like miniature galaxies expanding and contracting, continuously adrift and directionless. It *was* falling, though, as you could see if you watched it crawl perceptibly up your window-pane, shutting the room, the house, in. Day or night, it did not matter.

The first sign that not all villagers were occupied in this sort of ocular activity was the noise. Muffled by the snow but distinguishable: shouts, cries, groans, squeals, mass exhalations of indrawn breath, mass inhalations of rather soggy night-air. Sounds of excitation? Terror? Triumph?

Then the lights. Blinking up through the down-falling snow, a great ring of them. And in the larger ring of illumination thrown by them, first bumpy outlines of a rectangle. It is clear now that both the bumpy outline and the noise emanate from a common source — human beings, villagers to be precise. Gathered in this incipient rectangle, three or four deep, and venting their breath (with certain vocalizations of rage, frustration, ecstasy) towards a series of rapidly moving shadowy figures.

Here at last underneath the lights and looking cross-wise through the snow you will recognize an open-air hockey rink, surrounded by bleachers, now filled with cheeks, toques, gesticulating hands. And on the somewhat snowy ice the usual complement of hockey players making the gestures and moves appropriate to the intricate rules of that game — with an awkward gracefulness, a rough-edged fluidity. (Though admittedly a bit more awkward than graceful, here, almost two hundred miles from Maple Leaf Gardens.)

Strange, you might think, to find almost the whole population out on a Friday night like this one, with the village beseiged by snow, windows buried, the very doors blocked. But in truth they were: grocer, butcher, druggist, policeman (the only one), housewives, young-wives, dock-workers, day-labourers from the pool room, a foreman from the Refinery, the Reeve and those who voted for him, and some who didn't — young or old, wet or dry, you could not find a larger single gathering of villagers anywhere else except at Church on a Sunday morning, and since there were three houses where God dwelt (or visited on Sabbath) it was not nearly as unanimous a conclave as Friday night at the hockey rink. And one suspected, alone with a certain trinity of clerics, the level of devotion was not so high nor so deep as it was here, with the score three to nothing in favour of the hometown Flyers and less than two minutes to play.

Despite the comfort of an assured triumph over the deservedly despised enemy, there remained in the air an unusual tension. Most of the several hundred pairs of eyes were not trained upon the puck nor the players who swooped awkwardly around it, but rather upon two players who only occasionally came in contact with it. Indeed, most of their vocal encouragement, somewhat strained after fifty-eight minutes and three spectacular goals, was now directed toward two of the twelve players on the ice.

"Watch it, Bill, watch it!"

"Don't take any crap from that guy!"

"Oooh ... ! did you see that? Brute! Brute!" (A decidedly feminine voice.)

"Get the Yank!"

"Board him!"

"Kill him!"

The Yankee player alluded to *was* a huge brute of a player, all shoulders and hips, craggy face, black arrogance in the eyes, with the distinctly un-Yankee name of Danulchuck. How this alien came to play for the Wanderers from Landsend was still a smouldering mystery in the village, and his unamerican name did little to diminish the anxieties of the local fans. That he was American was condemnation enough: the foreign flavour of his appellation merely intensified the mystery and thus the level of resentment. And never was the resentment so deep as it was at the moment: with Danulchuck cruising the ice like a bear in full stride, with an ambling ferocious elegance — his prey in sight.

The prey provided a suitable contrast: slim but muscularly so, and tall: moving gracefully on skates that were mere extensions of the leg. And speed, muscular speed, and quickness, as he darted with apparent ease — here, there, just beyond the reach of the cumbersome lunges of the bearish Danulchuck. Now and then a blur of light brown hair, a flash of blue eyes wary but not fearful. Certainly not scared. If this were prey it was a kind who seemed secure in his swiftness, seeking pleasure in the quick strides of escape so that, for a moment, the partisan lookers-on were not sure who was pursuing, who was pursued. Just moments before this same striding had brought the Friday night village crowd to its communal feet (for the third time) — speed and elegance generating more power than beauty, but the thrust of energy in control, endlessly practised muscular movements (which led the local sportswriter to call him a "natural").

This natural — the local fans knew him as Bill — had just scored his third goal of the night, had virtually won the game and tied the series single-handedly. All of which may seem hyperbolic when viewed from this distance and this age — of TV hockey and commercialized enthusiasm. But it is not exaggerating to say that during the two-minute standing ovation (most of them stood anyway since there were no seats, but the ovation was genuine) accorded to their hero, the people of the Point came alive — individually and collectively — as they did on few other occasions. (Six years later when the bells began to ring out again over Europe there was dancing in the streets of the Point and a triumphal tolling of bells, but for now this triumph would do very nicely.) For this was their team and their boys: Bill's father worked at the Refinery, MacDonald was the druggist's son, Murphy the butcher's boy, and so on. So the victory was to be shared, the triumph communal. And in the sharing and the spontaneous approbation of their applause, all the petty human divisiveness, the pain of ordinary days, the long dream-distorted nights, the memories of wars on far-away ground, the half-healed scars — all that divides us from each other and ourselves faded with the blending voice, the harmony of the universal cheer. The momentary shout of triumph which gives, however illusory or fleeting, a sense of fusion and permanence. There was meaning in it. And if they did not know it they felt it.

How lucky, you think? To be the object of such praise, the source of this omni-healing enthusiasm? To be chosen not only hero of the hour, but 'saviour' of your people? To be nineteen years old: with strength and power and grace? To feel the praise of your peers and your elders come down upon you like a blessing? But you (lucky or unlucky) are not Bill Underhill.

Oh he was feeling the weight of that applause all right. He yearned for it. Every time he guided the black disk to its assigned destiny, he would wait, not breathing in or out, every muscle rigid, until the first wave of their cheering struck him like a bodycheck and even his bones vibrated with their mutual joy. Nevertheless, at this moment, he had only two thoughts running through his head — not in parallel, but alternately: *Watch out for Danulchuck*, and *I want out of this!*

Now the first one we might have expected. After all, the Landsend Wanderers had lost the game, but not the series, and so all that could be reasonably gained from this Friday evening's combat was to stop (injure, maim, harass, embarrass) the Flyers' star winger, the one who had scored three goals against them. In that way he would be less likely to score three more next Saturday at Landsend, they reasoned. Or if they could make him lose face with his own fans a sort of Pyrrhic victory might yet be salvaged. Bill, of course, had discovered this reasoning for himself and knew that Danulchuck, though awkward and slow, was the natural killer among the Wanderers. And though he himself was tall and strong, he had not honed these muscles for the purpose of brawling. Besides, Danulchuck had forty pounds on him and swung his stick recklessly — "like a berserk bruin with an assful of bees" (Old Charlie's epithet?).

Thus the peculiar tension alluded to earlier, as the fans, complacent in victory, nonetheless had to watch apprehensively as bear and his prey did their ritual dance beyond the regular circumnavigations of the game now winding down toward the final whistle. Thus far it had been no contest. Bill stuck to his position, made his plays, stayed out of corners, and when in danger, turned on the nervous speed which had become his trademark. Much to the delight of the fans who cheered each miss and near-miss. This was even better than goals, than winning, than sending the team off to the finals at the Gardens. They were delirious, intoxicated with victory beyond even *their* simple belief. To be blunt, they were drinking themselves silly on this last Friday, this last home-game of the year, with the snow coming down like a shroud around them and their village.

"Get Danulchuck! Get Danulchuck!" Male voices, in unison, more or less.

"Back to Michigan! Back to Michigan!" Descant, very feminine.

"You play better on your ass, Danulchuck!" (Old Charlie?)

The second thought running through Bill's mind, even at this point (Danulchuck *had*, as intimated, just slid thirty feet across the blue-line on both posteriors), is more difficult to explain. A nineteen-year-old about to be canonized by his elders does not normally cry, however silently, 'I want out of this!' But this sentence had been running like a continuous exclamation point through Bill's mind since the beginning of the game. It had been a thought long before it took shape as a sentence, growing, as it were, syntactically more articulate during the past few weeks, this longest of winters. Like most human thoughts when they finally give birth to the words, the phrase, the sentence toward which they are continuously striving, this one surprised its maker even more than is usual. To Bill, as to those now cheering him in their drunken delirium, there seemed no reason why he should indeed "want out!" But he did.

When the game first began he had thought it merely a natural reaction to the tension. After all, they were losing the series; he had played well (according to the Country Reporter) but several marks below his reputation. So for a minute he had resented and feared the cheering which greeted his first appearance on the ice. It was precisely at that point that the sentence had burst, fully-formed and grammatically unequivocal, from his brain. He had assumed it would dissolve with his first goal, the reassuring praise of applause. It didn't. Even though he had scored unassisted on the first shift. The applause was no help either, though the vibrations still hummed in his bones. He looked helplessly up at the falling flakes, everywhere, on all sides, and the sound of applause seemed like the snow itself, coming down unendingly, with a smothering and terrible inevitability cutting him off like the village. A desolate peninsula. Every bone in him rang like a tuning fork: "I want *out* of this!"

Nor was it any different when he scored the second goal and the third and realized with his worshippers that the game was won, the series tied. True, 'Watch out for Danulchuck' had forced its thoughtful way in, but was at best a minor theme. He wanted out for a long time. What terrified him even more was that this feeling was accompanied by no sense of shame or regret. It was there, and he wanted it.

In fact, there had been only one moment during the entire game when the old feeling had come back. His third goal. The hat trick. Scored on one of his patented end-to-end rushes. The constantly falling snow had slowed the ice considerably and hampered Bill's stickhandling, but halfway through the third period they stopped the play and cleared the ice so it was smooth. Bill wanted to rush, to cradle the puck as it was meant to, to hold his strides in the familiar, long-rehearsed pattern. He felt new power gathering in his legs, flowing up into his arms, wrists, stick. The puck laying in front of him: suddenly obedient. Around his own net: half a dozen red jerseys blurred in the snow. That other net barely visible. When it went well it was like a dance. A shift to the right, all power channelled to that side, bursting back to the left, and the red jerseys, it seemed, merely playing their part in the intricate dance. One, down on his knees, unbelieving: a second, too clever, tangled in his own amazed skates. The speed was there now: red-line, three more jerseys behind him; the puck jumping to his muscled command. Net in sight, waiting, its role assured. Old feelings coming back; as if he could fly — skates like a breeze on the ice, speed alone would do it, would carry him up and over, he was rising, floating with the puck, into or over the goal, above the smothering applause, the suffocating snow, he was above it all, knowing the puck had found its own way, the applause secure, but high and floating now through the snow which had a beginning after all, here, high over it, floating and free with a peace shared only by a quiet cold audience of stars.

Such moments are reserved for our dreams. And we are probably poaching on Bill's private preserve, for it will be evident by now that the puck did go in the net, and Bill, rather than flying over the defence, simply skated past them and blasted a shot so powerful the Wanderers' goalie didn't move (on home-ice he would have made a suitable gesture, but why bother, here?). The first wave of anticipated applause, however, did not come, for young Bill, moving so fast, faster than anyone had seen him skate, seemed unable to stop, almost (they said after) as if he were in a trance, until the end-boards kindly untranced him. As soon as he stood up, shaken but unmarked, the cheers poured down from the heights of the five rows of bleachers.

Dream or reality, illusion or not, Bill *had* been flying, the old feeling in him. The exhilaration that only power and speed and youth can give. It was the reason, he had always thought, for those late afternoons on the marsh-ice below the River, for the Saturday mornings, winter and summer, shooting pucks at potato sacking till hand and eye become one motion, one will. And when there was no one to play against him, he would take a beaten-up kitchen chair and push it before him, hour after hour, till the calve-muscles ached and the ankle-bones rebelled long before his desire gave way and he limped home hurting all over. But dreaming of applause falling endlessly like snow around him; dreaming, too, of a real arena where every shift, every glistening shot, was rewarded with cheers, was recorded and sent winging on air-waves over all the snows of all this country's towns and hamlets.

As always he had waited for the crowd's reward, even this bumptious hometown crowd, hoping that the familiar feeling would remain. But the end-boards had jarred it loose, for the snow was coming down harder now, mingling with the applause and the fading cheers. Then the inner voice: "I want out of this! Away from *them*, from *him* (Danulchuck? father?), from *her*, yes, even her (mother? Penny?)." And, for a second, a twinge of shame. For which he was grateful.

But as we have noted that was the only moment during the game in which this second thought was not upper-most in his mind. Bill was beginning perhaps to recognize how close he *was* to getting out, yet at the same time was proportionately close to being trapped here *forever*. In a sense, hockey had been a way *in* — success, approval, local fame — and could now be a way *out*. For everyone knew a scout from the Leafs was in the stands — no one had actually seen him yet, but the rumour was too persistent to be anything but true. And why not? Had not the Flyers, led by their star winger, won the C Championship last year? Were they not moved up to and contending for the title of the B League? Everyone, and particularly Bill, knew the provincial final would be played in Maple Leaf Gardens where every other seat was occupied by a National League scout. The big time. And at some point over the course of this endless winter he had realized he was moving inevitably toward it. Toward that arena which none of the boys had ever seen except in their mind's eye — boyish imaginations fed only by a famous voice riding the radio waves across the hills, the valleys, the vast plains, to every village in every corner of the land, even to this last point where the water began.

If the scout were not here tonight, he would be there next Saturday for the final, or, failing that, for the playoffs in the Gardens. He *would* be there, so it was important for Bill to play well, for the team to make it. How puzzling, then, that the familiar exhilaration did not overwhelm him, despite his three goals and flying skates. The louder they cheered, the more he wanted out of it all. The snow fell impartially on both.

"Look out, Bill!"

"Ooooh, my Goooood!" Female fear. Thrill of danger. Sexual sound.

A near-miss that time. Danulchuck just grazing his quarry, jolting the end-boards with a furiously un-intentional bodycheck.

The crowd cheered his accuracy. To the Echo.

Bill didn't hear it, vaguely felt the body lunge past him. (There are times when thought becomes the swiftest, all-encompassing kind of action, even to those whose flesh habitually sucks the brain outward to the nerve-ends, the consuming muscle. Thoughts with the power of voices: wafted like radio waves unimpeded through the high air, carrying his name into strange spaces beyond the lakes, the mountains even, to the bordering seas.)

At this point, another, more familiar kind of action took place — Danulchuck's thwarted, avenging elbow found relief at last against our hero's thoughtful brow. Then the fleshy thud of a stick butt-ended against bone. Bill saw or heard none of this. Pain flashed through him, he was falling, he was on his knees, struggling to get up, a fire on the left side of his head. And here, on the smudged ice, a patch of blood, a scarlet badge of defeat oozing into the snow, spreading and visible. His blood. Sudden shame. He stayed on his knees, dizzy, not wanting to get up.

There was no external reason for this fear, for the beleaguered referee (a neutral from the City) and his linesmen were endeavouring to keep the blue-shirted Flyers from skinning alive the avenging bear (now somewhat subdued and much less awesome). The crowd was attempting to assist them.

"Skin him alive!"

"Kill the bastard!"

"Cut out his Yankee guts!"

In fact they were becoming almost nasty and not a little dangerous, for Bill had struggled shakily to his skates, blood streaming down his left cheek, the scarlet pool at his feet widening, so that even those in the fifth row at the far end could see it despite the encompassing snow.

"Are you all right, Bill?" Baker's voice. Concerned. Genuine. He resented it.

"I'm all right. I'm all right. C'mon, let go of my arm, you guys."

"Christ, that's a helluva cut!" Macdonald. What a stupid remark. He was like that.

"I'm okay. I can skate. Okay? so lay off —"

"All right, for Christ's sake!"

"We'll get him, Billy. Don't worry." Baker meant it.

Meanwhile, the referee had given up the idea of getting Danulchuck into the penalty box. In fact, he had given up continuing the game —only forty seconds remained — because the crowd was turning nasty. Redmond, the intemperate grocer, was trying to get over the boards to assist the referee. Only his own drunkenness and the desperate clutchings of his more temperate (i.e. sober) wife, preventing him from doing so. Danulchuck was surrounded by red jerseys at the north end, taking verbal blows with as much grace and goodwill as his terror would allow. The exit to the dressing room was at the south end, however, and the main problem for the referee was how to get the Wanderers and their beleaguered bruin to it before the villagers decided to participate in the game en masse. One could see him glancing helplessly around for the half-dozen constables normally required for the operation-at-hand. What he found was a solitary Chief, one Michael Piersall, who at that moment was standing on top of the boards beside the penalty box (where he normally sat, feeling at home no doubt) with a most unconstabularly expression on his face. From which issued forth an unbroken string of polite compliments directed at the gathering of red jerseys. Law and order are relative commodities, a fact which, despite his apparent lack of sophistication, was well understood by the Chief.

"Kill him! Kill him!" In unison now. The true rhythm of rage.

"Let Piersall at him!"

The dozen or so Landsend fans had quietly slipped through the snow to their cars.

What ultimately saved Danulchuck from immolation or worse, was his victim. At the precise moment when this Christian mass was about to re-enact its oldest ritual, the victim found his skating legs, and, shaking off any help from his teammates, began to skate wobbly towards the players' bench. The blood was stopped now. But the wound, bright and visible, drew all eyes toward it. The rage changed dramatically to a renewal of the cheering, stronger, more passionate, more sustained and genuine than before. For another minute the old unity was there again, intact, the fallen hero revived, the brand of his triumph brilliantly visible.

This time, Bill felt it too: the shared pride. And underneath, a whelming sense of shame, of regret, for a loss not yet really lost, but somehow gone, before the event. For the moment this wound would serve as the badge of his loyalty, this pain as proof of his worth, deserving of adoration. But what lay beyond the moment?

Although not exactly sharing in this adoration, Danulchuck and his red-sweatered comrades took advantage of it by slinking out the south end to the protective cover of their dressing room in the shanty. No one noticed or cared. And though there was some brave talk of staying around until the enemy should re-emerge to board their bus, the plot never materialized. By the time the Flyers had been cheered, one by one as they left the ice, the rage had dissipated, swallowed as it usually is by the insatiable human appetite for joy.

So, within minutes, the bleachers and the rink, which had held this congregation of villagers spellbound for two hours, emptied themselves. Clumps of people, shadowy in the continuing snow, dispersed to their separate private places, dissolved slowly into white blurs. Several lingered yet outside the shanty. Small, female figures. The only movement, that of the omnipresent snow.

The Wanderers have long since filed out to their bus. It has found the road some way, moving off into the blinding storm, north along the Lake to Landsend.

The bleachers are bare. Not a footprint remains. The rink a hollow rectangle once more. The snow comes down, covering the boards, the nets, washing out the blue-lines, the red-line. Every sign of human motion blotted out by this soft, insistent, immaculate falling.

Only the keenest of eyes, looking straight down through the vertical maelstrom, could discern a tiny crimson spot, fringed with white and fading with each second — like the slow bleaching of a scar.

The Sportive Centre of Saint Vincent de Paul

❖ HUGH HOOD

Snow. Moist, heavy, fat flakes melting as they hit, down your coat collar, in your boots, underfoot, piling up in eaves-troughs and on outdoor Christmas trees, shorting their ice-blue, silver, yellow and red strands of light. Snow everywhere this mid-December, not a heavy fall this time — we haven't had much yet — but irksome on Friday night at 6:15 because of the traffic. If snow, then snow-removal equipment and crews, the salt trucks lugging slowly up the hill on Van Horne, growling in low gear. Whish ... whish ... whoosh ... the salt tumbles out behind in crystals, melts, and electrolizes the body metal of fifty thousand cars.

When we got into the car that Friday night, the windows clouded over immediately, and we both began to swear as we threw the goalie equipment and my kitbag and skates into the back, conscious of the half-hour drive ahead, and wondering how long it would take to traverse the level-crossing on Rockland. I spun the wheels backing away from the garage, which made Seymour, the goalie, turn and stare at me.

"Gotta do it in second."

We sunfished up the driveway. After two minutes in the car, our breath made it impossible to see out. I hate cold weather, even moderate cold, so I usually keep the windows shut, but a little cold air on the glass works wonders, so I nodded when Seymour glanced at me.

"All right, open the damn things." We went down the street, around the corner and hit bad traffic as soon as we tried to get onto Rockland; we were a couple of hundred yards short of the level-crossing, just by the park, and the bells were ringing, the red lights swinging, the combined efforts of two wealthy suburban municipalities, Outremont and the Town of Mount Royal, having succeeded for years in denying the plain public interest of the rest of Montreal. They don't want anything done to the level-crossing that will increase heavy traffic on Rockland, so to the detriment of the needs of the citizenry in general, they have put off from one year to the next the creation of an overpass or underpass, from planning council to engineering study, until the issue has evolved from scandal to joke to folklore.

They claim they're going to do something about it next summer, but I'll believe that when I see it.

Only ten minutes to get across this time, though, and from Rockland to L'Acadie, where we turned north towards the Metropolitan, was another five minutes. Half the time for the ride out of town spent on the first half-mile, such is the obduracy of the flourishing suburbanite.

Sometimes, working my way along beside the park towards the level-crossing in winter twilight or blackness, I used to have an infernal vision of the place as an immense and horrid ash-pit. There are piles of ashes and discarded rubbers, old tires, dead cats, at the back of the park where the snow-removal men heap tumuli of grey slush to await the coming of spring. It seemed ashy, grey to black, infinite, that stretch of obscurity along the railroad right-of-way, where now and then a truck might be seen, its body tilted at a dangerous angle. Spectral muffled figures prodded at lumps of packed snow and ordure as one came by; it was always mysteriously saddening to observe their dauntless activity.

Not too bad on L'Acadie, a bit of a tie-up trying to get into the far right lane for the Metropolitan turnoff, but after fifty cars had passed on my right somebody finally slowed and waved me on. I don't think he saw my grateful salute because my car, a degraded Volkswagen bus, allows little visibility in or out from abaft the beam. We pulled up to the green arrow and headed east, neither of us with much to say, concentrating on the coming game.

Seymour won't eat before a game. He takes a light lunch about two-thirty and dines afterwards, natural in a goalkeeper, I suppose, whose tensions are great. I play defence, and Seymour makes me look good or bad depending, so I can perhaps afford to do as I do and eat around five-thirty. After the game we have drinks and sandwiches. We don't talk much on the way out; that comes later.

"You left the front of the net on their second goal."

"I did, hell. Polsky should have been there; the play came in on my side."

"Anyway don't keep doing it."

We play in an informal two-team league, the Sportsman's League, organized a dozen years ago by some men who had played hockey all their lives and wanted to keep up with it as they got into their late twenties and early thirties. There is one strict rule: no board checking. There's a seasonal series of twenty-five games, and scoring records are kept; we have an elaborate and convivial end-of-the-season dinner.

"Shibley has taken up curling Friday nights," mumbled Seymour. "Curling!"

I eased up the ramp onto the Metropolitan and at once began to drive as fast as possible, which isn't all that fast. We crept up to fifty-five and the bus began to shudder a bit in the wind, always strong on the elevated highway. I couldn't get over fifty-six or seven, but that speed will heat the car slightly, and I got much better vision as our breath stopped condensing on the windows.

Past Place Crémazie, spic and span in black and white and grey brick, all lit up for the Friday night shoppers. Past a parish church of daringly advanced design, its big front window radiating pale yellow and apple-green bars of light over the snow. Over and past myriads of streaking lights. Then a wide sweeping turn coming down towards Saint-Hubert and Christopher-Colomb, whizzing on towards D'Iberville and the last Pie-IX, pronounced 'peanoof'. I looked at my watch as we came down off the Metro.

"Quarter to seven."

"I've got my equipment anyway," said Seymour. "I can dress in plenty of time." It takes him around twenty minutes to get it all on; he has pads for very unusual parts of the body, and rightly so. His face-mask, a strange plastic structure of his own design, closely resembles the death mask of Keats. He said, "We'll be there before seven," as we took a right onto Pie-IX.

Here the prospect of the city changes as you go north, heading off the island. The lights of the Metropolitan recede, a pale stippled line away behind to the west. On your left there's nothing but dark space belonging to Saint-Michel de Laval, half-developed industrial park, I think, with spur lines jutting off into fields, and here and there an occasional abandoned boxcar, and a taxi park or gas station. Pie-IX was just a ribbon development a few years ago but now there is beginning to be a bit of a spread eastwards towards Ville de Saint-Léonard. There are Dairy Queens, closed for the winter, on our right, and used-car lots, small restaurants and raw new shopping centres all the way to Rivière des Prairies.

The name Pie-IX always makes me think of the first Vatican Council of 1870-71, and the promulgation of the dogma of Papal Infallibility. It isn't very long since the tone of Catholicism in the city was much in the spirit of the lamented Pius the Ninth. What he would have said about contemporary Montreal church architecture, or about *aggiornamento* or the opening to the left, or Vatican Two, confounds me as I think of it. I don't believe anyone would name a *ruelle*, let alone a six-lane main artery, after Pius the Ninth, at this time. John, yes: Pius, no. Things are moving fast.

We cross the bridge fast because it has only two lanes and there's always a press of traffic behind, the river wide and black and very cold beneath. Swing to the right, right again along the north shore to Saint Vincent de Paul, left here, stop at the grocery store for a dozen Black Horse which will be drunk in the dressing room after the game, win or lose, and on to the edge of town to the *Centre Sportif* where, according to local legend, the Rocket and some of his life-long friends have played pickup hockey on Sunday afternoons since he retired five years ago. He still has his shot, they say around the arena, and from the blue line in, his legs.

The arena is shaped in what seems to my ungeometrical eye to be the arc of a parabola described by beautifully curving, powerful steel beams covered by crimped steel roofing and terminated by brick walls. It's about the size of a dirigible hangar and is surely the most useful building in the community, churches and schools apart. There's a parking lot at the main entrance, accommodating maybe fifty cars, and just past the building a flat expanse of ground which might be a soccer or football field. I've never seen it in daylight. Away off to your right, a very dim shape in this darkest week of the year, looms a building of unmistakably institutional shape, a college or an orphanage, evidently not a convent school because of the heavy predominance of males in the neighbourhood. Its presence probably explains those lurking grey-headed Christian Brothers with their collars like divided spades, who pace in the runway around the ice-surface at all times, keeping an eye on their students' development.

"*Il a quitté son aile, l'idiot.*"

"*Jeu de position là-bas. Position!*"

Strictly speaking, this is the Laval Community Arena, but since Laval is so expansive and sprawling a collection of suburbs, I prefer to associate it with the small township where it lies, named for a Saint of very charitable reputation.

LIGUE DE FRANCS COPAINS

	W	L	T	P
GARS:	5	1	2	12
CHUMS:	3	3	2	8
AMIS:	2	2	4	8
COPAINS:	1	5	2	4

I'm sorry but amused to note that the Guys, the Chums and the Pals are still beating hell out of the Comrades. I'd have preferred it otherwise — this is a local French league, much like ours, but on a grander scale. They play a devastatingly good brand of hockey and have no prohibition on board checking and other impolitenesses. One time a couple of seasons back a disgruntled forward in their league, objecting to a bad call, struck the referee — his close friend — in the eye with his stick. He got carried away, I suppose, and so in another sense did the official, who lost the sight of the eye permanently. *Les Francs Copains.* There's a big sign hanging inside the main entrance giving the current standings in their league, the Comrades securely in the cellar. In the foyer are hung dozens of photographs: the blessing and opening of the arena fifteen years ago, this year's local Junior B team, a championship Pee-Wee team ranked behind an enormous trophy as tall as anyone on the club, the Rocket in a referee's striped shirt kneeling in the middle of a crowd of autograph seekers.

There are arenas like this all over Montreal and the suburbs, with a foyer much used for ping-pong, for meeting your girlfriend, for loitering. In this one anyway I've never seen any rough stuff, no rowdyism, no delinquents. Often a lad of thirteen will hold the door open for you if you're carrying kitbag, sticks, skates. Plenty of long hair, and some remarkably chic girls of twelve or thirteen, but nothing even close to criminal.

We pass one of the gangways as we go to the dressing room. Two Pee-Wee teams are on the ice, working out at either end. Their hour, six-thirty to seven-thirty, seems to be devoted to shooting and play-making practice, not to league games which are likely played through the week or on Sunday afternoon. The players don't look at all like little boys dressed in outsized equipment. They look like hockey players, having played the game for seven or eight years, since they could stand up on skates. They have moves that I, who never played the game seriously growing up in Toronto, will never acquire: they shoot better than I do, feed a pass better, head-man the puck. They have the game in their legs and arms and hearts from the cradle.

Waiting for our league prexy to unlock the dressing rooms, I watch what the kids are doing. Tonight they're working on faking the goalie out, a line of forwards at the blue line carrying the puck in, one after the other, with a spindly defenceman rapping it out to the next man after the goalie has moved on the play. They don't shoot from the blue line on this exercise, but skate in close, perhaps take a head fake or a stick fake, move to the right or left to persuade the goalie to commit himself, so they can swing with the puck and shoot behind him as he goes the wrong way. At the west end of the rink, the team is dressed in green, apple-green sweaters with yellow trim, which makes me think of the church

121

we passed coming out, a broad band of yellow around the mid-section, and pants in a darker green; most wear headgear. Two defencemen, not taking shooting drill, are skating backwards from side to side of the ice, practising passing the puck forward while moving back, necessary for a defenceman and not as easy as it looks when done right.

Groaning behind me. Carpenter. The dressing rooms must be open now, time to dress so as to be on the ice the moment it's been reflooded at seven-thirty. We only have an hour's ice-time this year, but hope for an hour and a half next season.

Carpenter was taking a drink as I came past, filling himself with ice-cold water, glugging, not a good idea before the game. He straightened.

"Sixty minutes tonight, kid?"

"Sure," I said, "I'm in shape, Fred." I shouldn't have said that. He looked ashen. He could have been a good player too, lots better than me. He said, "I play, vomit, play. You know."

"No you don't. Not in this league." We went on down to dressing room Four to get ready. Paul Bowsfield had a dozen sticks he'd picked up in a job lot, good ones, and some of us took a look at them. Brian Tansey, an insurance man of twenty-nine, our best defenceman, who more or less keeps an eye on Carpenter, had a small dig for me.

"You were using Number Seven last week."

"So what? I'm getting the puck into the air."

"Yeah, but you're missing passes, and the puck keeps hopping over your stick, damn you. Try a Five."

He had a point. I bought two Fives from Bowsfield, cost me four bucks, and I didn't notice any improvement. I missed passes just the same.

In this city hockey is the chief social cement. The sportsman's League plays pretty poor hockey because most of us are in there once a week for fun. But there are five or six really good players, all of whom play in other, better leagues. Seymour plays in the Town of Mount Royal Senior. One week he was complaining to me about the play there.

"I'm getting beat where I shouldn't get beat. There's this guy Gary Paxton, he had three goals on me last night."

"Yeah?"

"He's pretty good. He played a couple seasons out west."

That got my ear. "Where out west?"

"In the Western League. Where else?"

I thought somebody might be kidding somebody, because the WHL is a very fast minor league, full of guys like Charlie Burns who had three seasons with the Bruins, or Andy Hebenton who holds the NHL ironman record, around seven hundred consecutive games with New York and Boston. One season he had over thirty goals, which means that at that time he was one of the best hockey players alive. So if Paxton played in the WHL he was bound to be damned good. When I got home that night I checked him out in the record book (I have record books going back a good long way) and there he was, PAXTON, GARY. Born 1940, and the rest, and he really did play for Los Angeles, 1963-64, 1964-65, and he had fifteen goals last year, which means that he wasn't just hanging on.

He probably realized that he was twenty-five and about at his peak. If you haven't made it at least to the American League by then, you likely won't ever make it to the NHL. I suppose he figured he'd gone about as far a he could and decided to come back to Montreal to settle into some kind of career, playing amateur hockey on the side. This happens in all sports; the phenomenon is familiar in sandlot baseball. You go out to throw the ball around and some guy is cruising back of second in that unmistakable way. Or get up a weekly game of touch football among friends in a park, and one fine summer Saturday somebody shows up who suddenly fires the ball seventy yards with a nice easy arm motion, and it turns out that he played for NDG and had a tryout with the Alouettes, that he might have had a football scholarship to Arizona State but chose to stay home and look after his mother.

Seymour could have signed with the Rangers' organization when he was seventeen, but his parents didn't want him to turn into a hockey bum. "If they'd only known how I'd turn out," he says, "they'd have signed, they'd have signed."

"My son, the painter," I say, and we laugh. But he keeps wondering how things would have worked out if he'd turned pro. I tell him he'd never have made it; they had Worsley and Marcel Paillé, and some other guys, but he keeps wondering.

"You're better off where you are."

"Yeah, but I'm not playing well. It's the quality of the competition."

He's quite right. Playing behind me isn't doing him any good. He gets a lot of shots but all from the wrong places, because I'm not good enough to jockey the forwards over to where they should be. Still, I'm playing with Seymour who was wanted by the Ranger chain, and he's playing with Gary Paxton who had fifteen goals in the WHL last year, see what I mean? And Paxton was playing with Hebenton and Burns who once upon a time played with Andy Bathgate and Johnny Bucyk. I feel as though I belonged to the club in a small way, and it's relations like these that give society its meaning. Me and Andy!

There's a dining and conversation group in the city called the Veterans. *Not* an ex-service club, which can be awfully tedious, but a collection of types who have been associated with hockey as player or coach or even as owner. Every year they give a big dinner with speakers, newspaper coverage and awards. Elmer Ferguson always comes and gives the function a fine advance write-up; they tape some of the speeches for the sports shows. This year their big award went to Claude Provost who beat out Gordie Howe for first all-star last season; everybody was there. Newsy Lalonde was there, who used to live a block away from me back of Maplewood. King Clancy was there, sitting with a lot of hockey men from Ottawa. Hooley Smith is dead now, but some of the old Maroons got to the dinner, Jimmy Ward, whose son has made it in major-league ball. Men like these have associations going back before 1910, the Arenas, the Wanderers, the Silver Seven, Montreal A.A.A.

In the Forum Tavern after the game, talking to Léon the waiter, we ask him to tell us who is the greatest player he ever saw, and he tells us the story of the time Maruice scored five.

"Gordie Howe is a better hockey player," he says generously, "and Bill looked better than anybody. But the Rocket…There was never anybody like him. One time the Rangers hired this boxer, this heavyweight, Dill. The Rocket flattened him with one punch. If it hadn't been for injuries, he could have played three or four more seasons."

"He cut a tendon," somebody says, "and he was putting on weight. They were calling him *pépère*."

"He's still playing. He plays ever Sunday out in Saint-Vincent. They say he can still score."

"Sure he can score."

"He could score," says Léon, "on the Devil himself. If Maurice was dying and the goalie gave him the angle, he'd get up and score. I saw him carry Earl Seibert in from the blue line on his shoulders and score with one hand. I saw him …"

He goes off for more beer talking happily to himself.

Before our game Fred Carpenter was babbling loosely and happily about a set of irons he'd picked up, a steal. I didn't follow what he said because I was concentrating on dressing and taping my sticks, and thinking about the game, wondering which line I'd be on against, Leo's line, or Kenny, Eric and Eddie? A lot of the quality of your play depends on your checks. I'd sooner be on against Leo's line because the forward coming in against me will be either Pierre or Chaloub, depending on how we line up and which side I'm playing. I turn best to the right and should play on that side, but as we often have somebody missing we shuffle our alignment every time out.

Playing against their other line, I'm too slow. All I can do is try to jam the wing on the boards, while avoiding the appearance of sin. Tactics,

tactics and ritual; hockey isn't a game but a complex set of rituals. That night Carpenter violated them all. He wandered up and down, smoking, which you never do before a game, and he was talking too much, in a disconnected way. Once or twice I saw Paul Bowsfield, who more or less captains our side, give him a strange evaluating look. Seymour seemed upset about something too.

The silent lines of communication that develop in a dressing room before a game are subtle, tight and unsmiling. They don't vary. Years ago some individual pencilled the single word 'Boisvert' over the hook where I hang my clothes. Boisvert, if that was his name, may long ago have died or moved away, but nobody will remove the name, and that's simply where I sit, facing Seymour. Tommy sits on my left by the door to the showers and George sits next to Seymour facing me. George and I take turns bringing the beer, twelve cans, one for each player and one over for the man who brings it. Watch how the Leafs come on the ice behind Johnny Bower. Shack is always the first man out. When the Canadiens take their warm-up, Terry Harper is almost always the last man to go off. At the start of the game, you skate back and say something to the goalie, whacking his pads. After the game, if you've won, you meet the goalie coming to the bench and congratulate him, whether he had a good game and kept you in there or was just lucky, or even if he was lousy and you had to outscore the other team eight to seven. You just do this.

When Carpenter kept on horsing around, getting up, sitting down, smoking, getting in people's way, he was violating many silent agreements.

That night I was first out of the dressing room as usual. When I'd been on the ice, which was very fast, fresh and new, for a couple of minutes, the others came on, we took the goalie's warm-up and then Paul gave us the line-up for the night and the game started. We only had three defencemen out. Polsky hadn't turned out, so the arrangement was that Tansey and Carpenter would start and I would spell them off alternately; each of us would get some short shifts and some doubles. Brian was playing strong rushing game, as he always does, and we kept the puck in their end for the first minutes. Soon Carpenter hollered, and I hopped over the boards and took him off, and things were all right for another three minutes.

Then the roof fell in. Brian had played around six or seven minutes, which he can do because he skates strongly and knows how to pace himself. But when Carpenter came on with me, and I had to change over to the left side where I'm uncomfortable, we gave up three goals, bang, bang, bang, with the game still young. The first was my fault. I got beat on the play but good and told Seymour so, as he fished the puck out of the net. But on the second I was nowhere near the play, and I was glad, because Seymour was pretty red-faced over it. After the goal he said something to Carpenter which was evidently fairly blunt. It was a funny play — the last thing I saw was somebody's glove deflecting the flying puck. The third goal was a clean play, a two-on-one situation where I had to play the puck carrier or anticipate a pass, and I made a wrong guess.

When you get down three in the early part of a game, two things can happen. Either you play stronger, hold them and come on when they tire towards the end, or you fall apart, lose your cohesion and stop skating. This night we fell apart. Oh, we got one goal to bring it up to three to one, and it looked for a second as if we might pick up, then they got it right back and led at the end of the first period, four to one. We only have ice-time for two periods, and the second was worse than the first. Nothing rolled right for us, the forwards weren't skating, and they weren't coming back. I took to falling all over the place out of haste and lack of confidence. Midway through the second period, Carpenter went off and could be heard some distance back of the bench vomiting into a fountain. We got bombed, seven to one. Trooping into the dressing room after the game, we saw the clogged fountain loaded with expelled matter; it was a dismal sight, but appropriate.

Silence, oh, boy, like you could spread it on pumpernickel, thick, heavy. I put the dozen Black Horse in the middle of the floor, and nobody dived for it, very unusual, that. Finally I popped it open, took one myself, handed out a few. Somebody took off a jersey; somebody fiddled with his skates. Tommy looked soberly at a cracked stick.

You could hear singing from the next dressing room.

After a couple of minutes of this Seymour rose and addressed the meeting: "I don't mind losing," he started off, gathering steam as he proceeded. "I think I can say that. I've lost a lot of games in my time. I've had my off nights, but this wasn't one of them, and I don't want to lose any more like that one. If there are guys here who don't care enough about the league to turn up sober — I'm not naming any names and I'm not talking about any one person — I don't want to play behind them. It's dangerous. You can get hurt on a goal-post or in the corners, playing like that, and you can injure somebody else permanently, and you might just as well take the game and hand it to the other team. A beer in the dressing room afterwards, that's fine, everybody likes that, but nobody but a fool, and I mean a fool, drinks before the game. That's all." He sat down and started taking off his pads.

Carpenter looked up from his skates — he'd had his head down while Seymour was talking — and said briefly, "I quit." He got the rest of his things off, didn't bother about a shower, and went out, shutting the door quietly.

Bowsfield said, "I was going to talk to him about it."

"Does anybody think I'm wrong?" Seymour said. "He could hurt any of us. He put their second goal in the net himself, just batted it in with his glove. I suppose he was trying to clear it, but what the hell, a goalie has no protection against that."

"He'll be back," somebody said.

"I think he'll be back," I said.

"Sure, after Christmas." We have to take a break at Christmas.

"Did he come up with you, Brian?"

"Naw, not tonight; he got away from the office early. I think he caught a ride with Yvan."

"Does he drink in the office?"

"Not in the office, no. Right after."

"I didn't think he looked so bad," I said.

"You could smell it."

"Ah."

I collected quarters from the few who had taken a beer, picked up the remaining cans and my equipment and hustled out to stick them in the car. Carpenter was standing at the coffee counter under the *Ligue des Francs Copains* sign. I joined him; he looked bereft.

"See you after New Year's," I said cheerfully.

He said nothing, just drank his coffee, shivered and went outside. I don't know who drove him home; he certainly didn't come with us. After he left there was the usual kidding around at the coffee counter.

"Tonight you couldn't make a wrong move," Seymour said jovially to Leo, "the way you hang around that red line."

Leo grinned at me. "You want to play with more confidence," he said. "Try charging the forwards. I don't mean so as to hurt anybody."

There were exchanges of holiday greetings, kind of a line-up in which we all shook hands and wished each other a good Christmas. Tansey looked around, wondering where Carpenter was.

"He's gone," Seymour said glumly. "I didn't catch him. I meant to."

"After Christmas," I said.

"That's it."

When we went out to the cars, it had stopped snowing; there were solid wet cakes of white on every car, oozing water down windows. It was growing colder. The sky had cleared, and you could see the clouds moving and the stars back of them. Car doors slammed. People joked about the lopsided score, gradually the parking lot cleared. When Seymour had had his weekly argument with the league president, about who should trans-ship his equipment to the Town of Mount Royal Arena, we drove away.

"Ron is taking care of it?"

"What?"

"Your pads."

"Oh, that." He lit a cigar Ron had given him, and a rich vapour filled the car. I coughed critically. "That's all right, now," said Seymour, "this is a good cigar. I wish I had Ron's dough."

"You will when you're dead."

"I suppose so." We drove in silence through Saint Vincent to the highway, through the underpass, up the ramp, onto the approach to the bridge. Coming back into town, the approach slopes sharply down and there is a fine wide view of the river and the lights along the dark shore. You almost seem to swoop down like a plane, and the lights of the town rush to meet you and the dark water somehow draws your eyes. You have to take care. Coming off the bridge, as the traffic divides into streams headed for various suburbs across the northern part of the city.

Tonight, perhaps because of the snow, there was much bright reflection from the river, white on dark, with faint moving pin-pricks of red and green here and there. I felt cold, and the cigar smoke was oppressive. Down Pie-IX in the centre lane southbound, we were bowling along pretty good, catching the lights in sequence, heading for the Metropolitan West, and a few beers and some sandwiches in a tavern on the Main called *Le Gobelet*, where we always go. By the time we were across town, the cold had become intense and we were glad to get out of the car and into the clatter and warmth of *Le Gobelet* where we sat watching colour TV, going over the game, eating, till it was time to go home.

Three weeks later the shoe was on the other foot; we got off to a grand start, got the right roll from the puck every time. I played my first decent game of the season and the rest of the club was hustling too. We won it, three to one, which started us off on a winning streak that lasted quite a time.

Tansey, Posky and I played defence; the other fellow never came back, although we hear of him sometimes through Brian. Once, after a game we won really big, Seymour and I stood around the foyer for a while watching the kids come and go around the ping-pong tables. Just by the entrance there's a little door which might lead to the building superintendents' office, and over it stands a big grey plaster statue of the Blessed Virgin with the Child in her arm; the statue has a circular electric halo. It all fits in.

Seymour took me by the arm for a second. "We have a lot in common, you know."

I agreed with him silently.

He said, "We take a pretty high moral line, don't we?"

I said I thought we did.

"You know," he said slowly, "if the position has a defect — I'm not sure it has — it would be self-righteousness, wouldn't it?"

I thought he was right, and said so.

Teeth

❖ FRED STENSON

Sixteen minutes and seven seconds are gone in the third period of this hockey game. We are behind four to three. The score might suggest to some that we have had a titanic struggle here, but we have not. Of the seven goals scored, five went in accidentally off skates and legs. Our goalie slipped and fell on one of the other two.

If the technicians who are steadily creeping into this game ever equip players with a device for clocking average speed (an innovation I suspect and dread), this would show up as a far slower than average game. It's a Tuesday night, not long after Christmas, and all around me I see that fatigued, glassy look that tells me that the rest of the players, like myself, are lapsing into a low energy coma. At the end of the game, they might have to move all this meat off the bench with a stock prod.

They say that some people play this game for fun. I personally can't imagine it and suspect this of being something cooked up by the owners and the press. I do have a foggy recollection of thirteen-year-old kids flailing away on corner lots in the freezing cold for reasons other than money or coercion, but I also know that I was never one of them.

My parents gave me no choice in the matter. They drove me to the rink late at night or at dawn and counted themselves the finest parents in the land for doing so. The fact that I didn't like hockey was unimportant. I was taught to believe that it was something you did whether you liked it or not — like school and community clean-up. For some parents, it's religion or music lessons; but my parents wanted neither Christian nor concert musician. They wanted a big, mean pro hockey player who would wish them toothless Happy Birthdays during the Hockey Night in Canada intermissions of their autumn years.

"Burns! Go on! C'mon, get the hell out there!"

Amazing. For a moment, I totally forgot where I was. All the hockey rinks and benches of my life merged into one and I didn't know whether I was twelve, eighteen or twenty-five — a bantam, a junior or an NHLer.

I am an NHLer of course. And I am on our toasty warm home bench. The man yelling at me is Chip, our manager, all crimson with rage. And, he is yelling because my line didn't go on when the other line came off. For many seconds, there has been no one on the ice but our goalie and six members of the other team.

One of them shoots. Carrasco, our goalie, gets a leg on it. Another one shoots. He stops that too. We are all cheering now, like mad; but, still, NOT ONE OF OUR PLAYERS CLIMBS OVER THE BOARDS TO PLAY!

"Goddamn you, Burns! Get out there before I break your leg!"

There is a blood vessel on Chip's forehead big and beating like an exposed heart. I climb over the boards and my linemates follow. Just in time to see the third rebound come off our goalie, Carrasco's pad right onto the stick of one of the five players buzzing around his net. The stick flicks, Carrasco dives; but the puck pops over him and into the net. The red light goes on just as we, the cavalry, arrive.

Fishing the puck out of the net, I look through the eye aperture of Carrasco's mask. He has drawn stitch marks on the plastic each time it saved him from a killing blast to the face. The mask looks like a railway map of Southern Britain. From a distance this motif is ghoulish, but from this close, I can see Ronnie's eyes behind. They are red, watery and scared.

"Where were you guys?" he croaks, a dribble of water running out the bottom of the mask onto his padded chest.

I hand him the puck. "A souvenir, Ronnie. You were terrific." I whack him on the pads and skate to centre ice.

Later, after losing the game 5-3, we sit in the dressing room. We grunt orchestrally. A few tubas, a bassoon; I am more of a French Horn. There is no mood to this music, happy or sad; it is just there. Heavy, heartless breathing in a thought vacuum.

Again I slip quietly off the ice-bound years of my adolescence. I was on the verge of rebelling, of telling my parents to varnish my hockey stick because it was my last. I was thinking about joining a tribe of travelling potters. I was about to do all that when a scout appeared after one of our play-off games. He took me to the best restaurant in own and told me to order as much of whatever I liked. While I ate, he mentioned several multi-digit money figures and I felt a sudden urge to take my hockey a little more seriously.

But, lately, something has gone wrong. I can't concentrate, not even on money. I just drift off. I start seeing the fifteen-year-old girls who hung around our hockey practices. I can see their faces and my memory has edited out every zit. The shy way they used to lurk in the shadows when we came out of the locker room with our hockey bags over our shoulders. I can hear them giggling, but I can't hear my own manager when he's screaming, "Go on, Burns! For the sake of sweet Jesus, go on!"

Chip enters and slams the door. His hair is sticking up valiantly from its sea of grease. His cheeks are flaming and he brings the smell of whiskey in to do battle with the robust aroma of sweat. He stomps up and down between us, his every movement ferocious.

"You guys stunk out there, tonight!" he shouts at last, relieving the tension.

Smitty Smith, the cornerman on my line, wrinkles up his smashed nose and gives an attempt at a loud sniff which winds up being a thunderous snort. "Still do," he says, laughing and snorting. "Smell," he adds for the slow ones.

Chip whirls, his coattails winding up like a propeller.

"Who said that?"

"I did, coach," says Smitty.

Poor Smitty, or should I say lucky Smitty, because, surely, hockey is keeping him out of an institution for the criminally stupid. He is regular cannon fodder for Chip's postgame rages. Chip walks up to him and levels a finger at the still snorting nose.

"Remember when I told this team that the next time we got scored on because of a slow line change, some lard asses were going to find themselves in the minor leagues?"

"No."

(Chip chooses to ignore this.) "Your line, Smith, was scored on tonight when you weren't even on the goddamn ice!"

"But, Burnsy ... "

"Screw Burnsy!" I can't say I care for the sound of this. "It was your line and I might just decide to put all three of you idiots down for a while. Maybe down there you could remember how to play hockey!"

This is a fairly idle threat. Obviously Chip would love to send most of us to the minor leagues and would except for the total lack of better players there to bring up.

"I'm telling you guys this team's on the verge of shake-up! Nobody's job is secure as long as we keep losing. There's three things wrong with you: No hustle! No brains! No speed! And NO GUTS!!"

"That's four," Smitty grins with happy idiocy, not a tooth in his giant head. He is so proud of his deduction.

The effect on Chip is quite fascinating. He begins to sag slowly like a pin-punctured inflatable couch. Frowning at the floor, he mutters in a vague monotone; something about the plane we have to catch to Montreal in the morning. He finishes by saying, "If we play like this against Montreal ... " but his voice trails off into silence before he can entirely tell us what we're in for. He shuffles to the door, still sagging. Smitty really can't help himself; he has to give the old coach just one more helping hand.

"They'll kill us," he offers cheerfully.

Chip is at the door by now, with his hand draped on the knob, a rag. Hearing Smitty, he finds one last nerve of fury, yet unexploded. He swings around. His eyes travel the bench on which we sit. His eyes meeting ours. I wouldn't be surprised if there are tiny cross hairs in the middle of his vision. When his eyes reach mine, they stop. His mind pushes the button marked Torpedo.

"Burns. In my office after you shower."

When I step into Chip's office a half hour later, he is gnawing on one of his hands. A lonely cannibal. I feel something for him close akin to sympathy: disgust, I think. If Chip's stomach was a garbage bag, you wouldn't want to carry anything wet or heavy in it.

"You took your sweet time."

"Heavy dirt and grime."

I move a dog-eared scouting file off a chair and sit. Chip waits deliberately hoping the suspense will fill me with regret for my many wrongdoings.

"You're not putting out, Burns."

"I'm the team's highest scorer."

"Look, Burnsy," 'Burnsy' means an appeal to my sporting side. Chip is still under the impression that I have one. "You could do a hell of a lot more for this team. You're a great little hockey player when you want to be. You were a first-round draft pick."

"Fire the scout."

"But, cripes, just sitting there during the line change."

"I think it was my inner ear acting up again."

"Okay, alright. Water under the bridge." Such is Chip's obsession with this game, I'm sure he sees ice on the water and kids with great potential playing shinny on the ice.

He looks up, past my head, at a yellowing photograph of his last winning team; juniors he coached to a national final.

"You could lead this team out of the doldrums." His voice has taken on that misty monotone again, as if he was talking from the cockpit of a time machine. "We wouldn't have to be in the cellar if you played your

best game. Take charge. Like Bobby Clarke. The players look up to you."
He pauses, frowns, takes a bite out of his hand and glares at me crazily.
"They look up to you and you infect the whole bunch of them with a
lack of desire!"

I feel this is a bit strong. I try to instill in them a sensible lack of hope.

"Don't you ever want to be on the all-star team, Burns?"

The answer to this question is no, but I won't break Chip's heart by
telling him. The all-star game is sixty minutes of hockey I presently have
the luxury of taking or leaving.

"The point is this, Burns, if you don't start putting out, I'm going to
trade you."

I shrug.

Chip looks heavenward and grasps the air. Maybe God is lowering
him a ladder.

"This rotten damn game! I can remember juniors I coached; big kids,
tough as nails, crying their eyes out because they didn't get drafted. And
you. Big fat contract. Commercials. Endorsements. And you couldn't care
less if we trade you."

Chip rips open the bottom drawer of his desk and pulls out a whiskey
bottle. He spins off the top and it bounds across the carpet. He drains off
a couple of inches from the neck of the bottle and scrapes his hand vi-
ciously across his mouth. His eyes are those of a cornered pig.

"What about me? What the hell do I do when I get fired off this tail-
end team?"

Perhaps Chip could sell endorsements for ulcer milk.

*It was the third period of the game. We were behind and stinking the
place out. It would be our sixth loss in a row and I could already hear the
management baying for my blood. I can tell you, my ulcers were giving
me hell. I reached for the mickey of rye in the inside pocket of my sports
jacket; but my wife had taken it out and replaced it with a bottle of
Abdomal the Ulcer Milk. My first thought was, I'll break that bitch's face;
but when that Abdomal got down there and started to soothe ...*

"Get out of my sight, Burns! You make me sick."

A speedy jaunt in my Porsche and I am home to my luxurious two-bed-
room condo by the river. The kitchen faucet exudes a thin stream of boil-
ing-hot water which in former times was a simple drip. The dirty socks,
the Kentucky Fried Chicken bones, the cones of cigar ash on the carpet,
the beer bottles lying on their sides ...

I had a cleaning lady once. She clucked her tongue and said how dis-
gusting. A monkey wouldn't live like this and you a big-shot hockey player

too. As a helping hand to a better life, she stole my liquor.

In the midst of all this filth, I sit in almost abject misery. If I was someone else looking in I would sneer. How dare you be abjectly miserable with a salary the size of yours, I'd say. And all I could say back at me would be a lot of whining about too many practices and road trips, about our grueling schedule. I would also plead my peculiar belief about the women of this world.

According to the popular myth, there are a million women in this land who are dying to take care of and slip between the satin sheets with me, a national sporting hero. I believe in this ghostly batallion of beauties with a kind of desperate fervour. I do my best to keep myself attractive for them. For instance, all thirty-two of my teeth are still straight and solid in their gums — a rarity if not a total exception among hockey players.

My secret is regular brushing, flossing and a total avoidance of anything resembling a fight, an elbow or a high stick. It was once said of me by a smart-ass reporter that I could go into the corners with fresh eggs in my hockey pants and never break a one. So what? It's true.

But where are these women? This is the greatest mystery of my life. Maybe they are in a bed with my toothless teammates but I doubt it. I have a feeling that they are already married to lawyers and carpenters and accountants and that they limit their goings-on with pro athletes to a sly lusting after our brutishness in front of the colour TV Saturday night. Oh, please. Just one of you. Come to me!

But really, as I sit here in my bathrobe, sipping an orange juice past my perfect, mint-flavoured teeth — my jock strap drying on a chair between me and the national news — I look at my purple shins, the scars on my knees and ask, who in their right mind *would* be interested in this body?

Less than twenty hours later, the gate swings open and the Montreal Forum ice gleams ahead of me under the TV lights. Yes, for the first time all year, we are going to be displaying our talents on national TV. At last, our Moms and Dads across the land will have the opportunity of watching their favourite sons being thrashed by one of the nation's most powerful hockey machines.

We emerge to a chorus of jeers and boos from the rabid Forum fans. Our team name is the Bisons. That name always seemed like a prophetic and fitting title for our team. I devised my own little cheer from it to motivate me across dull spots in the play. It goes like this:

Go Bisons go!

Big, stupid and slow;

Onward to'rd extinction,

Go Bisons go!

The game begins and before it is a minute old, the Canadiens star right-winger has picked the puck from Steve Burke's skates, gone in alone on our goalie Carrasco and popped the puck past his internationally famous weak spot: low, to the stick side.

Soon after, we take a penalty and the Canadiens have us all hemmed into our own end again. It looks like just a matter of time until they bang another one in. I'm staying out of trouble by the blue line. It's safe and quiet there and a nice, short skate to centre ice after the goal.

All of a sudden one of our defencemen takes a wild swipe at the puck, connects and knocks it rolling up the ice. The Montreal defencemen have all closed in on our net for the kill and, as a result, I am the closest person to the puck by about twenty yards. I skate for it and have perhaps the cleanest breakaway of my life.

I try hard to concentrate. I haven't scored a goal in six games and Chip may just be getting serious about trading me. A new team might mean pressure, extra practices, or, God forbid, the playoffs.

The goalie is coming out to meet me. I should really deke and go around him, but I might screw up and lose the puck if I did. Better to shoot now. I pick a spot in the right corner and fire. Somehow I fan. I get practically no wood on the shot at all, but the goalie, seeing what I was planning to do, moved to cover the right hand corner. This opens up a little hole between his legs and, through that hole, my meagre shot trickles. It has just enough momentum to get over the goal line into the net. The period ends 1-1.

During the intermission, Chip tries to tell us that the Canadiens aren't that tough. We'll take 'em boys, he says. This is such a good one that several of us cannot stifle laughter.

Halfway through the second period, pucks start streaming past Carrasco's stick side. Every time we make a big effort to stop this shelling, we take a penalty and they pot another one. After the fifth goal, Carrasco comes skating over to the bench like a man possessed. He tries to open the door into the bench but Chip holds it shut from the other side.

"What's wrong with you? You're not hurt."

"Lemme in," Carrasco whimpers. "I saw it again."

He jerks his mask off. His face is white. A drop of sweat jiggles crazily on the point of his chin. "I saw the ghost again. He had on a white uniform. He skated in on me laughing. His teeth were all black. He slapped the puck and it went right through me! Right in one side and out the other!"

"You stop talking like a nut and get the hell back out there!"

Bond, our captain, leans over. "Jeez, coach, let him come out. He won't stop nothing like this. It's a mental problem."

"You're damn right he's got a mental problem. He can't stop a G.D. thing on his stick side. That's the problem!"

Carrasco stops yanking on the door. He throws his goalie stick up into the crowd and climbs over the boards. He beats his way past Chip and runs on his skates down the alley to the dressing room.

"Fart!" screams Chip. "No one else in this league has half the crazy bastards I do. Bordeaux, get in there."

Bordeaux is our back-up goalie, a fuzz-faced kid from Montreal. His hometown is the very last place on earth he ever wanted to appear — on TV yet — playing behind a cheesecloth outfit like the Bisons. But fear drives him to brilliance and the second period ends without further scoring. 5-1 Canadiens.

In the third period, I score again. If the TV colour man was to discuss my goal after the game, he might describe it this way:

Burns was parked out in front of the net jostling with a defenceman and keeping up a constant stream of chatter. 'Watch it, you bastard you almost got me in the eye. Hey, ref, this guy's trying to hack my head off here!' All of a sudden a defenceman on Burn's team winds up for a slapper from the point. It comes in like a bullet and, well, nobody could jump higher on skates than Burns when he thought he was going to get hit by the puck. So, there it was, the puck doing about a hundred and Burns up in the air this high; the puck hits his skate blade, whango! and it's right in the net. Heck, I must have seen Burns score five goals that way over the years.

But, the colour man won't be discussing my goal as it only serves to make the Habs mad. They come storming back scoring on poor Bordeaux almost at will. Soon, the Montreal crowd is cheering wildly every time the kid stops a dribbler.

Then, it happens. Steve Burke, who has been on the ice for every Montreal goal, goes nuts. He boards the Canadiens' superstar right-winger so hard a pane of plexi-glass falls out into the crowd. The super-star drops as if shot and does not move.

The rest is axiomatic. Two of the Montreal players go for Burke with sticks up and threatening. One of our boys goes in to even up the odds. The referees race over to try and prevent total war. Fat chance. The super-star still isn't moving. His eyes are closed. He may be dead. All the Montreal players come storming off the bench which means that all our players must storm off the bench too.

I am on the bench and would love to stay here. But it just isn't done.

All these things are as pre-ordained as the order of events at a Vatican high mass. I file dutifully onto the ice with my gloves held by the gauntlets and skate around the perimeter of the six fights now in progress, trying to look as unmenacing as possible.

The super-star is up now. Unhurt, and forgotten. The crowd that was gasping in fear for his career seconds ago is now too busy watching the fight to notice him up and skating off the ice. Right now, he's unimportant. One fight is busy spawning another. Oaths wing hither and thither in need of bilingual translation. Fans are up on their feet, clinging to the plexi-glass and crying for blood.

In the midst of all this bloody hubbub, it happens again. I begin to drift. I drift down the thousand or so benches I have sat on and pick up not a sliver. I drift right back to Buffalo Flats, the Alberta small town where I was allowed to live for a few years before I had to move on to bigger centres and better coaches. I am with a girl I had forgotten existed. Her name is Paulette. We're thirteen and we're in the dark beside the rink. She is letting me put my hand up under her heavy woolen sweater. It is the first time I have ever done this. It is freezing cold out. One of my ears is totally numb, but I don't own a hat. Hats are sissy. It's so cold that Paulettte is afraid we might freeze solid. I think one part of me is already afflicted, but I don't tell her this. She may be able to feel the evidence anyway. She is most worried about freezing solid because it would mean that we would be found as we are; with my hand up her sweater.

I am so far gone, so absorbed in these philosophical matters, with Paulette and her sweater, that I hardly notice the kid who races over to me, screeches to a halt in a spray of ice and grabs hold of my sweater. I hardly see his pimply, writhing face, his madman eyes. I hardly hear the stream of abuse from his toothless mouth. While I am in Paulette's sweater, he is trying to pull mine over my head. Unable to do this and frustrated to total insanity by the faraway, seraphic smile on my face, he lowers his head and drives the top of his helmet into my mouth.

This, I feel.

Suddenly, Paulette is gone. Her sweater. Buffalo Flats. All banished back to the foreign past. The crazy kid is gone somewhere too. Dragged off by a referee or maybe by one of my teammates. I am back in the Forum. Standing at centre ice. I look down at the red dot and it is getting redder by the second, dyed by a stream from my mouth. A quick lick tells me that one of my two perfect, well-flossed and brushed front teeth is no longer occupying its traditional place in my healthy gum. I don't remember swallowing it. Slowly, I skate around the ice looking. It's got to be here somewhere. Teeth don't just vanish.

Then, I am corralled by our trainer and two of our players. I keep telling them I must find my tooth, but they are pushing me along toward the gate.

On the narrow bench in the dressing room. Mouth wadded full of cotton batting. The muffled roar of the crowd as the game peters out to its lop-sided conclusion.

The game ends. The team trudges in. Chip follows, raving about a shake-up. I am not around to be raved at, however. I am off in the near future this time, rather than the distant past that I so often visit. In this near future, there are sticks but they are all embedded in weinies or the soft belly of an ice-cream bar. There are pucks too, of bacon. Body checks come annually at the doctor's office and he always announces that you are in great physical condition. Afterwards you go home to your pad, an old fashioned but modest and clean apartment. Meeker is someone more meek than someone else.

Somehow, every time I lick up under my swollen lip, I am reminded of this near future and the many sources from which money can come. Money, unlike teeth, can be replenished. A missing tooth is a hole in your head for life.

excerpts from the novel *The Last Season*

❖   ROY MacGREGOR

Even in the forty below weather of Pomerania, I always had to be the
first one to the rink. And I kept it up in Vernon. Coach Bowles — to me
he deserved being nicknamed Sugar — he got so tired of seeing me standing around the side entrance when he arrived to set up that he slipped
me my own key so I could come and go as I pleased. The day Poppa
came to watch I left Riley's about noon, even though we weren't playing
until seven. I'd told Poppa I'd see him after the game, that I needed the
time before to unwind and get ready, and he seemed to understand. And
I took the same crazy route to the arena I've followed since we won our
opening game of the season against Orillia, shortcutting across the curling rink parking lot, hopping the chainlink fence around the war memo-
rial — wreaths just now starting to wilt after a week in the cold and
rain — then over across the field back of the Legion Hall, through the
lane between the houses, down the slope by the river and up again to
the rink. Someone down toward the docks was burning wet leaves and
the smoke was rolling along the river, sharp and delicious. For some reason it made my stomach growl.

Sugar was already there, sharpening in the skate room. I could hear
the stone and smell the dry grind, and though I loved to watch him work,
I passed and went directly to the dressing room. The lights were on over
the ice and I could hear Bull Tate tripping the tank levers as he began his
first flood. Usually I loved to watch that too, the water spreading wet and
glimmering behind him, the steam rising from the spread rag and the
taps, but this I passed on too.

It was not a matter of trying to be first, I *had* to be first. And far worse
in Vernon than back home. At our very first skate in Vernon we all dressed
together, and Tom Powers, who had already been made team captain by

Sugar, stopped right in front of me, pointed straight at my drawers and shouted: "Christ, if you're going out there in *that*, forget the equipment — no one's going to come near *you!*"

No one had ever said anything like that in Pomerania. I'd been expecting to be called "Polack," had even specially remembered the great line Jaja's hero, Wally Stanowski, had when he played for the Leafs, so I could use it, too: "I train on Polish sausage, the breakfast of champions." But they weren't laughing at my heritage — it was my underwear! I couldn't just jump up and paste Powers, so I leaned over and pretended I'd lost something in my duffel bag, scrounging around till I felt some of the burn leave my face. So I didn't have nice, new, bright white insulated underwear — big goddamned deal! I was angry and I couldn't shake it. I carefully checked out Powers during the warm-up, the way he'd skate in over the blue line and then let the puck drop back from the blade to his skate, kick off over onto the other skate and then kick the puck back up to the blade, the illusion being that he had lost it. I skated around memorizing his move and gathering myself, enjoying the season's first waft of arena air on my face, giving my little extra kick as I rounded the net so I came out of the turn with pants hissing and the ice behind me making a sound like I'd just been withdrawn from a scabbard. And then, when scrimmage began, I simply waited for Powers to try that little suck move on my side, aiming for his head rather than the puck, and I put him up so high he did a complete somersault in the air and came down so hard on his brand-new Tackaberry skates that the left blade bent and Sugar, smiling rather than angry, had to go off with him into the skate room and pound it straight with a mallet.

After that I never had a moment's trouble from Tom Powers. After that, though, I never failed to be the first one dressed either. Not that I had to any more. At the very next practice I arrived to find a brand-new cellophane-wrapped set of Stanfield longjohns resting on my seat. The only other person in the rink was Sugar Bowles, sharpening, but he never said a word about the underwear, and I never mentioned it either. But it had to be him.

I could hear Sugar coming along dragging a new bundle of sticks and I got up and caught the door for him. I'd been imagining I was Tim Horton sitting there yakking up a storm with Stanley and Bower before we took to the ice. But it was hard to think of Sugar as Punch Imlach. Sugar had more hair sticking out one ear than Punch had on his entire head, I swear, about an inch above his eyebrows, hair like Poppa's, black and thick and dry-looking like he'd just washed it, though I doubt Poppa and he had a half-dozen washes between them over their lifetimes. Punch looked like a bank teller; Sugar like the holdup man. Sugar had this huge scar on his face running from the corner of his right eye down across his cheek and sliding off his jawbone. The right eye seemed to look at you but was cloudy, the left one nearly as black as his hair. Tom Powers put it about that Sugar had lost his eye in a hockey fight, kicked by a skate when he was down, but Sugar hadn't verified this story. Powers also said Sugar was once a prospect himself, but when Danny pressed him on the way back from a North Bay game, Sugar denied he'd even played the game and told us all to shut up and try and get some sleep.

"Batterinski."

"Yah," I said, looking up. The cloudy eye seemed to have me fixed. Sugar was still taping, but not thinking about it.

"What do you think of Fontinato?"

"He's okay."

"You ever hear of Sprague Cleghorn?"

It sounded like a disease to me. "No. Why?"

"Cleghorn'd eat Fontinato for breakfast."

"He played?"

Sugar nodded and spit. "Five times they arrested him for hurting players. Five times."

I shook my head. I didn't know what else to do.

"Newsy Lalonde," he said, letting it hang.

I looked at Sugar, unsure.

"Sent more'n fifty guys off the ice on stretchers."

Sugar finished taping the first stick, bit off the tape and picked up another, his head turning so the left eye could catch me directly. "Who do you like in the NHL, Batterinski?"

"Horton," I said.

"You take a look at Fontinato," he said. "And maybe even this new guy Eddie Shack. You understand?"

I didn't. Sometimes no one could figure out Sugar or his crazy riddles. Talking with him was always like breaking an oar halfway across the lake. But I did like some of his sayings. He really pissed Powers off one practice when he said: "You don't have enough talent to win on talent alone," and when Powers came up after practice and asked Sugar if it was meant for him in particular, Sugar just said: "If you have to ask, you must have a question." Beee-utiful.

One of the sayings was meant for me in particular, and I knew that for certain because he gave it only to me, all folded over and placed in an envelope with my number on it. "The unforgivable crime is soft hitting," it read. "Do not hit at all if it can be avoided, but *never* hit softly." Underneath was this name, Teddy Roosevelt, which sounded vaguely familiar to me, but I didn't have the nerve to ask.

The other guys straggled in, Terry LeMay, the goaltender, Powers and his sidekick, Bucky Cryderman, then Danny.

"Hey, Bats," Cryderman said, laughing, "you want I should call your old man in here to tighten your skates?"

"Screw off." I said, closing the issue. Danny was a loudmouth.

Ten minutes before warm-up Sugar was ready for his talk and slammed a stick into the equipment box for our attention. "All right, then," he began. "We should be ready. You all remember Parry Sound from the exhibitions, so you forwards know if you get a chance you shoot. Goalie's weak on long ones to the stick side; but don't try to suck him because he's good in tight and flops well. So keep it simple and make your first shots count. I'll be juggling lines to keep Powers' line away from their checkers, so if I touch your shoulder that means *you* are on, not necessarily your line, so just keep track of yourselves, okay?

"These guys like to carry the puck and they like to make the pretty play, but they don't seem as keen when the going gets rough. Batterinski?"

"Yah?"

"You set the pace, you understand?"

"Uh huh."

"Sprague Cleghorn, remember. Now the rest of you are going to be seeing a very small player out there and though he's a defenceman they'll probably play him up front 'cause he's only peewee age."

"A *peewee?*" Powers said, falling into giggles.

"Laugh once and get it out of your system," Sugar said, eyeing Powers with the black left ball. "His name is Orr and I've seen him and he's already a better player at twelve than any of you are at fifteen. Understand that? Don't let his size fool you and watch him. Defence, I want you to stick to him like snot to an oven door, understand?"

All around the room we grunted that we did.

"Cryderman," Sugar called, kicking at Bucky's skates stuck out in front of him like he was about to take a nap. "What's the toughest fish in the ocean?"

"Huh?"

"Come on. You guys think you're all big fish in a little pond. What is it?"

"I dunno," Bucky said. "A shark, I guess."

"That's very good, Cryderman. Now there's something special about sharks that I want you all to consider. There's one thing that makes sharks different from all other fish ... anyone care to guess what it is?"

"The fin," said Powers.

"Nah."

"The teeth," Danny shouted, showing his.

"No."

Sugar waited, scanning the room, then he smiled.

"A barracuda's teeth are just as nasty, maybe worse. What makes a shark truly unusual is what he *doesn't* have. And that's a swim bladder."

Someone laughed. Powers, probably. Or Bucky.

"Go ahead," Sugar said. "Laugh. But let me tell you first what it means. A shark has to keep moving constantly. A shark does not float, like other fish. A shark can't float. He has no swim bladder, see. He can't let up for a minute and that's what makes him top dog. You think about that awhile, okay?"

Sugar walked out the door and closed it silently and no one said a word. No laugh, no burp, no fart. No one would dare destroy Sugar's pregame silences because they worked. We were leading the league.

Danny and I could hardly believe it when we first got here. We were used to Father Schula's prayers that no one got hurt, but so far this year we had had Sugar read aloud from *Tom Sawyer*, quote John Kennedy and Winston Churchill and some Chinese guy I'd never heard of and give lectures on everything from why water droplets scoot on a hot pan ("Keep the puck away from the traffic") to how vultures in Egypt break open ostrich eggs by dropping small stones on them ("You can't do it all yourself").

By tradition, I went onto the ice first. Number seven was the first sound in the arena always, first scrape on the ice, first slice of the corner, first stick on a puck, first crash of puck against the boards. In a way I created the game, just as I so often finished the game. With my hands.

I didn't see Poppa until "God Save the Queen." The record always skipped slightly and Al Willoughby, the arena manager, had piled so many pennies on the arm the record had slowed to a near growl. But no one sang along anyway, so it didn't matter. I quickly scanned the seats, skinny Wilemena Bowles, Sugar's wife, in her usual seat, clutching the gong of her cow bell so it wouldn't sound, and behind her a plastic golf hat held over a heart. *Poppa.* And he was singing along, or trying to. The only one in the arena fool enough to even try.

Powers won the first face-off and got it straight back to me. I circled slowly, shifted, then doubled back and cut across ice when the winger charged me. At their blue line I hit Powers with a perfect pass and he stopped, a give-and-go play. I followed through, slipping up the far wing and into the clear, and Powers put on the shift I figured he would, a shoulder dip, but when he tried to thread the pass through the defenceman's skates the puck was suddenly stopped and Powers was standing there looking like a fool.

It was the *kid!* They'd *started* him for Christ's sake, and on defence too. He looked like a mascot out there, but suddenly the puck was sailing off his stick high through the air and perfectly into the glove of the winger who'd originally rushed me. I was caught up ice. Parry Sound came in two on one; a deke, a flick pass and a stab, and poor old Terry didn't have a prayer. Parry Sound 1, Vernon 0.

Sugar let into us on the bench. What had he said in the dressing room about floating? Why did Powers stop? What made me so sure I could just walk away from my position? We took it all, heads down, not saying a word. Sugar waited through ten minutes of stopped time before he tapped my shoulder again.

At the start of the second period Danny got the puck back to me at the point and I slammed a low, hard one, and Danny, just like we used to practise back home, skated in front and let his stick dangle so it just ticked the shot straight down onto the ice and suddenly it was 1-1. I slapped Danny's pads and went straight back toward the face-off circle, skating bent over, stick riding both knees, looking up from the ice just once to see how much time was left. I wanted to look at Poppa, but I couldn't. But I could imagine what he must have felt hearing his family name crackling out over the P.A. System. Had a Batterinski ever before known such glory?

A minute left in the second period and I was last man back with the blond kid breaking over centre, intercepting a bad Bucky pass over to Powers. He looked like an optical illusion coming in on me, too small, too compact, rushing in a near sitting position, but still accelerating too fast for me to simply ride off into the corner. I forced him slightly to my left, then stepped right, where he came, and stopped and thrust out my hip with a little bit of knee I hoped the referee wouldn't catch. I had him clean. But then I didn't. All I felt was the wind from his sweater on my face as he somehow stepped yet another way and was gone. I turned and lunged, sweeping his feet out from under him, but even that was too late. The red light came on even as he flew through the air past Terry, and before he landed I could see him smile and raise his hands in victory, as if he'd somehow had control even as he sailed through the air.

I knew it wasn't right, but it felt great. I could feel my defenceman on my knuckles and when I touched them they stung with his jaw, just as I knew when he moved this week he would feel me and I would be with him, his better, for weeks to follow. He had my mark on him. I too had swelling and redness, but on the knuckles it shone with pride. Where his swelling made him less, mine made me more. I tried to feel his fear of me, and in trying this, my respect for myself grew. I went to the half-shattered mirror but saw no pimples. Just *Batterinski*, hulking in his pads, solid from blade to brush cut, a man oddly at ease while others about him panic.

Danny always talked about how quickly things take place. "He never even saw the puck," he'd say. But it was never so with me. I was like Willoughby's recording of "The Queen." When attention was on me, time slowed down. In a fight, I relaxed. I could sit in the dressing room in the hours before a game and twitch so bad sometimes a foot would jump right off the floor. But when my defenceman charged I was aware even of my own breathing. He came in flailing, but to me it was like watching someone swim toward me doing the crawl. I could sense his intention and I could feel his blind fury. When I had him about the waist it almost felt as if I was comforting him. That I didn't just keep squeezing until his insides poured out his mouth was an act of charity. I put him down and I ended his humiliation quickly for him, even hiding his face under his sweater when it happened. He should have thanked me.

The horn went to signal the end of the game and Danny was first in to confirm what I already knew.

"Ugga-bugga!" Danny shouted. His victory call. "Five-four for us, Bats."

I smiled. The rest poured in, shouting, slapping, tossing sticks and gloves. As they passed by they looked with the respect of the leeches but had no fear in touching, which I was glad for. I felt their hands and their sticks praising me.

"You fucking near killed that twit, Bats!"

"I heard the ambulance."

"Best check of the season."

"You turned it around, Bats old fart."

I said nothing in return. I sat there, completely dressed but for my gloves at my feet and felt no different than if I was lying in bed on a Saturday morning. The trainer, Biff, came in with a tray of Pepsi and made sure I got mine first. Then came Sugar, making like he was scribbling the final score down on his clipboard in case he'd somehow forget. He stopped, looked with the good black eye and winked it.

"Teddy Roosevelt," he said.

I said nothing, just smiled and looked down and began undressing slowly. Not undressing, more like dismantling: sweater, elbow pads, shoulder pads, lift off the braces, take off the skates, pants, undo garter, socks, shin pads, jock. Each piece dropped off with reluctance. If only the people who saw me on the street could see me in uniform, the big

"A" over the heart, the number 7, the tuck of my sweater into the back of my pants. I knew the uniform spoke better for me than I did myself.

Coming out of the shower Sugar reached out and caught my arm, turning me toward him. He whispered: "That your dad waiting out there?"

Danny! The son-of-a-bitch.

"Yes."

"You want me to call him in?"

I shook my head. Sugar hung his thick lower lip out and nodded his understanding.

When I was dressed though, Sugar insisted on leaving the dressing room with me. Poppa was outside, leaning on the nearest edge of the snack counter, chewing on a Coffee Crisp like a little kid. There were chocolate and wafer crumbs all over his chin and front.

"Mr. Batterinski?" Sugar said before I could say a word.

Poppa looked like he was about to get into trouble with the law. "Yes?"

"I'm Ted Bowles, sir. Felix's coach. Delighted to meet you."

Poppa took Sugar's hand like it was some sort of trick. I began praying he would say nothing with "th" in it.

"How'd you like the game?" Sugar asked.

"Yes." Poppa said, brushing the crumbs off his chin like he hadn't properly heard the question. "Some of it."

"Your boy here," Sugar said, smiling, "he turned it around for us."

Poppa looked startled. "He did?"

"Sure he did. We were flat as pancakes before he shook things up." Sugar smacked me on the back of the head, reaching up to rub his knuckles into my brush cut. I knew I was turning red. "You got any more like this back home, Mr. Batterinski?" Sugar asked.

In hockey it is called a "rep," short, of course, for "reputation." Mine grew out of North Bay: one game, one moment, the clock stopped, the game in suspension — and yet it was this, nothing to do with what took place while clocks ran in sixty-eight other games, that put me on the all-star team with more votes than Torchy. Half as many, however, as Bobby Orr. But still, it was Orr and Batterinski, the two defencemen, whom they talked most about in Ontario junior.

Bobby Orr would get the cover of *Maclean's*. I almost got the cover of *Police Gazette* after the Billings incident. My rep was made. The *North Bay Nugget's* nickname for me, Frankenstein, spread throughout the league. I had my own posters in Kitchener; there were threats in King-ston and spray-paint messages on our bus in Sault Ste. Marie; late, frantic calls at the Demers house from squeaky young things wanting to speak to the "monster."

They didn't know me. I didn't know myself. But I loved being talked about in the same conversations as the white brush cut from Parry Sound. Orr they spoke of as if he was the Second Coming — they sounded like Poppa praising the Madonna on the church in Warsaw; for me it was the same feeling for both Orr and the Madonna — I couldn't personally see it.

Orr had grown since I'd seen him first in Vernon, but he was still only sixteen in 1964 and seemed much too short to be compared to Harvey and Howe, as everyone was doing. He'd gone straight from bantam to junior, but Gus Demers still said he was just another in a long list of junior hockey's flashes-in-the pan. Another Nesterenko, another Cullen.

We met Oshawa Generals in that year's playoffs, and the papers in Oshawa and Sudbury played up the Batterinski-Orr side of it. "Beauty and the Beast," the Oshawa *Times* had it. The *Star* countered with "Batterinski's Blockade," pointing out that the Hardrocks' strategy was to have Batterinski make sure Orr never got near the net, though no one ever spoke to me about it. I presume it was understood.

On March 28 we met on their home ice, the advantage going to them by virtue of a better record throughout the season. I said not a single word on the bus ride down, refusing to join Torchy in his dumb-ass Beatles songs, refusing even to get up and wade back to the can, though I'd had to go since Orillia. My purpose was to exhibit strength and I could not afford the slightest opening. I had to appear superhuman to the rest of the team: not needing words, nor food, nor bodily functions.

If I could have ridden down in the equipment box I would have, let-ting the trainer unfold me and tighten my skates just before the warm-up, sitting silent as a puck, resilient as my shin pads, dangerous as the blades. The ultimate equipment: me.

I maintained silence through the "Queen" and allowed myself but one chop at Frog Larocque's goal pads, then set up. Orr and I were like re-flections, he standing solid and staring up at the clock from one corner, me doing the same at the other, both looking at time, both thinking of each other. We were the only ones in the arena, the crowd's noise simply the casing in which we would move, the other players simply the setting to force the crowd's focus to us. Gus Demers had advised me to level Orr early, to establish myself. Coach Therrian wanted me to wait for Orr, keep him guessing. I ignored them all. They weren't involved. Just Orr and me.

His style had changed little since bantam. Where all the other players seemed bent over, concentrating on something taking place below them, Orr still seemed to be sitting at a table as he played, eyes as alert as a poker player, not interested in his own hands or feet or where the object of the game was. I was fascinated by him and studied him intently during the five minutes I sat in the penalty box for spearing some four-eyed whiner in the first period. What made Orr effective was that he had somehow shifted the main matter of the game from the puck to him. By anticipating, he had our centres looking for him, not their wingers, and passes were directed away from him, not *to* someone on our team. By doing this, and by knowing this himself, he had assumed control of the Hardrocks as well as the Generals.

I stood at the penalty box door yanking while the timekeeper held for the final seconds. I had seen how to deal with Orr. If the object of the game had become him, not the puck, I would simply put Orr through his own net.

We got a penalty advantage toward the end of the period and coach sent me out to set up the power play. I was to play centre point, ready to drop quickly in toward the net rather than remaining in the usual point position along the boards and waiting for a low shot and tip-in. Therrian had devised this play, I knew, from watching Orr, though he maintained it was his own invention. I never argued. I never even spoke. I was equipment, not player, and in that way I was dependable, predictable, certain.

Torchy's play, at centre, was to shoulder the Oshawa centre out of the face-off circle while Chancey, playing drop-back left wing, fed the puck back to me, breaking in. A basketball play, really, with me fast-breaking and Torch pic-ing. The crowd was screaming but I couldn't hear. I was listening for Orr, hoping he might say something that would show me his flaw, hoping he might show involvement rather than disdain. But he said nothing. He stared up at the clock for escape, the numbers meaningless, the score irrelevant. He stood, stick over pads, parallel to the ice, back also parallel, eyes now staring through the scars of the ice for what might have been his own reflection. Just like me, once removed from the crowd's game, lost in his own contest.

The puck dropped and Torchy drove his shoulder so hard into the Generals' centre I heard the grunt from the blue line. Chancy was tripped as he went for the puck, but swept it as he fell. I took it on my left skate blade, kicking it forward to my stick, slowing it, timing it, raising back for a low, hard slapper from just between the circles. I could sense Orr. Not see him. I was concentrating on the puck. But I could sense him the way you know when someone is staring at you from behind. I raised the stick higher, determined to put the shot right through the bastard if necessary.

I heard him go down, saw the blond brush cut spinning just outside the puck as he slid toward me, turning his pads to catch the shot. His eyes were wide open as his head passed the puck; he stared straight at it, though it could, if I shot now, rip his face right off the skull. He did not flinch; he did not even blink. He stared the way a poker player might while saying he'll hold. Orr knew precisely what my timing was before I myself knew. I saw him spin past, knew what he was doing, but could not stop; my shot crunched into his pads and away, harmlessly.

The centre Torchy had hit dove toward the puck and it bounced back at me, off my toe and up along the ankle, rolling like a ball in a magician's trick. I kicked but could not stop it. The puck trickled and suddenly was gone. I turned, practically falling. *It was Orr!* Somehow he'd regained his footing even faster than I and was racing off in that odd sitting motion toward our net.

I gave chase, now suddenly aware of the crowd. Their noise seemed to break through an outer, protective eardrum. There were no words, but I was suddenly filled with insult as the screams tore through me, ridiculing. It seemed instant, this change from silently raising the stick for the certain goal, the sense that I was gliding on air, suspended, controlling even the breath of this ignorant crowd. Now there was no sense of gliding or silence or control. I was flailing, chopping at a short sixteen-year-old who seemed completely oblivious to the fact that Batterinski was coming for him.

I felt my left blade slip and my legs stutter. I saw him slipping farther and farther out of reach, my strides choppy and ineffective, his brief, effortless and amazingly successful. I swung with my stick at his back, causing the noise to rise. I dug in but he was gone, a silent, blond brush cut out for a skate in an empty arena.

I dove, but it was no use. My swinging stick rattled off his ankle guards and I turned in my spill in time to see the referee's hand raise for a delayed penalty. I was already caught so I figured I might as well make it worthwhile. I regained my feet and rose just as Orr came in on Larocque, did something with his stick and shoulder that turned Frog into a life-size cardboard poster of a goaltender, and neatly tucked the puck into the corner of the net.

The crowd roared, four thousand jack-in-the-boxes suddenly sprung, all of them laughing at me. Orr raised his hands in salute and turned, just as I hit him.

It was quiet again, quiet as quickly as the noise had first burst through. I felt him against me, shorter but probably as solid. I smelled him, not skunky the way I got myself, but the smell of Juicy Fruit chewing gum. I gathered him in my arms, both of us motionless but for the soar of our skates, and I aimed him carefully and deliberately straight through the boards at the goal judge.

Orr did not even bother to look at me. It was like the theory you read about car accidents, that the best thing you can do is relax. Orr rode in my arms contentedly, acceptingly, neither angry, nor afraid, nor surprised. We moved slowly, deliberately, together. I could see the goal judge leaping, open-mouthed, back from the boards, bouncing off his cage like a gorilla being attacked by another with a chain. I saw his coffee burst through the air as we hit, the grey-brown circles slowly rising up and away and straight into his khaki coat. The boards gave; they seemed to give forever, folding back toward the goal judge, then groaning, then snapping us out and down in a heap as the referee's whistle shrieked in praise.

I landed happy, my knee rising into his leg as hard as I could manage, the soft grunt of expelled air telling me I had finally made contact with the only person in the building who would truly understand.

If it would stop there, the game would be perfect. But I knew, having taken my best shot, I would have to deal with the rebound. My hope was to clear it quickly. I pushed Orr and began to stand, only to be wrapped by the linesman trying to work a full nelson around my shoulders. I went to him gratefully, shifting with false anger, yanking hard but not too hard, according to the unwritten fighter-linesman agreement. He was taking in my ear the way one does to calm down a dog who has just smelled porcupine.

"Easy now, fella. Just take it easy now, okay?"

I said nothing. I pulled hard; he pulled back hard. He twisted me away; I went with him, scowling, delighted.

"Get the trainer!" I heard the referee shout to one of the Generals.

I twisted back. Orr was still down on the ice. The other linesman stood above, waiting to embrace him, but Orr just lay there, eyes shut, face expressionless.

"Chickenshit!" one of their larger players yelled at me and then looked away quickly, afraid to own up to his words. I lunged toward him, but gratefully let the linesman reel me in.

"Just easy now! Easy, easy, easy," he said in my ear. I felt like barking, just to throw him off.

The referee signalled to the linesman to get me to the box, and I let him wrestle me over with only a few stops and twists. Some of the crowd was hanging up over the glass and screens, throwing things, spitting, screaming. They looked like the muskrat Danny had once taken on a tip trap and failed to drown; we'd put it in a box and stabbed cattail stems through the cardboard at the little fucker until it ran at the screen we'd placed over top, screeching and spitting at us as if it would have torn us to pieces if it hadn't been blocked from us. These rats seemed voluntarily caged. Unlike the muskrat, they welcomed their confinement. If they broke through and got me they'd have trouble finding the courage to ask for my autograph.

Orr did not return to the game. We won 4-1 on Torchy's hat-trick. I scored the fourth on a desperate empty-net attempt by Oshawa, and the slow slider from centre was booed all the way into the net, making it as sweet as if I had skated through the entire team and scooped it high into a tight corner as the last man back-slashed my feet from under me. I even asked the linesman for the puck, just to rub it in.

But such sweetness never seems to last. The x-rays went against us, Orr returned for game three and after six we were out of it, retired for the season. Orr scored or set up seventeen of the Generals' twenty-two goals over this stretch. I scored twice, set up three and spent sixty-two minutes in the penalty box, twelve of them for boarding him. But Orr and I did not make contact again until May 19, 1974 when Eddie Van Impe, Moose, the Watsons and I set up the defensive minefield that even the Great Orr with perfect knees couldn't have penetrated. Philadelphia 1, Boston 0. The Flyers take their first Stanley Cup in six games.

Truth

❖ W.P. KINSELLA

No matter what they say it wasn't us that started the riot at St. Edouard Hockey Arena. The story made quite a few newspapers and even got on the Edmonton television, the camera showing how chairs been ripped out of the stands and thrown onto the ice. There was also a worried-looking RCMP saying something about public safety, and how they had to take some of the twenty-five arrested people all the way to St. Paul to store them in jail. Then the station manager read an editorial about violence in amateur hockey. None of them come right out and say us Indians was to blame for the riot; they just present what they think are the facts and leave people to make their own minds up. How many do you think decide the white men was at fault?

There was also a rumour that the town of St. Edouard was going to sue the town of Hobbema for the damages to the arena. But nothing ever come of that.

Another story have that the trouble come about because my friend Frank Fencepost own a dog named Guy Lafleur. Not true either. Frank do own a dog named Guy Lafleur, a yellow and white mostly-collie with a question mark for a tail. And Guy Lafleur the dog *was* sitting on a seat right behind our team players' box. That dog he bark whenever our team, the Hobbema Wagonburners, get the puck. And every time he bark Frank would shout the same thing, "Shut up, Guy Lafleur you son of a bitch." A lot of heads would turn every time he said it, because, as you maybe guessed, St. Edouard was a French Canadian town. But it was something else that started the riot.

We never would of been there anyway if Frank hadn't learned to read and write. Someday, I'm going to write a story about the time Frank go to an adult literacy class. Now, just to show off, he read everything in the

Wetaskiwin Times every week, even the ads. One day he seen a notice about a small town hockey tournament that offer a one thousand dollar first prize.

"I think we should enter a team, Silas," he say to me.

"What do we know about hockey?" I say back. Neither me nor Frank skate. I played a little shinny when I was a kid, but I don't much like ice and snow up my nose, or for that matter, hockey sticks.

"Let's go see Jasper Deer," say Frank, "there's a two hundred dollar entry fee to be raised."

Jasper is employed by Sports Canada. All the strings on Sports Canada are pulled from Ottawa. Jasper he have an office with a grey desk big as a whale, in the Consolidated School building. About fifteen years ago Jasper was a good hockey player. I'm not sure what Sports Canada is, but I know they figure if they give all us Indians enough hockey sticks, basketballs and volleyballs, we forget our land claims, quit drinking too much, get good jobs so we can have the weekends off to play games.

Jasper is glad to have anybody come to see him. He was Chief Tom's friend, was how he come to get this cushy job, though he would rather be trapping, or cutting brush than sit in an office. He is already bleary-eyed at ten o'clock in the morning.

"You want to enter a team in a tournament, eh?" he say to us, pushing his desk drawer shut with his knee, the bottles rattling.

Hobbema has a team in the Western Canada Junior Hockey League, so once guys turn twenty-one and don't get signed by any NHL team, they got no place to play.

"It'll be easy to get some good players together," Frank say, "and playing hockey keep us young people sober, honest and religious."

By the time we leave Jasper is anxious to put his head down have a little sleep on his desk, but he agree to pay for uniforms, loan us equipment, and rent us a school bus to travel in. I write down all those promises and get him to sign them.

Trouble is, even though a thousand dollars sound like a lot of money to me and Frank, the guys we approach to play for us point out it don't even come to a hundred dollars each for a decent sized team. So the players we end up with is the guys who sit in the Alice Hotel bar bragging how they turned down NHL contracts ten years ago, plus a few of our friends who can stand up on skates, and a goalie who just got new glasses last week.

The uniforms are white as bathroom tile, with a bright red burning wagon on the front, with HOBBEMA in red letters on the back. Some people complain the team name is bad for our Indian image, but they just ain't got no sense of humour.

Frank is team manager. I am his assistant. Mad Etta, our four-hundred pound medicine lady is doctor and trainer, and Guy Lafleur is our mascot.

St. Edouard is way up in north-east Alberta, a place most of us never been before. Gorman Carry-the-kettle drive the bus for us. We have a pretty rowdy trip once we get Etta all attended to. She squeeze sideways down the aisle and sit on the whole back seat.

"I'm surprised the bus didn't tip up with its front wheels about three feet off the ground," say Gorman.

"Don't worry, you'll balance things out," we tell Gorman. He is about two hundred and eighty pounds himself, wear a red cap with a yellow unicorn horn growing out of the crown.

We stop for lunch in a town called Elk Point, actually we stop at the bar, and since most of the team is serious drinkers, it is three p.m. before we get on the road again. I have to drive because Gorman is a little worse for wear. When we get to St. Edouard, a town that have only about ten houses and a little frame hotel gathered around a wine-coloured elevator as if they was bowing down to it, we find we already an hour late for our first game. They was just about to forfeit us.

The game is played in a hoop-roofed building what is a combination curling rink and hockey arena. It sit like a huge haystack out in a field half a mile from town. Being February it is already dark. All I can see in any direction is snow drifts, a little stubble and lines of scratchy-looking trees wherever there's a road allowance. The countryside is not too different from Hobbema.

Soon as our team start to warm up, everybody, except maybe Frank, can see we is outclassed. We playing the St. Edouard Bashers. Their players all look as if they drove down on their combines. And they each look like they could lift a combine out of a ditch if it was to get stuck. Most of our players are hung over. And though most of them used to be hockey players, it easy to tell they ain't been on skates for years.

The St. Edouard Bashers is young, fast and tough. Someone mention that they ain't lost a tournament game in two years. There must be four thousand people in the arena, and they all go "Booooo," when our team show itself.

"I wonder where they all come from," says Frank. "There can't be more than fifty people in the town; sure must be some big families on these here farms."

They sing the national anthem in French, and after they done with that they sing the French national anthem. Then about a half a dozen priests, and what must be a bishop, he got a white robe and an embroidered quilt over his shoulder, come to centre ice where they bless a box of pucks. The priests shake holy water in each goal crease. The players all cross themselves.

"We should of brought a thunder dancer with us," says Frank. "Make a note of that, Silas. We do it next time."

I don't bother to write it down. I'm already guessing there won't be a next time.

Right after the puck is dropped St. Edouard take hold of it, carry it right in on our goal. They shoot. Our goalie don't have any idea where the puck is; by pure luck it hit him on the chest and fall to the ice. The goalie, Ferd Tailfeathers, lose his balance fall forward on the puck.

About that time a half-ton St. Edouard defenceman land with a knee on Ferd's head, smash his mask, his face and his glasses about an inch deep into the ice.

Guy Lafleur stand up on his seat and bark like a fire alarm.

"Shut up Guy Lafleur you son of a bitch," says Frank. Then looking out at the rink where Ferd lay still as if he been dead for a week or so, he say, "That fat sucker probably broke his knee on Ferd's head."

But the St. Edouard defenceman already skating around like he scored a goal, his stick raised up in the air, his skates making slashing sounds.

It is Ferd Tailfeathers get carried from the ice.

"Who's buying the next round?" he ask the referee, as we haul him over the boards.

"They take their hockey pretty seriously up here, eh?" says Frank to a long-faced man sit next to Guy Lafleur. That man wear a Montreal Canadiens toque and sweater, and he have only four teeth in front, two top, two bottom, all stained yellow, and none quite matching. I notice now that almost everybody in the arena, from old people, like the guy next to Guy Lafleur, to tiny babies in arms, wear Montreal Canadiens sweaters. Somewhere there must be a store sell nothing but Montreal uniforms.

"You think this is serious," the old man say, "you ought to see a wedding in St. Edouard. The aisle of the Catholic Church is covered in artificial ice, at least in the summer, in winter it freeze up of its own accord. The priest wear goal pads and the groom is the defenceman," he go on in a heavy French accent.

"I didn't see no church," says Frank, "only big building I seen was the elevator."

"You seen the church," say the old man, "elevator got torn down years ago. You guys should stick around, there supposed to be a wedding to-morrow. The bride and bridesmaids stickhandle down the aisle, careful not to be off-side at the blue-line; they get three shots on goal to score on the priest. If they don't the wedding get put off for a week."

Another old man in a felt hat and cigarette-yellowed mustache speak up, "We had one priest was such a good goaltender there were no weddings in St. Edouard for over two years. Some of the waiting couples had two, three kids already — so the bishop come down from Edmonton and perform a group ceremony."

Knocking Ferd out of the game was a real unlucky thing for them to do. I'm sure they would of scored ten goals each period if they'd just been patient. In the dressing room we strip off Ferd's pads, look for somebody to take his place.

Frank tell first one and then another player to put on the equipment.

"Put them on yourself," they say to Frank, only not in such polite language.

"You're gonna have to go in goal," Frank say to me.

"Not me," I say. "I got some regard for my life."

"Put your goddamned dog in the goal," say the caretaker of the dressing room. We can hear the fans getting restless. They are chanting something sound like "Alley, alley, les Bashers," and stomping their feet until the whole building shake.

"You guys should go home now," the old caretaker say. "They just looking for a bad team to beat up on. The way you guys skate it will be like tossing raw meat to hungry dogs."

"I think he's right," I say. "Let's sneak out. We can fend off the fans with hockey sticks if we have to."

We are just about to do that when Frank get his idea.

"It's why I'm manager and you're not," Frank say modestly to me that night when we're driving back toward Hobbema.

We hold up the game for another fifteen minutes while we try to find skates big enough to fit Mad Etta.

Etta been sitting the corner of the dressing room having a beer. Her and Frank do some fast bargaining. End up Frank have to promise her nine hundred dollars of the thousand dollar prize money before she'll agree to play. Frank he plunk a mask on Etta's face right then and there.

"Not bad," say Etta, stare into a mirror. The mask is mean looking, with a red diamond drawed around each eye and red shark teeth where the mouth should be.

When we ask the Bashers to loan us a pair of BIG skates, they tell us to get lost.

"We've got to default the game then," we tell them, "guess you'll have to refund all those fans their money."

That make them nicer to know.

"Yeah, we didn't bring them all the way up here not to get in a few good licks."

"Besides, the fans are in a mean mood. They want to see some blood. We're going to get even for what happened to Custer," say their biggest defenceman, who is about the size of a jeep and almost as smart. He give us his extra skates for Etta, then say, "We'll score four or five goals, then we'll trash you guys for a full hour. Get ready to bleed a lot."

We sat Etta on a bench with her back to the wall. Me and Frank get one on each side of her and we push like we was trying to put a skate on a ten pound sack of sugar.

"I'm too old for this," puffs Etta. "What is it I'm supposed to do again anyway?"

"Just think how you'll spend the nine hundred dollars," says Frank, tie her laces in a big knot, "And everything else will take care of itself."

Three of us have to walk beside, behind, and in front, in order to steer Etta from the bench to the goal. The fans are all going "Oooh," and "Ahhhh."

I get to walk behind.

"If she falls back I'm a goner," I say.

"So keep her on her feet," huffs Frank. "I figure you value your life more than most, that's why I put you back there."

"That's one big mother of a goaltender," say one of the Bashers.

"More than you know," says Etta, but in Cree.

"Alley, alley, les Bashers," go the audience.

Once we get Etta to the net she grab onto the iron rail and stomp the ice, send chips flying in all directions, kick and kick until she get right down to the floorboards. Once she got footing she stand with an arm on each goal post, glare fierce from behind that mean mask what painted like a punk rock album cover.

Soon as the game start again the Bashers get the puck, pass it about three ways from Sunday, while our players busy falling down, skate right in on Mad Etta and shoot … and shoot … and shoot. Don't matter where they poke the puck, or how often, there is always some part of Mad Etta blocking the goal.

After maybe ten shots, a little player zoom in like a mosquito, fire point blank; the puck hit Etta's shoulder and go up in the crowd.

"That hurt," shout Etta, slap with her goal stick, knock that little player head over heels as he buzz by the net. She get a penalty for that. Goalies can't serve penalties, but someone else have to. The Bashers take about twenty more shots in the next two minutes.

"You're doin' great," Frank yell from the bench.

"How come our team never shoot the biscuit at their goal?" Etta calls back.

"We're workin' on it," says Frank, "trust your manager."

Things don't improve though, so Etta just turn her back on the game, lean on the net and let the Bashers shoot at her backside. There is more Etta than there is goal; even some shots that miss the goal hit Etta. I think it is a law of physics that you can't add to something that is already full.

There is no score at the end of the first period. Trouble is Etta assume the game is only one period long.

"I got to stay out there how long?" she yell at Frank. "I already earn more than nine hundred dollars. That little black biscuit hurt like hell," she go on. "And how come none of you guys know how to play this game but me?"

The players is all glassy-eyed, gasp for air, nurse their bruises, cuts and hangovers.

As we guide Etta out for the second period, Guy Lafleur go to barking like a fire siren again. He always hated Mad Etta ever since one day he nipped at her heel while she huffing up the hill for Hobbema General Store, and Etta punted him about forty yards deep into the mud and bulrushes of the slough at the foot of the hill.

When she hear the dog Etta spin around knock a couple of us to the ice, make Frank afraid for his life, and go "Bow-wow-wow," at Guy Lafleur, sound so much like a real dog that he jump off his seat and don't show his nose again until after the riot.

The way we dressed Etta for the game was to put the shoulder pads on, then her five-flour-sack dress, then tape one sweater to her chest and another to her back.

Soon as she get to the goal she have to guard for the second period, she don't even stomp the ice, just fumble in the pocket of her dress, take out a baggie with some greenish-looking sandy stuff in it, sprinkle that green stuff all across the goal line. Frank rush off the bench, fall twice on the way 'cause he wearing slippery-soled cowboy boots.

"What are you doin'?" he yell at Etta, who is waddling real slow, force each skate about an inch into the ice every step, and is heading for the face-off circle to the left of her goal.

"If I stay in front of that little closet I'm gonna be so bruised I'll look polka-dotted. I've had enough of this foolishness."

"But the goal," cries Frank.

"Hey, you manage the team. I'll do what I do best," and Etta give Frank a shove propel him on his belly all the way to the players' gate by our bench.

As the referee call the players to centre ice, Etta sit down cross-legged in that face-off circle, light up a cigarette, blow smoke at the fans who stomping their feet.

The St. Edouard team steal the puck on the face-off, sweep right over the defence and fire at the empty goal. But the puck just zap off to the corner as if there was a real good goalie there. After about ten shots like that the Bashers get pretty mad and the fans even more so. It is like Etta bricked up the front of the goal with invisible bricks.

The St. Edouard Bashers gather around the referee and scream at him in both of Canada's official languages, and all of Canada' swear words.

The referee skate to the net, test with his hand, but there is nothing to block it. He stick one skate into the net. He throw the puck into the net. Then he borrow a stick from one of the Bashers and shoot the puck in, several times.

"Stop your bitchin' and play hockey," he say to the St. Edouard players.

"I bet I could sell that stuff to Peter Pocklington and the Edmonton Oilers for a million dollars an ounce," Frank hiss into my ear. "You're her assistant, Silas. What do you think the chances are of getting hold of a bag of that stuff?"

"It would only work when Etta stare at it in the right way," I say.

"Hey, Edmonton Oilers could afford to buy Etta too. She's more valuable than Wayne Gretzky. And we'd be her agents ... "

"Forget it," I say. "You can't buy medicine."

Les Bashers keep shooting at our goal all through the second period and into the third, with no better luck.

It a fact of hockey that no matter how bad a team you got you going to score a goal sooner or later. At about fifteen minutes into the third period, Rufus Firstrider, who skate mainly on his ankles, carry the puck over the St. Edouard blue-line, try to pass to Gorman Carry-the-kettle, who been wheezing down the right wing.

The goalie see the pass coming up and move across the goal mouth to cover it, and there's a Mack truck of a defenceman ready to cream Gorman if the puck even gets close to him. But Rufus miss the pass entirely, fall down and accidentally hit the puck toward the net and score. That is all the goals there is: Hobbema Wagonburners 1, St. Edouard Bashers 0.

It was them and their fans who started the riot. We all headed for the dressing room, except for Frank, who jump into the stands looking for Guy Lafleur, and suffer a certain amount of damage as a result.

After the RCMP cooled everyone off and escorted us to our bus, Frank show up with a black eye and blood on his shirt, while Guy Lafleur have a notch out of one ear but a big mouthful of Basher hockey sweater to make up for it.

They got carpenters screwing the seats back in place and men busy resurfacing the ice. The Bashers decide to start the tournament over the next day, playing against teams they can beat. They agree to pay us twenty-five-hundred dollars to go home and never enter their tournament again.

And that's the truth.

excerpts from the novel *King Leary*

❖   PAUL QUARRINGTON

I was found guilty in the juvenile court of arson (I wasn't charged for killing the chicken) and sentenced to spend time at the Bowmanville (Annex) Reformatory for Boys. My crime was judged a serious one, and the judge shook his jowls somberly and said he thought it would be best if I stayed at the reform school until my sixteenth birthday. The judge kind of implied that when I turned sixteen he'd throw me into a real grown-up slammer.

Clay Clinton attended the court proceedings, dressed in a blue suit with short pants. He nodded judiciously throughout and seemed to think the judge's verdict was a wise one.

So they took me on the train down to Bowmanville, Ont. I was accompanied by a correctional officer, a fat man who smoked cigars and didn't say a solitary word to me. The general feeling was that I'd turned out bad, but this fellow seemed to think I was headed for the gallows. When he noticed people staring at us, and quite a few people did, the correctional officer would say to them, "Arsonist," and tip his head in my direction.

The first few times I tried to say, "I didn't know Rex's dung would explode!" but every time I said that, the correctional officer would give me a cuff on the side of the head.

At the Bowmanville train station, I was turned over to my new keepers. I thought things had gone from bad to worse.

They were *monks.*

There were four of them, all dressed in long black robes like they were waiting for a funeral to pass by. And as if them being monks wasn't bad enough — if the old man saw a monk he'd cross his fingers and wouldn't uncross them until he'd seen a horse sneeze — they were the oddest assemblage of monks the world has ever seen.

One was a great big cusser, ugly as all get-out. He looked like what dogs are dreaming about when their back legs start twitching. Another of the monks looked like a fireplug, short and squat, even to the extent of having a bright red face with a little yellow top, that being his blond hair. If this man of the cloth marched into any seaside groghouse, the drunken sailors would back out politely. The third monk was just barely there, that's how slight he was. He looked like something was eating him up from the inside. The skin on his face looked as thin as tissue paper.

The fourth was a regular enough goon, except for his eyes. They were crossed and bossed and weird in every way, a strange milky blue colour. This was Brother Isaiah, about whom there were two schools of thought. The most popularly held position was that Brother Isaiah was blind as a bat. The other school (Brother Isaiah himself being practically the only adherent) had it that Brother Isaiah could see perfectly well. To add fodder to this case, Isaiah was always saying sentences that began, "I see" or "You look." That's what he did now. He leant in real close to me and rested those egg blue eyes on my chest for a few seconds and then said, "I see you have arrived safe and sound, Mr. Leary."

I grunted, my old mother's admonitions of politeness be damned.

The ugly one made a big show of puckering his mouth. Speech took some preparation in his case. "Did you have a nice trip?" the monster demanded.

Next the tough little fireplug monk wanted to know if I was tired, and the skinny one asked, "Are you hungry?"

I didn't say anything. I was thinking of asking the correctional officer if he might be interested in adopting me.

The monks lined out (they couldn't walk to the icebox, I was to find out, without forming into a single file), and they led me to an old cart that was full of farming equipment, groceries and gewgaws. There were two old horses hitched up front, and they seemed to get uneasy on our arrival, snorting and shifting their trembling legs around. I found out why. The blind monk, Brother Isaiah, climbed up onto the box. It took him upwards of two minutes to even find the reins, him groping with his hands, those two bossy-milk eyes of his no use at all.

Then the monk made a sharp chicky sound with his tongue and the side of his mouth. The old nags started moving forward and this Brother Isaiah started steering. If you want to call it steering. The wagon kept going back and forth across the road, and a few times we came within an ace of tumbling into the ditch. I was the only one who seemed to notice or care. One time the blind monk drove the horses straight for an old oak tree. I watched the two ancient beasts exchange glances, and I guess they decided that the time had finally come for rebellious action, because they pulled away just in time.

The three others sat with me in the cart and paid this wagoneer no mind. They kept trying to make conversation, but I wasn't having none of it. Instead, to keep myself occupied, I started digging around in all the junk, looking to see if there was anything interesting.

I found a hockey puck. It seemed a strange thing to find in a cart full of monks. I rooted around some more and came up with a pair of skates and a couple of sticks.

The ugly one, who'd told me that his name was Brother Simon, puckered up his face truly gruesome in order to ask, "Do you play hockey, Percival?"

I shrugged juvenile delinquent-style, but managed to sneak a little nod into it.

The fireplug, Brother Andrew, grinned and said, "Most excellent." He had a nice smile, except for the lack of teeth. He had the same amount of teeth as I do now, approximately one.

The skinny one — sunlight passed through the man — whose name was Brother Theodore, he asked, "What position do you play?"

"Mostly the centreman, but I can play the point or the cover-point. I can play the rover. I could play the wings. It none of it makes any difference to Little Leary. You could stick me in goal for all of that."

Brother Isaiah all of a sudden swung around and aimed his strange wally eyes somewhere in my general vicinity. "Mr. Leary," he said, "your new home."

Ahead of me, sitting at the end of a road and the top of a hill, was a castle. It looked like a picture ripped out of one of my brother Lloyd's storybooks, *The Knights of the Round Table*. The first time I saw it, the reformatory was golden in the autumn sun, all covered by clouds and ivy. It had turrets and round windows and even a moat, except for the moat was just an ambitious ditch. We had to cross a small bridge to get over, and then we had to pass under a gateway. I looked up and saw that someone had burned these words into the wood:

TO KEEP A BOY OUT OF HOT WATER, PUT HIM ON ICE

It was sometime in late October when the brothers started putting together the boards. They were usually a quiet bunch, but they got even quieter, all of them rushing around with hammers in their hands and nails sticking out of their mouths. The only thing us lads heard from them was pounding out in the playing field, pounding and the occasional grunt. I personally thought the monks were crazy, and I'll tell you why: they laid out the boards in a circle. A huge and, as far as I could tell, perfect circle. I even asked Brother Isaiah about it. He just grinned and fastened his strange eyes on my left shoulder. "Have ye no known?" he asked me. "Have ye not heard? It is he that sitteth upon the circle of the earth that bringeth the princes to nothing." That's the kind of answer I used to get from Brother Isaiah. So anyway, they laid out the boards in a circle, and around the beginning of December they raised them. The monks took the old horses off the cart. It took the horses and sometimes six or seven brothers to raise each section of board. The weather stayed pleasant for a week or two, the sun all biting and bright even though the trees were naked as firewood. We all waited; the monks prayed.

On Christmas Eve the temperature fell about forty degrees. The brothers rushed out with buckets and hoses. They stayed out there all night, and to keep themselves amused they sang. They sang strange songs with words I didn't understand. All night long the monks watered the world, and the winter air turned the water to ice. Blue-silver ice, hard as marble. On Christmas morning the round rink was ready. Brother Simon was out there skating, his face even uglier, reddened by lack of oxygen, his carbuncles polished by the stinging wind. For a huge, monstrous man he sure could dance out there on the ice! He had some figure-skating moves, dips and twirls, his arms raised slightly, the hockey stick acting as a balancing pole. And as I watched him, Brother Simon the Ugly became airborne. It seemed he was up there for a whole minute, and during that time he pirouetted lazily. This stunt robbed me of my breath and made my knees quiver. I determined right then and there to learn how to do that. It would be some months before I did, and it would take a couple of years for me to refine it and come up with the spectacular St. Louis Whirligig.

Brother Andrew, the one who looked like both the fireplug and the bulldog that might employ it, was streaking up and down, dodging invisible opponents. Whatever he was doing, it made my hardstep look like a cakewalk. I said to myself, if you could do that, no one could ever stop you. It took me some months to learn to skate like Brother Andrew the Fireplug. I call it Bulldogging. Miles Renders, who is currently coaching the Toronto Maple Leaves, calls it "achievement through perseverance and mental imaging," and I say that one of the reasons the Leaves are faring so poorly is that Renders would call Bulldogging something like that. All it is, is, you are at point one. You want to be at point two. The shortest distance, as every schoolboy knows, is a straight line, but there are no less than four big johnnies blocking the way. The secret is, don't give a tinker's cuss, just go, man. Just go.

Brother Theodore the Slender, who seemed on the verge of evaporation with all the rink-building activity, stood in the centre of the round rink, his eyes half closed, his pale lips moving slightly in silent prayer.

And some of the other monks (there were twenty-odd monks at the reformatory, regular fellows, especially in comparison to the four I knew best) were taking shots on Brother Isaiah.

I have never in my life seen such a good goalie as Brother Isaiah, and I have seen everyone from the Chicoutimi Cucumber to that tall slender fellow who looked like a schoolteacher and played so well for the Montreal Canadiens in the seventies. Yet I am convinced to this day that Brother Isaiah was blind as a bat, though he denied it. Isaiah might occasionally admit to being "a tad shortsighted," but you'd have to catch him walking into a brick wall. But the other monks couldn't get a shot by him. Isaiah would just reach out and grab them in his glove (and gloves back then didn't amount to much), or else he'd get the toe on them, or the chest in front of them, or bang them away with his stick. Brother Simon the Ugly tried to jimmy one by him, dancing right up to the goal crease, flipping the puck off his backhand as he made one of his ballerina twirlabouts. Brother Isaiah flicked it away with his wood. Then Andrew the Fireplug comes barreling along the wing, taking out a couple of bystander brothers just for style, and he unleashes a slapshot even though the damn thing isn't even invented back then! Brother Isaiah the Blind raises his left shoulder maybe a quarter inch and the rubber is dancing harmlessly behind the net.

But there was Brother Theodore standing in the centre of the huge silver circle, and his eyes were popped open all the way and his mouth had ceased working. In front of him was a puck. Brother Theodore the Slender brought his stick back real slow, and then, with a motion that cut the air like a knife, Brother Theodore whacked the rubber. I swear to Jesus he hit that puck harder than Bobby Hull ever hit one, and it didn't even look like he was trying. Brother Isaiah didn't hear it or feel it, or however else he detected pucks, as I believe with all my heart that the man couldn't see the sun if it tumbled into his back yard.

There was a small smile on the face of Theodore the Slender.

I learnt how to do that, too. Some people (like scrawny Hermann over on the next bed) say that shooting was the weakest part of my game, but in my prime I could whistle the rubber like nobody's business. I scored on every goaltender there was in my day, and they'll tell you that I had one of the hardest shots going. Unfortunately you can only ask Hugo "Tip" Flescher, because he's the only one still breathing. What's more, you better hurry. But Theodore the Slender gave me the gam on shooting, which is this: shooting is more mental than physical. You just practise so much that you can feel the puck, like the blade of your lumber was the palm of your hand, and then you just inner-eye that puck into the back of the net. "Set it there first," Brother Theodore was wont to say, "and then put it here." In other words, *wham, bingo.*

The monks left off playing long enough to tell us that there were plenty of skates in the recreational hall cupboards, so us puppies ran off to lace up. I had my own pair with me, of course. I'd brought them from Bytown, even though I'd had to leave out most of my clothes to get them into my suitcase. I was the first one on the ice with the Brothers of St. Alban the Martyr, and I commenced to hardstep. I flew around the circle. I got my speed up so that ice formed in my eyebrows. When I finally stopped, I saw that all of the other delinquents, and all of the black-robed monks, were staring at me.

Brother Simon the Ugly puckered hideously and made the following pronouncement. "It would seem," he said, "that Percival is something of a natural!"

The phrase just tickled me. One time I even asked my wife, Chloe, to put that on my grave marker: PERCIVAL H. LEARY, SOMETHING OF A NATURAL. But Chloe died many years back, done in by more diseases and ailments than I could count. I can't recall what it says on her gravestone.

Andrew the Fireplug divided us boys into two teams, and we had some shinny scrimmages. Periodically Isaiah would stop us and give us such coaching tips as, "Who through faith wrought righteousness, he quenched the violence of fire and waxed valiant in fight!" We quickly learnt how to nod politely (us little boys nodding at a blind man!) and then we'd get back to playing. I was the best pup on the ice, scoring four or five goals in as many rushes. Then I stole the puck from a boy named Billy and smashed him into the boards. Theodore the Slender rendered a two-finger toot that almost ripped the ears off my head.

"Leary," he intoned somberly. "Expulsion!"

"What?" I screamed.

All of the monks droned "Expulsion" in unison. It sounded like their strange singing.

"You mean I can't play anymore?"

Theodore the Ugly said, "You *weren't* playing."

I was mortified. I threw away my stick and left the ice.

You see what they were trying to tell me, don't you — that hockey is a team sport. I had forgotten that, because I was so damn much better than anybody else.

It was in Montreal, March 13 of one-nine one-nine, that I made my first move to become the King of the Ice. I did that by deposing the previous King, Lalonde. He was called Newsy, although his right name was one of those French affairs with too many vowels. Lalonde looked like God wrought him out of stone — except really Lalonde looked like God had thought better of the idea halfway through and gone out to a movie. In the middle of Newsy's face were two eyes, as black as a nun's habit, and when Lalonde was angry — all of the time — they acquired a distinct lunatic sheen. Many a player was beaten just by a look at those eyes. Mind you, Newsy Lalonde could play. He was what you might call a talented and sound hockey player, and when you combine that with largeness and the ability to scare the holy bejesus out of people, then you got something. In 1919 he was thirty-two years old, and that's when I went after him.

I was Little Leary, the heart and soul of the Ottawa Paddies. I wore the Letter *C* over my heart, captain of the shinny-playing Irishers. I had the ginger back then, brother.

We were tied up in overtime.

Patty Boyle called for a time-out. The Paddies crowded around him at the bench.

Manfred looked at me and smiled that long crooked grin of his. "Let's do it, Percy," he said with a wink. "I'm getting hungry."

I nodded, stuff stirring in my guts.

"Here," said Manfred, and he stuck something in my gloved hand. It was his crucifix, the huge one. I noticed that Our Saviour was not dying, He was stone dead. "Carry that," said Manny.

"You figure that's gonna help, do you?"

"You know what Brother Isaiah would say."

Manny had an uncanny knack for remembering the blind monk's drivel. I shrugged.

"Brother Isaiah would say, 'It couldn't hurt.'" Manfred winked again. "The Magic Stone, Percy."

"The Magic Stone?"

"Percival!" shouted Clay from the stands. He was sitting in the front row, having used some of his Bytown timber baron connections to get the ticket. "Score a goal, my prince! We're wasting valuable drinking time!"

"Go, you Lucky Number Seven!"

I dropped the crucifix inside my jersey. The metal felt cool and soothing on my belly.

We set up for the face-off. Newsy Lalonde was staring at me.

"Hey, newsboy," said I, "don't stand there. That's where I mean to skate with the puck."

"You are horsemeat, O'Toole." Lalonde always affected to disremember my name, or maybe he really did, and he just used any Irish moniker that popped into whatever he was using for a mind.

"Come on, guys," said Manfred, "let's not fight."

"Mind your own business, chief," said Lalonde.

Manny crossed himself.

I crossed myself, too, and I touched the crucifix.

The rest is historical.

I heard Clay Clinton shout "Yes!" with all of his heart and soul. Clay had just won a lot of money — this was the start of what is commonly referred to as his "vast financial empire" — but his shout had a lot more to it than that. And I heard Manny cry, "Hey!" — that big delighted bellow of his. I realized that I'd scored, that we'd won the Stanley Cup. For that instant, we were three young men alone in the universe.

The rink that the Brothers of St. Alban the Martyr built was round. Hockey rinks are curved in the corners, as you likely know, but basically they should be squared. Our rink was a circle.

One night, I couldn't sleep. I didn't usually have that problem (I do nowadays, in my dotage — I have actually snoozed for periods of seven seconds and been wide awake for the rest of the night) but that evening, there in the reformatory, I was restless. There was a full moon, and it filled the window across from my cot, and for some strange reason I could make out all the mountains and craters. The moon was a strange colour, too, a silver like a nickel had been flipped into the sky.

Then I heard the sounds, the soft windy sweeping of hockey sticks across ice. At first I thought I was dreaming, but then I recalled that I never did dream to speak of. I moved across to the window, soft on my feet so as not to wake the other delinquents. The moon was so bright that I do believe I squinted up my eyes. I have never seen it like that since.

I could see the rink, and I could see the shadows moving on it. The monks were playing a little midnight shinny. It quickened my heart. I threw on some clothes and flew outside.

There were five of them. I watched from a distance at first. I couldn't understand what sort of game they were playing. The action would move erratically within the circle, and sometimes the five would split so that three men would rush two, or four would rush one, and then sometimes the five of them would move in cahoots, the idea seeming to be to achieve a certain prettiness of passing. Then a man would break from the pack, and another man would chase him around the circle, and as quick as that happened they'd rejoin the three in the centre. There were no goal nets on the ice. Just five men, a puck and a lot of moonlight. They played in silence. I moved closer.

Simon the Ugly was the easiest to pick out, because he was the biggest. He was dancing, jumping into the air, and sometimes I could see his monstrous frame silhouetted against the trout silver moon. Theodore the Slender cut a shadow so fine that it was hard to pick out, but I could tell him from the quick, precise movements of his twiggy arms as he took a shot. And Andrew the Fireplug, it was he who was likeliest to make a break for the boards, to drift like gun smoke around them. I watched him scoot off with the puck, and then I watched a man slip up easily behind Andrew and relieve him of the rubber. That was Isaiah the Blind. I could scarcely credit it. Playing goalie is one thing — I mean, at least Isaiah was standing still between the pipes, and you could always convince yourself that he was simply the luckiest son of a bee *ever* — but here he was skating around like a madman, stealing pucks, passing and receiving, and the moonlight was sitting on his dead eyes like it does on the still surface of a lake. I crouched down behind the boards. Brother Isaiah had an aerial maneuver that made the Whirligigs look like tumbling down a flight of stairs, he had dekes and fakes that would have baffled God! Whatever the hell game they were playing — and I never did come close to figuring it — Brother Isaiah was the best. In fact, Brother Isaiah was the best I've ever seen, bar none. That includes me, Duane Killebrew, and the fifth man out on that moon-washed rink, Manny Oz.

excerpts from the novel *Peckertracks*

❖   STAN DRAGLAND

Arena

The arena is dimly lit and cool inside, and smells of new lumber. The shell of the arena has been up for three years, but it's been used as a huge granary to help pay the cost of construction. The last of the wheat was only trucked out three weeks ago, and already the boards of the new rink are in place. There are player's boxes at one side and a penalty box at the other. Percy hops over the boards and gives the door of the penalty box a push. It's locked from inside so he reaches over and slides out the bolt. The door swings open. The two by six top of the gate has been cut diagonally where it meets the two by six of the boards, so it won't be able to put any strain on the hinges, or swing out onto the ice. Percy slams the door. It closes with a chunk, like the doors of the Pontiac. *Body by Fisher*. Percy notices that the edges of the two by six that runs all around the rink have been chamfered and sanded smooth. There's a one by twelve baseboard that sweeps around the bottom of the boards. *Get most wear there, I guess*. Percy wonders how the men of the town found out how to build a rink. They don't seem to have left anything out. Everything is incredibly solid. It makes Percy feel really good.

"That you, Perce?" Percy looks around. He can't make out where the voice came from.

"Over here." Percy locates Ben at the north end of the rink, where some men are working on the dressing rooms and the waiting room. He walks over.

"Really sumpin, eh?"

"Jeez, I'll say."

"Makes Excelsior's look pretty rickety. Say Pearce, didja know the

Merchants're gonna be playin Intermediate C next year?"

"No, ya mean in a league?"

"That's right, with playoffs, the whole works. There's, lessee, there's gonna be Excelsior, Bures, Credit and … One other, oh yeah, Kuziar. N Depot."

"Ya don't mean the Credit Hornets."

"No, they're still Intermediate A, but there's gonna be another team."

"Hey, should see some good hockey."

"Merchants're gittin new uniforms too. Ya know, green n white, with sweaters that lace up in front. Really sharp."

"Zat right? Howja find out?"

"I wuz over't the Cockshutt n Art Darby n Al Goring wuz lookin through a catalogue."

"God, makes ya sorta wish it wuz winter already, doesn't it?"

Ord and the Merchants

Fairview is in town for an exhibition game against the Merchants. They play in a Saskatchewan league. Intermediate B, but, as Art Darby says, they're "suckin the hind tit" in their league, and the Merchants are on top of their own, so it could be a good game.

It gets around that Fairview has a rough player called Ord, who's been suspended from play in their own league. Nobody knows what for, but the Depot fans take a dislike to him during the warm-up. For one thing, he's obviously a good player. He skates with style. But also he looks uppity. As soon as the game starts the fans start to ride him.

Depot scores first. Art Darby. *One of his patented slap shots.* The Fairview goalie fishes the puck out of the net with his stick and slaps it at the boards in disgust. He leans on his pads a minute, looking down at the ice. Then he looks up and says "fuck!" Nobody can hear him for cheering, but Percy's been watching his face.

"See that?" he says to Ginny, who's standing beside him.

"Yes." She's half-smiling. It's their own joke. Percy feels as bold as if he'd said fuck himself. It's great to have Ginny next to him, pushing close. Against the cold? Bob Raft isn't with her. Does that mean something?

It isn't long before Ord starts to respond to the crowd. He smiles at them satirically and spits towards the boards at face-offs. Once he takes off a glove and blocks one nostril, then the other, and fires a couple of gobs on the ice.

"Well, the *fil*thy! Ja ever see anything so dis*gus*ting!"

"BOO! Wipe the ice with*im*!"

Halfway through the second period Ord gets into a fight with Paul Craig. He goes wild, hitting like a windmill, and Paul can't do much more than cover up. Ord has to be dragged away by his own players. Is there something wrong with this guy? Percy starts to watch his face as he skates by. Now that he's stopped smiling he only looks about half there.

Ord is getting all the razzing now, which is even kept up after the whistle blows and play stops. The Merchants start to get the message, if they needed any. The bigger ones, like Neely, are starting to lay for Ord. The game is getting rough. There are a lot of penalties. In fact Percy sees that the Merchants are getting dirty. Nobody seems to care. Neely skates behind the Fairview net and conks the goalie on the head with his stick. A cheer goes up from that end of the rink. The goalie bellows and starts out of his crease after Neely, who's following the play up the ice, looking innocent. The referee and most of the crowd are watching the play, so there's nothing the goalie can do but skate back to his net, one glove off, testing his head for blood. After that he starts to take swipes with his stick at any Merchant who gets near him, trying to get them across the back of the legs.

Things are getting out of control. Percy isn't much for hollering, so he notices that some of the people who were shouting are quiet now, just watching. There's still plenty of noise though. Some people are yelling "Killim!" at Ord. A few are slapping the boards with pieces of broken hockey stick.

Ord gets cross-checked against the boards where Percy is standing. As he starts to skate away somebody grabs the end of his stick. He whirls around and chops as hard as he can into the crowd, hitting Ginny on the side of the arm. She falls against Percy, then to the concrete. Some people bend over her. Percy is speechless, torn between helping Ginny and watching what's going to happen on the ice. Some of the Merchants skate over to see who's been hurt. Somebody says "My God! He coulda killed somebody!" Neely says, "Alright boys, let's gittim."

The noise has built to a howl. Ord is skating around with a neutral expression on his face, like nothing happened. Now some of his own players grab him and start to shove him toward the dressing room. He tries to push them off. Neely crashes through and takes a swing at Ord, missing and falling down with his momentum. Paul Craig, right on his heels, sits on him till he cools off. A Fairview player has Ord's arm twisted behind him, and two or three more are forcing him out through the gate and down the walk to the dressing room. The spectators there are silent as he passes. Nobody wants to taunt him. He could get loose and go for anybody.

The game is held up. The players are all on the ice, standing in groups and talking. Paul Craig is talking to a Fairview player. *Good old Paul.* He's the oldest player on the ice, nobody knows how old, and still the best puck handler. He keeps his hockey pants up with a belt and makes it look natural. Art Darby is flipping shots at the net. Neely is skating around, looking hard at the dressing room door. Now it opens, and Ord comes out in street clothes. His teammates escort him out the side door, to hoots and jeers. Word comes around the boards that they've put him in a car and told him to get the hell out of here.

Finally the game resumes. There's still most of a period to play, and the hockey is very clean. But the spark is gone out of the game. Nobody has much to holler. Nobody cares much that Depot wins 5-2.

Percy walks home by himself. News of the game gets there ahead of him.

"What in Heaven's name goes on at those hockey games? Somebody hit Ginny with a stick? Her mother's really up in arms. Grown men! If that's what hockey's all about you'd better stay home from now on."

"How's Ginny?"

"Well there's nothing broken apparently, but really!"

There's not much use trying to explain. His mother never goes to hockey games, so she doesn't understand how the emotions get involved.

Percy tries to read, but he can't concentrate. He prowls around the house. Then he goes to the basement, gets his trapper mitt and rubber ball. He throws it against the wall, catches it, throws it against the wall.

"Stop that Percy! Everybody's going to bed."

Percy's a long time getting to sleep.

Blue Moon

❖ LIONEL KEARNS

Whenever Harvey hears the song he thinks of Sybil Chalmers, who in 1949 came into the Grade Seven class, and sang it, astonishing them all.

"We have a new face with us this morning," the teacher had said. "This is Sybil." She was a middle size girl with her red hair in a kind of page-boy perm, a common style in those days. "Sybil wants to sing us a song," added the teacher.

This was something out of the ordinary. No one sang songs to the class. It was unheard of. It was unthinkable. Even so, it might be better than getting into the morning's social studies lesson. So the boys did not jeer at this point, as they might have done, had they had more time to consider what was happening.

"What are you going to sing, Sybil?" asked the teacher.

"Blue Moon," said Sybil, and after a little pause, she began to sing: "*Blue Moon/ You saw me standing alone/ Without a dream in my heart/ Without a love of my own,*" and so on, right through the whole song, including the choruses.

Sybil belted it out in a deep, rich, sexy, crooning voice that should have been coming over the radio or out of the mouth of a movie star, but should definitely not be occurring here in this time and place. The class was stunned. What was happening? One of themselves, even though she was a newcomer, was standing there revealing herself to be something very strange and threatening — a non-child, a young woman, a sexual being, or was it a kind of parody? No one knew how to respond, so they stared at her, noticing her small breasts pushing out her sweater front as she sang with all that husky-throated self-assurance and conviction about the unmentionable, about romantic love.

When she finished there was silence. The class was in a state of shock.

Even the teacher was upset. She had agreed to Sybil's suggestion, thinking that it would be a children's song, executed in the customary thin high pitch of a schoolgirl. But Sybil's rendition of "Blue Moon" seemed almost obscene. After a long pause someone began to clap, and then there was general applause. But that Grade Seven class was never the same again.

Three years later Harvey is on a train with the other members of his Midget B hockey team. They are headed for Regina, the site of a minor hockey tournament. Walking through the train with some of his teammates on the way to the diner, Harvey sees Sybil Chalmers. Wham! He passes her without speaking, pretending he does not recognize her. She is sitting with her mother. "*Blue-moon-blue-moon-blue-moon,*" the words race through his mind's ear as he moves quickly on through the door at the end of the train car. His friends behind him have also noticed her, and one of them gives a whistle before Harvey can close the door and move quickly on through the next one into the diner.

"Did you see that cutie?" someone says, as they are shown to their seats by the dining car steward.

"Hey, Stupid, that's her mother she's with," says one of the others.

"Let Harvey have her mother," says someone.

Harvey, of course, does not let on that he knows her, though he can feel his cheeks turning hot. He has a sudden moment of terror, thinking the others will notice his blush, but this passes. While he eats his lunch he tries to convince himself that he has been mistaken. The girl in the next coach is much too beautiful to be Sybil Chalmers. But the song is going through his head. "*Blue moon/ You saw me standing alone ...* "

"You watch me," says Ed. "I'm going to make a date with her when we go back through her coach. I'll bet she's getting off at Regina too."

"Bet she ain't," says someone.

"Five bucks says you don't even speak to her," says somebody else.

"Ten bucks she doesn't speak to him!" says one of the others.

Harvey is feeling a bit sick. What should he do? He is not participating in the merriment of his teammates. "The stupid bunch of jerks," he thinks to himself. "If I was alone I'd speak to her for sure."

When they finish their lunch Harvey is the first one up and through the door at the end of the diner. He knows that Sybil and her mother are facing the other way, so if he walks through fast enough she won't have a chance to recognize him. He can hear the laughter and loud remarks of the others behind him.

"Excuse me, do you know the time?" Ed is saying, trying to sound serious.

"What's the matter with your watch, Ed?" someone shouts.

"Hey Lady, you have to watch this guy. He's got lover's nuts," someone is hooting amongst the uproar.

Harvey is at the end of the train car and shutting the door on their noise and laughter. Sweating and cringing, he is relieved to be out of that space and finally into the safety of his own seat. He sits there alone, asking himself why is he such a chicken. If he played hockey like that he certainly would not be on this team or this trip. By now the others are coming through the door and down the aisle in quick succession.

"Boy, did she ever tell Ed," says one of them, a little subdued.

"That's five bucks you owe me anyway," says Ed.

"Bullshit! You didn't talk to her. You talked to her mother! Ha ha ha, and did her mother ever put you down," says one of the others.

"You're a bunch of jerks!" says Harvey.

For the next two hours Harvey sits looking out the window at the monotonous prairie landscape. The train comes to several stops, once at a siding, twice at small prairie towns that seem to have no more than a few empty box cars waiting on sidings, one or two grain elevators, and a cluster of houses.

"Can you imagine living in a dump like that?"

"They don't even have a rink."

"Prairie kids skate on ponds, Stupid. They use magazines stuffed in their pants for shin pads. Wait till you see them on the ice in Regina."

"But they sure have classy women."

"She ain't from the prairies, Stupid."

All afternoon Harvey looks out the train window and thinks about Sybil Chalmers, and the words of the song keep going through his head " ... *without a dream in my heart/ Without a love of my own* ... " in time to the rhythm of the wheels of the train on the track. He wonders whether she recognized him. Of course she did. Then why didn't she say something? Because he didn't give her a chance. Was that all? No. Maybe she was embarrassed too? Not if she was the Sybil Chalmers from Grade Seven. Nothing seemed to embarrass her. Was that true? He remembers how he avoided her at school. Everyone avoided her. Did she have any friends? Harvey remembers seeing her once or twice on the street with her mother. He too referred to her as "Blue Moon," as everyone did, even when she could overhear it. Sometimes they called her "Blue Moon" to her face. That must have hurt. What finally happened to her? Harvey remembers that she did not return to school in Grade Eight. She and her mother must have left town.

These are the thoughts that are going through Harvey's mind as he sits quietly looking out the train window. When he thinks of Grade Seven he feels sad and ashamed, but when he thinks of Sybil Chalmers sitting one train car away from him he feels excited. Perhaps he will be able to somehow wipe away all that teasing and ridicule she had to endure. And Harvey begins to think that he should walk back there and apologize to her. Wouldn't his teammates be amazed if they saw him sitting there chatting to her and her mother like old friends? But Harvey decides that it would be safer to do it when they are not around. He begins to rehearse the scene in his imagination.

"Excuse me, but didn't you go to Kootenay Junior Secondary one time?'

"Why yes, how did you know?"

"Well, I'm Harvey Santini, and I used to be in your class."

"Why you're not the Harvey Santini I used to know. I mean he was just a little fellow."

"Yes I am, and I want to apologize."

"Oh don't be silly, Harvey."

"We treated you very badly ... " Harvey spends the rest of the day trying to get the dialogue to go right, and to generate enough courage to put his plan into effect. By late afternoon he has made up his mind. His plan is to stay behind when the rest of the team goes down to the diner for dinner.

"Not hungry right now," he says. "Maybe I'll go later."

So Harvey sits alone for twenty minutes, and then gets up and moves towards the door at the end of the train car. He is frightened. His heart beats fast and loud. He pushes open the first door and stands waiting in the noisy platform area between the cars. Then he draws in his breath and pulls open the second door. He begins to walk casually down the aisle, keeping his eyes unfocussed until he is close to them, to where he thinks they are sitting. But when he looks at the seat where Sybil and her mother were sitting, they are not there. The seat is now occupied by an old couple. Harvey is relieved, and begins to breath easier. Then he wonders if perhaps Sybil and her mother are in the diner. This thought troubles him. The diner, full of his own teammates, is not the place to carry out this plan.

"Leave it till later," he says to himself, turning around and going back through the train to his own seat, where he waits for his friends to return.

"Ed must have driven that chick and her mother off the train," someone remarks after they get back.

"What, you mean she's gone?" asks Harvey. It is the first time he has mentioned her.

"Sure has, Harvey, and her mother too."

Some years later Harvey is blowing trombone in a local dance band. It's not a very good band, but it is the best one in the district, and so they play regularly every weekend. They play mostly tunes and arrangements out of the swing era; you know the kind of thing: "Tuxedo Junction," "Pennies from Heaven," ... "Blue Moon."

Of course that tune always makes Harvey think of Sybil Chalmers. He remembers how beautiful she looked on the train, and he regrets his cowardice in not speaking to her the first time he saw her. He wonders if he will ever see her again.

The band needs a female vocalist, and Harvey thinks of her singing "Blue Moon" whenever they play it, which is at least once a week. He has been thinking of her now for years. She grows more and more voluptuous and desirable in his imagination. And she is always connected with that song: *"Blue Moon/ You saw me standing alone/ Without a dream in my heart/ Without a love of my own/ Blue Moon ... "* Sometimes he dreams of her spontaneously, without the aid of the musical cue.

Harvey wonders how he can track her down. He worries that if he does not find her soon they will both be so old that they will be repulsive to each other when they finally meet. Already he is approaching middle age. What should he do? He has tried to forget her, but whenever he thinks he has rid himself of that troublesome memory, he hears the tune *Blue Moon*, and there she is, back in his head again.

Somehow he expects her to turn up as a famous singer in a big name band in the States, or maybe to surface suddenly as a star in a Hollywood musical. But he never hears of her. Perhaps she is dead. This thought makes him very depressed. It is as though part of his own life has been suspended. The idea of tracing her becomes more and more obsessive.

In a final effort to locate Sybil Chalmers, Harvey Santini writes a story and sends it to *New: West Coast Fiction* that publishes it. That story is what you are reading at this moment. The third person hero is only a literary device. I am Harvey Santini. That is why I know so much about this situation. My goal is to reach Sybil Chalmers, wherever she may be. Surely she will notice the title of this story and be intrigued enough to read it and find out that I am writing about her. Or, even if she does not see it immediately, someone else will read it and tell her about it, and she will eventually contact me. Surely she will. That is why I have gone to the effort of writing this story.

But Reader, I beg your indulgence to let me return again to the ease of third person narration, so that I may tell you in a more detached manner what happens next. Shortly after the story is published, Sybil Chalmers discovers it. However, instead of making contact with Harvey directly, she chooses to send her lawyer, who lays libel charges against Harvey and the editors of the magazine that contains it.

Why has Sybil responded in this way? Harvey has written this story as a tribute to her magnificent voice and her beauty. He has written it as an apology for the way he treated her in Grade Seven. He has written it to confess his cowardice on the train. He wants to tell her that her song has touched him more deeply than any other song has touched him. Yet she is bringing libel charges against him. She does not deny that the first part of the story is essential correct. She is the same Sybil Chalmers who sang "Blue Moon" in the Grade Seven class of the Kootenay Junior Secondary School. She is the Sybil Chalmers who travelled with her mother on the train through the Prairies three years later. However, the second part of the story is completely false. It seems that it has somehow looped ahead of itself, for she has not yet brought charges against the writer of this story or the editors of this magazine. It is this strangeness in the story that constitutes the grounds for her libel action.

Harvey has a number of possible responses open to him. He can claim that all names in the story bear no relation to anyone living or dead. He can change the names of the principal characters and the name of the song. He can even change the offending ending of the story. He considers these various alternatives and decides that none of them is feasible. This story does not have the freedom of fiction. It is a true story that has meaning only as it relates to the actual events. To change any part of it would render the whole work meaningless. Falsification would commit these words and images back to the flux and swirl of unorganized and unintegrated experience. It would push the song and the girl and the part of Harvey Santini himself into the oblivion of never having actually occurred, where no one stands alone among strangers without a dream, without a love of his or her own, where this feeling, where feeling itself, is unconnected and so unbearable.

There is also the other problem. If Harvey changes the name of the song, or the name of the girl, or the school, or even his own name, Sybil will not read the story and recognize herself and him and their situation. The pattern will remain incomplete and so the story will not make sense.

In the end he cannot change the story or retract the truth. Sybil sues Harvey and the magazine, winning a devastating court settlement. Neither he nor the magazine can find the money to pay. The magazine folds and Harvey changes his name and goes underground. What else can he do? Years later he starts a small literary magazine devoted to enigmatic reminiscence. The name of the magazine is *Blue Moon*.

My Career with the Leafs

❖ BRIAN FAWCETT

I'll explain how I came to play hockey for the Toronto Maple Leafs. It was surprisingly easy, and other people with similar ambitions to play in the Big Leagues might be able to pick up some valuable tips. I'm a poet, you see, and one of the things we do as part of our job is an occasional public reading. I had a reading to do in Toronto, and one of the first things I did when I got there was to drop down to Maple Leaf Gardens. The day I went, the Leafs happened to be practising.

As I sat in the stands watching the Leafs skate around the rink I got an idea. I walked down to the equipment room, and politely asked a man who turned out to be the trainer if it would be okay if I joined the practice.

"Sure thing," he told me, just like that.

I asked if I could have a uniform to wear.

"Sure," he said. "What number would you like?"

"How about number 15?" I said innocently.

The number belonged to Pat Boutette at the time, but he was injured and I knew he wouldn't be around. I felt a surge of ambition — maybe I could beat him out of a job! Minutes later I was out on the ice with the Toronto Maple Leafs.

I skated around for a while, carefully declining any involvement in the passing and shooting drills while I tried to get my floppy ankles to cooperate. Instead of cooperating they were beginning to hurt, so I drifted in the direction of the coach, Red Kelly, who was yelling instructions at the players. I leaned casually on my stick the way I'd seen Ken Dryden do on television, and looked down at my skates. I watched the drills for two or three minutes until the ache in my ankles started to fade, then edged closer to Kelly.

"Mind if I take a turn?" I asked as evenly as I could.

"Not at all," he replied. "Let's see what you can do."

Somebody pushed a puck in front of me and as I reached for it I tripped on the tip of my left skate and fell flat on my face. What to that point had almost been a dream turned abruptly into a nightmare. I lay on the ice for a second, peering at the puck as if it had tripped me, and wondered why I couldn't wake up. I thought about quitting then and there.

I had nothing to lose, so I didn't quit. I got up, picked up my stick, and looked Red Kelly in the eye. He didn't move a muscle — didn't laugh or anything. I pushed the puck forward and skated after it in the direction of the goalie — it was Gord McRae I think — slowly gathering speed. About fifteen feet from the net I deked to my left without the customary deke to the right. The deke took McRae with it, and I cut to the right. The net was wide open and I shovelled the puck into it on my backhand.

All of this is incredibly difficult for a left-shooting skater to do. In fact, the whole manoeuvre is an impossible one, and everyone who saw it knew, including Kelly, who was staring at me with his mouth open. For my part, I had no idea how I'd done it, except that it had been awful easy.

"Not bad," Kelly shouted. "Not bad at all."

If scoring that first goal had been easy, the rest of the practice wasn't. I'm not a great skater at the best of times, and I wasn't in shape. I seemed able to score goals almost at will, but I had difficulty with the defensive drills, particularly the ones that involved things like skating backward. I fell several times, and one time I went into the boards so hard that Kelly skated over and told me to take it easy.

As the practice ended, he asked me if I could drop by his office after I showered. I told him I'd be pleased to, and after a shower I can't remember at all, I was sitting in a stuffed red naugahyde chair staring across a big desk at Red Kelly and Jim Gregory, the General Manager of the Leafs.

Kelly was writing something on a pad of yellow foolscap. Gregory did the talking.

"You've got some interesting moves out there," he said. "I caught the whole thing from up in the box. Where'd you learn your hockey?"

I decided to tell them the truth.

"Well," I replied, "I really haven't played organized hockey since I was about twelve. I watch Hockey Night in Canada, of course, and I guess I've learned a lot from that."

"Where do you come from?" he asked.

"That's kind of a hard question," I replied, trying to figure out what the truth was. "I'm from the West Coast. Well, not the coast, actually. I'm from up north."

"What brings you to Toronto?'

"I'm a poet," I said, "here on business, doing a public reading."

"No kidding," he said, looking reasonably satisfied with my answer.

"I guess you know Rota. He's from up there."

I was stumped. I didn't know any writer from up north named Rota. Kelly saw my confusion.

"New kid," he said. "Plays for Chicago."

"I've heard of him," I shrugged. "But I never played with him. He's a bit younger than I am."

There was a silence, as if the two of them were trying to decide which of them should speak. Finally, Gregory stood up and cleared his throat.

"How would you like to play hockey for the Toronto Maple Leafs?" he said.

"I'd really like that," I said quickly. "I'd prefer to play just the home games, though. I hate travelling."

Gregory seemed puzzled by my request, but he agreed to it, probably because I didn't ask for anything else.

"We play Boston Monday night," he said. "We'll see you at the rink at six p.m." He paused. "Make that five-thirty, and you can get in an extra half hour of skating."

I stood up. "I can probably use it," I smiled.

Kelly grunted, and then grinned, and I followed him out of the office and down the long concrete corridors of Maple Leaf Gardens to the players' entrance. He shook my hand.

"Good to have you with us," he said, with a lot of sincerity.

"It's good to be a part of an organization that takes chances," I said, with even more sincerity. "Toronto treats its visitors well."

Kelly smiled and waved goodbye as I stepped through the open door into a fine early winter blizzard.

The next thing I knew I was sitting in the Leafs' dressing room beside George Ferguson, suiting up for the game. Kelly came in and announced the player assignments.

"Fawcett here is going to be playing home games for us," he shouted, pointing vaguely in my direction. "He'll play on the wing with Ferguson and Hammerstrom for a while, and we'll see how things go. Any questions?"

To my surprise, a fair number of the players knew who I was, and it turned out that some of them had even read my work. Out of the corner of my eye I saw the two Swedes, Hammerstrom and Salming, exchange glances. Maybe they thought having a poet on the team might take some of the heat off them. They were still relatively new in the league, and they were taking a lot of physical and verbal abuse from the rednecks and goons who were worried about foreigners changing the game and taking their jobs. The rap on the Swedes was that they were chicken, particularly Hammerstrom, who the papers were saying was allergic to the boards. Personally I thought his skating more than made up for those faults.

I wondered a little at Kelly putting me on a line with him, but decided that he was trying to compensate for my poor skating. Every team in the league would stick their goons on our line, that was certain. Kelly probably figured Hammerstrom would skate his way out of trouble, and I would talk my way out.

We'd see soon enough. It was nice to be able to play with Ferguson, who I thought was one of the smarter centres to come into the league in a while. I planned to do what any rookie should — keep my head up and my mouth shut. It would be a new way of working, that was for sure.

The first period of that game was nothing to remember. My check, predictably, was Wayne Cashman, probably the dirtiest player in the league. I went up and down my wing without incident, partly because Cashman wasn't much of a skater either. He cut me with his stick several times, but I didn't bleed much and I ignored it when he got me with the butt end just as the period ended. I waited until I could breathe again and skated off to the dressing room with the rest of the team.

Early in the second period Lanny McDonald and Don Marcotte were sent off for trying to remove one another's vital organs, and Kelly sent me out with Hammerstrom on a five on five. The Bruins sent out Greg Sheppard and Cashman. The face-off was in our end, and Hammerstrom won it, got the puck back to Ian Turnbull, and he banked it around on the boards to where I was waiting. I circled once, almost lost my balance, and headed up the ice. As I crossed the red line, I saw Cashman skating toward me with a gleam in his eye. I kept going toward Orr at the blue line, did the deke to my left as if to move between Orr and the boards, and then cut sharply right. Orr went for the first deke and so did Cashman, who by this time was right behind me prodding at my liver with his stick. When I deked to the right, Cashman ran into Orr and both of them went heavily to the ice. I had a two on one with Hammerstrom, and I slid the puck over to him. He drew Al Simms over, passed back, and I had only Cheevers to beat. I did it again; deked left, cut right, and plunked the puck over the bewildered netminder into the upper right corner of the net.

I stuck my stick up in the air the way I'd seen it done on television, and was trying to honk my leg when I ran into Hammerstrom and we both fell down. Turnbull came over to congratulate me and Salming skated over to dig the puck out of the net. He handed it to me, grinned, and said something in Swedish I didn't understand. Hammerstrom grinned at me the same way and pointed to Cashman, who was skating in small circles at centre ice with his head down.

It was a tight-checking game, and the score was still 1-0 halfway through the third period. That was as far as I got that night. I skated into the corner for a Ferguson pass, Cashman went in behind me, and only Cashman came out.

Eventually I came *to*, but that was well after the game was over. The Leafs had won it 2-0. Cashman got a penalty for hammering me, and Sittler scored on the ensuing power play. That's what they told me, anyway.

I made it to the practice the next afternoon, none the worse for having spent the night in the hospital to make sure I didn't have concussion. I didn't get much sleep because the interns kept coming in every half hour to see if I was going to go into a coma.

"Are you there?" they asked, and lifted my eyelids with one finger to flash their penlights at my pupils. About four a.m. A very young intern came in. He was a hockey fan.

"You're the new guy with the Leafs, eh?" he asked.

"Yeah," I croaked.

"Nice move you made on that goal you scored," he said. "Where'd you learn that?"

"Watching television," I answered, telling the truth.

"I hear you write poetry too," he said.

My head hurt, so I just grimaced.

"Pretty strange," he said. "Watch out for Cashman."

He checked my eyes so carefully I thought he was looking for poems, but he said I'd probably be able to leave in the morning.

At the practice the next day, Ferguson told me to watch out for Cashman too.

"You were lucky," he said. "Cashman spent two periods setting you up. We all knew it was coming, but I guess you had to pass the test like anyone else."

"Some test," I complained. "All I can remember about it is my bell ringing when it was over."

I played the three games in that home stand, scoring again in the last one against the Rangers, and setting up a goal by Ferguson. The team was away for the next three games, and then back for three more. While they were away I worked on my skating, circling the rink again and again until my ankles were too sore for me to move anymore. I tried skating without a stick, but found, as I had when I was a kid, that skating that way was beyond me. I needed the stick for balance and without it I could barely stand.

When the team came back, I confided to Ferguson that I couldn't skate without a stick.

"You're kidding," he said.

"No," I told him. "It's true. I only got skates every three years, and the first year they were too big and the third year they were too small."

Ferguson had a good eye for details. "What about the second year?" he asked.

"I had weak ankles back then."

"You still have weak ankles," he said.

"I use the stick for balance," I said, as we went on circling the rink.

Ferguson was skating backward to tease me. "Skating is easy," he laughed. "For me it's like breathing."

"I feel that way about some other things," I replied, "but not about skating."

"You don't look as if breathing is very easy right now," he pointed out.

While we unlaced our skates after practice, he asked me cautiously what it was like to be a writer.

"It's my way of breathing," I said.

"How'd you get into it?" he asked with genuine curiosity.

"I guess I was about thirteen," I said. "Right after I quit playing minor league hockey."

Ferguson and I became friends. He taught me a lot of the basics of pro hockey and I gave him books to read in return. I was interested in Rilke and an American poet named Jack Spicer at the time, and he pored through everything I lent him. I always had books in my equipment bag, and he dug through it regularly to see what was there. He asked me if Canadian writers were as good as Americans.

"The old guys are pretty tame," I said, "but there's a few writers under forty who might turn out to be interesting."

"Jeez," he said, "how long does it take to get good at it?"

"Usually about fifteen years of hard work," I said. "A few get good earlier than that because they have special attentions or come from environments that encourage them," I went on. "But that's rare. Most of us have to learn pretty well everything about the culture twice, and that takes time. After that, there's the job of keeping on top of it as it changes. A lot of writers get one good review of their work and they have to please their public, or, worse, they decide that they're geniuses, and don't have to listen to anything. So they imitate themselves until they lose their ability to learn. After that they just get drunk, or academic, or spend all their time trying to please the reviewers and filling out grant applications."

He wanted to know about the grants, so I explained to him the economics of trying to be a serious artist in a country that wants to have serious art without having to put up with the inconvenience and cost of paying the artists.

He looked skeptical. "Except for that, hockey is pretty much the same," he said after a moment's thought.

"Only hockey players get screwed up more easily and a lot faster."

"That's because there's more people paying attention," I said, "and there's more money involved."

That home stand was a good one. I scored my third goal, drew assists on one of Ferguson's, and another on the power play, passing from behind the net to Sittler in the slot. Only four goals had been scored while I was on the ice, and after seven games I was plus five. Then the Leafs were off again on a five-game road trip and I went back to my solitary skating, circling the ice over and over again until slowly, very slowly, my skating began to improve. I skated clockwise first, and then counter-clockwise. Going counter-clockwise was easier, maybe because on the corners my stick was closer to the ice. But I couldn't quite master skating backward, and stopping remained a problem unless I was close to the boards. But I developed reasonable speed skating straight ahead, and during games I combined my lack of stopping skill with my speed to provide the team with some excellent bodychecking.

Ferguson and I went out on the town the night after the team flew in from Los Angeles. He showed me the important sights of Toronto, like Rochdale and Don Mills, and later that night we walked down to Lake Ontario and threw rocks at all the empty milk cartons floating in the water. There had been a thaw, and it was like spring — dirty snow was piled up everywhere, abandoned cars were being towed off the streets, and the curious sensation I'd had of being in Middle Earth began to dissipate. There were lovers everywhere, discussing Parliament, and kissing and fist-fighting as the fog rolled in from the lake to meld with the darkness coming up from the East.

We played our only other home date of the season with the Bruins several weeks later. As the game approached, I got a lot of good-natured ribbing from the guys about what to do with Cashman.

"Check him into the boards with a powerful metaphor," advised Sittler.

"And then slash him with an internal rhyme," someone else chimed in.

I laughed at the gags, but deeper down I was worried. The press had picked it up and were amusing themselves, mostly at my expense. Alan Abel in *The Globe & Mail* wrote something about it being a test of whether the stick is mightier than the pen, and in an interview, Cashman noised it around that he not only disliked my style, he detested poetry. Anybody who wrote poetry, he said, had to have something wrong with their hormones. That wasn't all he said, either. He told the interviewer he was going to show the fans that there was something fishy about me, promising to make fillets out of me *and* my poetry.

As I skated out for the pre-game warm-up, Cashman gave me the evil eye, so I gave the fans a demonstration of how fast I could skate through the centre ice zone. Kelly, out of kindness I guess, kept our line away from Cashman's as the game began, but on the second shift I saw the Bruin right-winger head for the bench right after the face-off, and Cashman came over the boards. Somebody froze the puck, and as we lined up for the face-off deep in Bruin territory, Cashman skated up to the circle, and around me once with his stick about a quarter of an inch from my nose.

"I hope you got a nice burial poem written for yourself," he sneered. "You skinned my behind and I'm gonna carve yours off and throw it to the crowd."

I looked him right in the eye and mustered up all my powers of language.

"Suck eggs," I said.

On the face-off Ferguson drew the puck back to Salming and I skated to the corner to wait for a pass. Cashman ignored the puck and followed me. I ducked an elbow. It missed me, but the Ref didn't miss it, because I slid down the boards as if I'd been pole-axed. Cashman got whistled for an elbowing penalty, and then got a misconduct penalty when he tried to chase me into the stands. I skated away from him, and three of my teammates stayed between us to make sure I stayed alive. Kelly kept me on for the power play and I banged Sittler's rebound past Gilles Gilbert to make it 1-0.

When I got to the bench, Kelly told me Howie Meeker wanted to interview me after the first period. It was Saturday, and the game was being televised nationally.

I'd forgotten it was Hockey Night in Canada. You get like that in the pro's — you forget everything that makes the world tick for real people. You also pay a price. The price I was going to have to pay for my forgetfulness was an awful one. I hadn't brought any poems in my equipment

BRIAN FAWCETT

bag. I was being handed the largest audience any poet in this country ever dreamed of and I wouldn't have a thing to read.

A few minutes later I was sitting in front of several television cameras with the customary towel over my shoulder, watching Howie Meeker introduce me to the nation and thinking that the dream was going to turn into a nightmare if I couldn't think of something quickly. My mind was a blank.

"We've got Toronto left winger Brian Fawcett here in the Hockey Night in Canada studios at Maple Leaf Gardens," Meeker announced in a voice that sounded more nasal in real life than on television.

He was hunched toward the cameras and I noticed he sat closer to them than I did. I hadn't seen a brush cut for years or, for that matter, as much make-up as he had on his face, and I was sorting through all that novelty without listening to what he was saying. Luckily, he was babbling as inanely as usual at the camera and ignoring me completely:

" ... nice to see a young player come to the NHL with a good grasp of hockey fundamentals and play sound, heads-up positional hockey the way you've been doing. Gee whiz, but I just get thrilled when I see a young kid with his mind on the game skate away from a player like Wayne Cashman. And it pays off, don't you see? It must have been less than a minute before you scored that beautiful goal like you were born with a stick in your hand and skates on your feet."

He hadn't actually asked me a question, but he seemed to have finished.

"Actually, Howie," I said, too nervous to do anything but tell the truth, "I haven't played much hockey since I was twelve or thirteen years old, and I'm thirty, so I'm not much of a kid any more. I've been mainly concerned with language, and more specifically with disjunction in poetry, for the last few years. You might say I've been learning the tools of an extremely complex trade."

Meeker appeared not to have understood. Maybe he thought I was speaking French. He ignored everything I said, and went off on another rant.

"Well, Brian, how do you like being with a team like the Leafs, eh, with their tradition of ruggedness and hard work?"

"Well, Howie," I said, still not sure if he realized that I understood English, and pretty sure he didn't know I was a poet, "I find the ruggedness something of a problem. Northrop Frye and Margaret Atwood created a problem a few years ago by writing some books about the importance of Nature and the frontier, and a lot of similarly empty glamour nonsense about rugged Canadian pioneers, and as a result a lot of the writers in this country now go around wearing logging boots and punching people for no reason. I used to do it myself, actually."

Meeker was staring at me, his jaw somewhere down around his navel. I took this as a signal to continue.

"I mean, violence may be natural, but Nature isn't a very good model for behaviour. It's been really over-estimated."

I knew I was gesticulating too much, and starting to yap. I'd forgotten about the cameras — it was Howie Meeker I wanted to convince. I couldn't stop.

"Art is really about civilization," I said, "not about Nature. All Nature does is overproduce, then waste most if it, and then resort to violence when the garbage starts to stink. When human beings follow Nature, you get guys like Hitler."

I was really flying, so I went to Meeker's questions about hard work next.

"Hard work, like you say, is really important, Howie. The more I know about this game, the more I begin to realize that the real secret is hard work. I guess that goes for hockey as well."

Meeker, for some reason, seemed to have lost his voice, so I went right on.

"If you'd given me a little more notice, I could have brought some work here to read, but I guess these interviews are a bit too short to give the folks at home any real idea of what's going on, let alone a sense of the breadth and skill and variety of good writing going on in this country today."

"Ah, ahhh ... Yes, well ... Well, Brian, I wish you and the Leafs the best of luck in the upcoming second period," he said, regaining a measure of control that didn't show in his face.

"Back to you, Dave Hodge!" he said hoarsely.

I smiled politely at the camera until fade-out. I'd seen a few guys start to pick their noses when they thought they were off-camera, and I wanted people to remember what I'd said.

Meeker turned on me. "What was that all about, you crazy sonofabitch?"

I began to explain, but he walked out of the studio without listening to my answer.

The dressing room was oddly silent when I returned. I sat down next to Ferguson and pulled the towel from around my neck. He was sitting with his head between his knees, as if he were air-sick.

"Didn't you know about Meeker?" he asked incredulously.

"Know what?" I said, stuffing the towel into my equipment bag as a souvenir. "He seemed kind of ticked off when I talked about writing, but then he did ask those dumb questions, and he didn't stop me from answering them the way I wanted to."

"Geez, man, that's the unwritten law of hockey," Ferguson said. "You're supposed to pretend you're really dumb."

It was my turn to be incredulous.

"Darryl thinks there's some kind of agreement between the owners about it," he said. "When you get out of Junior Hockey, you're given a sheet of things you can say to the press. You talk dumb, talk about teamwork, and all that crap."

My head was reeling. When I was a kid I believed that the world was full of secret rules and conspiracies, but this was real life — the Big Leagues. I couldn't believe what I was hearing.

"I mean, a few years ago," he continued, "when Kenny Dryden started getting interviewed, he used all kinds of literate words like 'tempo' and so on, pronounced all the words properly, and there was a terrific uproar. But he was in law school and they had to accept it. I dunno. They may get him yet — force him to retire."

Ferguson shrugged, and a note of hopelessness entered his voice. "Rumour is," he said, "that this whole business about us being stupid and inarticulate is an explicit policy of the Feds — right from the top."

I looked around me to see if he was kidding. A couple of guys just nodded and looked the other way, but most of them were glaring at me. Kelly looked really angry.

"Aw, come on, you guys," I said to no one in particular. "Why put up with this? I've seen what's really true. Look at the books lying around the dressing room."

Several players slipped large hardbound books into their equipment bags. Sittler, everyone knew, was a big Henry James fan — said it helped his passing game. And Tiger Williams had come up from Junior already heavily into Artaud. The league had its share of jerks, it was true, but unless you noised it around, you were left alone if you had intellectual interests. I guessed they were mad at me because they thought I might have let the cat out of the bag. Hockey, Kelly told me later, was in enough trouble.

There was a TV set in the dressing room, and we watched as Meeker came on the screen to do the highlights of the period. My goal wasn't one of them. A few of the guys exchanged significant looks, but everybody remained seated, as if they were watching something very sad.

When a commercial came on, I asked Ferguson who'd died.

"You did, dummy," he said.

"Aw, come on," I said. "Why? Is it that bad? All I did was to get Howie Meeker mad at me."

"It's a lot worse than you think. You'll be blacked out," he said, grimly. "No radio perks, no television interviews, and as little newspaper coverage as they can give you. What you *will* see will all be bad."

"That's okay," I said, philosophically. "I'm pretty used to that."

I scored the winning goal in the third period by going around the defence in the usual way, and I didn't even get third star. I went up and down my wing against Cashman, took his checks, many of which were flagrantly vicious and should have drawn penalties, and I threw a couple of my own in his direction. Cashman was given third star, actually, and Meeker said he was the one Bruin on the ice who had dominated his opponent.

Ferguson and I had a few beers after the game. I invited the rest of the guys, but nobody seemed interested.

"You're really a goof," Ferguson said cheerfully. "Do you know that?"

"How was I supposed to know?" I said, irritably. It seemed like everybody knew the rules but me.

"Look," I said, "I didn't go through the system like you guys did. For me it was all watching the tube, and thinking about it. How was I supposed to know — I mean, I've never believed much of what I've seen on television, but I did think Hockey Night in Canada at least was for real."

Ferguson grunted. "Rules are rules," he said. "Nobody but you believes they're supposed to be just."

"I'd settle for knowing what they are," I said bitterly.

"Would you really?"

"I'm not sure," I admitted. "I guess I really want to know who the big shots are who make them."

I didn't find out who the big shots were, that night or on any of the ensuing nights that season. I played my hockey as well as I could and I played it in more or less the kind of obscurity I had been warned to expect. I scored nine goals and built twelve assists in twenty-seven games, and I was invited back for training camp the following season even though I played increasingly less often toward the close of the season.

As I was packing up to go home, the two Swedes came over and mentioned how much they'd enjoyed my presence during the home games, and asked if I'd be able to visit them in Sweden during the summer.

"I've got a lot of writing to catch up on," I told them. "My season's really just starting now."

Salming grinned that same grin I'd seen in my first game.

"I understand this," he said. "No fun to go to Sweden if you're interested in the Pros in English language."

"Something close to that," I admitted.

He and Hammerstrom left the dressing room laughing. They sure weren't like the Scandinavians I knew from watching Ingmar Bergman movies. I wandered over to where Ferguson was packing his equipment, and said goodbye. His bag was full of books, and he was having a hard time getting them all in. Finally, he had to give up, and he left with a pile of them under one arm. He turned at the door.

"I'm going to try to write some stuff myself this summer," he said. "Mind if I send you some of it?"

"Do," I replied. "You've got my address?"

"Sure have," he smiled. "Well, see you. Stay in shape."

"You too," I said. But I was talking to his shadow. He'd disappeared.

That summer passed in a flash, and by mid-September I was back skating and shooting again with the Leafs. The season started, and by December I had four goals and as many assists and, I thought, I was doing okay.

But the team wasn't doing well at all. We were fourth in our division, and Ballard could be heard snorting and snuffling all the way to Buffalo.

Then, before a practice right after a road trip that had gone badly, King Clancy walked into the dressing room, announced that Kelly had been fired, and that John McLellan was the new coach. Two days later Ferguson was traded to Pittsburgh. The day after that, McLellan called me into his office.

"Brian," he said, "I talked things over with Jim, and we, uhh ... "

He seemed to be stumbling for the right words.

"We don't think your heart is really in this game. You're not skating ... "

"I can't skate," I cut in, but he ignored that and went on.

"We want you to retire."

"I'm practically a rookie!" I sputtered.

"You're thirty-one," he said, "and you're not going to get any better. Meeker is still after your behind, and you're a target for every goon in the league. Both Jim and I spent some time over the summer reading your work. You're a better poet than a hockey player. You've got to go for that."

I fussed and fumed, but I ended up agreeing with him. I had two, maybe three years of good hockey in me. With poetry I had maybe forty years, and I would only get better. I'd miss the crowds and the attentiveness of the critics, even though they'd done a good job of ignoring me. But I wouldn't miss Toronto and its bars, and I wouldn't miss the poetics, which, try as I did to ignore them, are as venal and profit-oriented at

Maple Leaf Gardens as they are in the English departments of the nation's universities. If more poets were to play hockey instead of pretending flowers or vacant lots are really interesting, things might get better. But I wasn't going to hold my breath.

"You're right," I told McLellan. "I'll retire right now."

And I did. I walked out the way I had come in, gave back the blue on white and the number 15, and stepped out into the dull Toronto streets as if it were the next morning and not the next year I'd awakened to.

Three weeks later I got a letter from Ferguson, postmarked Atlanta. In it was this poem:

> It's cold in Pittsburgh, colder still
> in Philly. The north wind blows all night
> from Canada, and these raucous crowds
> that hoot and holler for our blood, Hey!
> They're the coldest thing of all.
> Skate and shoot, the coaches tell us
> Skate and shoot. But masked men block the goals
> and I am checked at every turn.
>
> Each year more miles to go
> More senseless contests of the will.
> My heart is like the puck; often frozen
> too often out of play, too often
>
> stolen by the strangers
> in the crowd.

Wives

❖ PETER BEHRENS

My friend Pierce Harkin lived with his wife on City Councillors Street in Montreal. I'd played hockey with Harkin at McGill, but I hadn't seen him in ten years. After graduating, I'd gone to Toronto and gotten a job on a newspaper. I married, was sent to Europe and then to Indonesia as a correspondent for the Canadian Broadcasting Corporation. My wife died in Indonesia and I came home.

I met Harkin on a Sunday afternoon while I was walking in Mount Royal Park. He was a good-looking man with sandy hair that was thinning on top, and a hard middleweight's build. When I recognized him on the carriage road beneath the Cross, he was wearing an old tweed jacket and a pair of English corduroys. It was the last Sunday in September and the carriage road was littered with red and yellow leaves.

I hadn't had close friends at McGill but I'd always liked Pierce Harkin. He had a cleanliness about him and he never lied. We used to sit in the locker-room after practice and talk of books we'd read. He spoke French perfectly and was aiming for a political career. He had good manners and behaved the same way to everyone, with easy, unconscious grace.

We walked along the road to the Chalet and he told me he and Luc Fortier, who'd also played for McGill, had started their own law firm. I told him I'd quit the CBC and was working as a correspondent for a group of British newspapers. Pierce wanted to go downtown and have a drink, but I told him I had other plans.

"We're having a party at Thanksgiving," he said. "Why don't you come?"

"I'd like to, but I might be working in Ottawa."

He was already scribbling his address on a piece of paper. "Not on Thanksgiving! Look, come if you get the chance. It's good to see you!"

We shook hands and I watched him walk away through the Sunday-afternoon crowds, with his soft, well-fitted jacket and his comfortable stride.

I was in Ottawa the week before Thanksgiving and almost forgot Harkin's invitation. I only thought of it Saturday night as the rain was coming into Montreal. I wondered whether or not I would go, as I walked out through Windsor Station. The station always affects my mood, particularly in the autumn, when the floor is strewn with leaves blown in from Lagauchetiere Street.

The next morning I spent a couple of hours reading the papers, then had lunch at a café on St-Denis street. I had a beer with lunch and a coffee afterwards, and sat until the shadows fell across my table and the air got cool. I went for a long walk on the Mountain and came down the carriage road as the light was fading. The dusk smelled of leaves and cold earth, and I made my way through the still streets to Pierce Harkin's.

He lived in the middle flat in a three-storey building. I climbed up an iron staircase and rang the bell. I could hear the sounds of a party, and when Pierce opened the door the hallway behind him was crowded with guests. We shook hands and he pulled me inside and introduced me to Katherine, his wife. She was wearing a red woolen dress.

"You're Jack McDermot," she said, placing her hand on my wrist. "I met you in once in Toronto, at a woman called Betty Wilder's, do you remember?"

"No, but I'm pleased to meet you."

She reminded me of women in Rome, with her wide shoulders and black hair.

"Do you live in Montreal now?" she said. "Didn't you use to work for the CBC?"

"I used to, I don't any more. I work for some papers in England. I live in Carre St-Louis."

"Good for you," she said. "I like it down there." She sipped some wine. "Pierce said you'd know these people."

I looked at the guests crowded in the hall. "I might know some of them, but I've been away from Montreal for quite a while."

"You met Pierce at McGill, didn't you?"

"We played hockey the same year. What do you do?"

"I'm a photographer. I knew your wife, you know."

"Did you?"

"Yes, I just wanted to tell you. Not well, but I knew her, we went to school together. In Toronto, you know. I think the last time I saw her was when I was seventeen. She was a year ahead of me. I always liked her."

"What do you take pictures of?" I said.

She took another sip of wine. "This week I was taking pictures of Haitian cab drivers downtown."

"Good for you," I said. "I'm glad to have met you. I like your dress."

She laughed. She had a soft, clear laugh that reminded me again of women you see in Rome, walking through the Borghese Gardens with their elegant boyfriends.

I recognized only one of the guests, a woman from the Ottawa press gallery who seemed surprised to see me. Most of the others were lawyers. Pierce offered me a bottle of Danish beer. "Got any skates?" he said. His face was flushed. The room was warm and smelled of nutmeg and furniture polish.

"What?"

"Skates. Do you still own any?"

"I haven't skated since college."

"There's a bunch of us playing Thursday nights at the Winter Stadium. We could use another player if you're interested."

"Thanks. I'm not in town very much. I don't have any equipment."

"We can always dig you up some gear. It's a terrific way to keep in shape, more fun than running or squash. That stuff's for masochists. You don't have to be a regular, either. I'll give you a call some time. Nobody gets hurt. We keep the sticks low and go easy on the checking."

Later in the evening while the party was still going on, Pierce led me to his study in the back of the house. The walls were lined with books and with photographs Katherine had taken. He took a bottle of cognac from a drawer in his desk and poured us each a glass. I began looking through his library and he pointed out a couple of books he thought I should borrow. My books were all in storage somewhere, I couldn't even be sure which continent. He leaned against the desk, sipping cognac. His eyes were triangular-shaped and coloured the bright, hard blue that makes you think of the Atlantic in July.

When I left some time after midnight they were out on the sidewalk, saying goodbye to their guests. Katherine kissed me on the cheek and Pierce said he'd phone about the hockey games. While I was walking away, carrying the books I'd been lent, I heard Katherine's clear, careless laughter, and looked back to see her and Pierce waving goodbye to a carload of guests. In the streetlight I saw how his arm held her around the waist and how she wore his tweed jacket gathered at her shoulders.

Pierce phoned two weeks later and asked me to play hockey at the Winter Stadium. Young lawyers are good at making arrangements and I found myself suiting up in borrowed equipment the next night and pulling on skates for the first time in ten years. Afterwards I bought skates and started playing once or twice a week. I was in poor shape but began doing conditioning exercises Pierce showed me. Pierce and Luc Fortier were the best players. When we'd played for McGill the League had been very rough — Fortier still wore a bridge in place of the teeth he'd lost at a championship game in Trois-Rivières. At the Winter Stadium, however, it was a gentleman's game. There were no set teams, we improvised by sorting through whoever turned up on a particular evening. Everyone got his share of ice time. The players reminded me of boys I'd known at private school. They played for diversion and for comradeship. All were married, and most had one or two young children. In the locker room they told jokes about their wives.

Pierce was hurt in December. By that time the ground on Mount Royal was hard as iron, the trees stripped of leaves. He was a good player, a fast, tough wing who wasn't afraid to chase the puck into the corners and usually came out with it on his stick. We were digging for the puck when the blade of my stick came up and caught him in the eye. The game stopped and all the players rushed over the boards.

There was no blood but the eyeball, milky-coloured, was bulging in the socket. Pierce kept cupping his hands as if he were trying to press the swelling down. It took two of us to hold him still while Fortier brought his BMW to the front door of the rink. We carried Pierce out to the car. Two men got in the back with him and I sat in front with Fortier.

We brought Pierce in to Emergency at the Royal Victoria. After he was wheeled away, Fortier went to phone Katherine. The other players began arriving with our street clothes. Fortier got hold of a staff doctor who knew Pierce, and who promised to find out what he could. A few minutes later the doctor returned to say Pierce wouldn't be released and there was no point in any of us waiting. Fortier said he'd stay until Katherine arrived.

I walked out to the hospital parking lot and watched the other players get into their cars. It was dark and had started to rain. I watched the cars drive away, then went back inside and sat in one of the chairs in the corridor.

A few minutes later Katherine came in at the other end. She stood by the nurses' desk talking with Fortier and the doctor who knew Pierce. She was wearing a navy blue overcoat and a scarf tied loosely at her neck. As I walked over, she was telling Fortier to go home, there was no reason for him to stay. He picked up his equipment bag and kissed her on the cheek. He brushed past me and walked away down the corridor.

Katherine asked the doctor when she could see her husband. She reached for my hand and squeezed it. The doctor said he'd find out where they had taken Pierce. When he had gone off, Katherine and I sat down on a pair of hard plastic chairs.

I had often thought of her that fall because she was the only person I still knew who had known my wife. We'd never spoken of my wife again, though. I described Pierce's injury. "You mustn't blame yourself," she said. An East Indian family sat facing us across the corridor. The mother was cradling a sick infant and the father and grandmother seemed to be arguing, quietly and bitterly.

The young doctor returned and took Katherine to see Pierce. She came back a few minutes later. "He's all doped up. He looks terrible. They're going to cut out his eye."

A nurse suggested we go to a waiting room in the surgical wing and we followed her down pale green corridors. The room where she left us was empty and smelled of floor polish. Katherine removed her coat and we sat in leather armchairs. There was music playing over invisible speakers. We sat without speaking and Katherine lit a cigarette. When the music stopped, I could hear the whirr of the electric clock above the door.

"You can go if you want to, Jack. There's really no reason why you have to stay."

I got out of my chair and went to the window that looked out over the mountainside. The rain smashed against the glass in big, angry pellets.

"Pierce is awfully lucky," Katherine said. "He'll pull through this all right. Hospitals are really funny places, aren't they? It would be a good place to spend a week with a camera, roaming the corridors. You'd have to be careful not to bother anyone, but you could get lots of powerful stuff. I hate these waiting rooms, though."

"The last time I was in a hospital was when my wife died," I said.

"I knew your wife, she was a very lovely girl."

"You went to school with her. You probably even knew her before I did."

"Probably. She was the year ahead of me, so I didn't know her well, but she was one of those girls I looked up to. When did you get married? Was she ill for a long time?"

"It happened suddenly. She died in Indonesia, you know."

"There was a notice in one of the alumnae letters."

I moved away from the window. She'd taken off her scarf and her neck was very white. "Hospitals in Indonesia aren't anything like this," I told her. "And it wasn't in one of the cities or the big towns — it was in a place you've never heard of. I'd never heard of it before. Maybe Pierce has heard of it, he reads a lot, he knows things like that. The hospitals are very dirty. No one speaks English."

Katherine glanced at the clock. "I'm so tired," she said. "I was up at six this morning, there was stuff in the darkroom I had to do. Then I was shooting all day."

"Don't worry," I said. "Pierce will be all right."

"Yes, he will."

She was being very brave, I thought. "Of course he will," I told her. "It'll take more than that to hurt him. More than a stick in the damned eye. You know what they did to my wife?"

"Excuse me," she said, "what did you say?"

"Do you know what they did to my wife?"

"No, I don't. I'm very sorry."

"She was run over by a bus," I said. "Doesn't that sound funny?"

"No," she said. "It sounds very sad."

"After she was hit they lifted her in the back of a truck. Her legs were broken, her pelvis, there were some bad cuts. She was in shock. When we got to the hospital, they just laid her down on the grass outside and went away. She wasn't talking but she was breathing, and she knew what was going on."

Katherine's face was very pale and beautiful.

"There were sick people on the grass — dozens. It wasn't even a real hospital, just a clinic sponsored by one of the political parties. I wanted to get her inside, out of the sun, but I couldn't find anyone in the compound who looked like a doctor or understood what I was saying. They have about a dozen major languages and God knows how many dialects. I didn't speak the right one. When I came back to her stretcher, there was an old woman squatting there pouring water on her lips. I suppose it was some gesture of mercy, but I knew she had injuries inside and shouldn't drink anything, so I knocked the ladle away and screamed at the old woman."

Katherine started to cry.

"What she actually died from was drowning — the lungs were full of water. I have all this in a report from the Canadian Embassy in Djakarta. They arranged an autopsy for some reason, autopsies aren't done in that part of the world, you know. Anyway, I watched some men carry her away."

Katherine was bent over and I saw the neat part in her hair, black as a raven's wing. She whispered, "They all keep their sticks low, those are the rules, those are the *rules*!"

I looked at her, thinking what a lovely wife she was.

"Don't worry," I told her, "it'll take much more than that to hurt him."

Number 33

❖ MARSHA MILDON

My name is Cal Mariner. You won't know me by that name, unless, of course, you've hired me to walk your dogs along with my two golden retrievers. And even then, you probably remember their names — *Great Golden,* that is *GG the Second,* and *Blue line* — better than you do mine. I suppose you might also know me if you've hired me lately to find a missing aunt or fortune for you; I do some "Private Investigator" work to supplement my dog walking business. But I only take cases I like, and, to be honest, there aren't that many of those. Thank goddess for dogs. In any case, don't be misled. This isn't a detective story or a dog story. It's my story this time, told my way.

My name is Cal ... Okay, okay, to be honest, it's Calliope, Calliope Mariner. Mother, who in 1945, the year I was born, was only fifteen and living in the Blessed-Mary-Mother-of-God's-Home-for-Unwed-Mothers, must be forgiven her flights of romanticism. But I shortened my name to Cal as soon as I could speak. When she heard my baby gurgles, she instantly became convinced she'd given birth to the first diva to hail from Southern Ontario, and so named me after the Greek muse of the *beautiful voice.* My infant cries were enough to change all her plans to give me up for adoption and retreat into the stern embrace of her Welsh forbears. Instead, she struck out to build her life as a pioneer in the twentieth-century version of women's liberation.

All through the *family-fifties,* my mother soldiered along, working first as a cleaning lady, later as the manager of her own cleaning firm, insisting to anyone who'd listen that life for her and her daughter was better by half than that of most women with a man around the house. Not, unfortunately, that her liberation was extended to me. Mother had great expectations for her Calliope. I was dressed in pink and frills from day one so I'd learn to appear feminine (for my hordes of adoring fans, you understand). I was traipsed (by bus, of course — Mother's spare money went towards lessons for me, not towards a car) across the blast-furnace-infested soot-drenched city of Hamilton to ballet lessons, acting lessons, piano lessons and, most important of all, singing lessons.

Mother was not deterred by an apparent lack of talent or progress on my part. When, after one full year of ballet lessons, I was given the important job of pulling the curtain for the year end show, this merely suggested to her that I showed a greater than average sense of responsibility. When, after two years of acting lessons, I played the part of the celery — *Celery is long and full of strings. It's one of the crispiest, crunchiest things* — in the acting-class pageant, she was certain I was given only two lines so as not to outshine the rest of the class.

The piano lessons were better. At least there was an instrument, which, left to itself, made good sounds. When I managed to push through my terror of those weird little black marks strung like lost sheep along the musical staff, I actually hit a few correct notes. I was in ecstasy when the *Song of the Volga Boatmen* — yo ho heave ho etc. — actually sounded vaguely European and exotic.

I was not so lucky with my singing lessons. Mrs. Duclos and I probably could have survived if I'd been a mere ugly duckling in a class of singing swans. To our sorrow, however, I was a small, black-haired crow complete with *caw*. After six months, Mrs. Duclos sent me packing and not a single other Conservatory teacher would take me on. Mother finally found a church organist who, for a fee equivalent to Mother's daily wage, allowed me to sing alto in the First Baptist choir, but it broke Mother's heart. By age seven, it was already clear I would not be a diva. Still, she was not completely put off her plans for my stardom. The lessons continued.

Now none of these lessons, you understand, reflected my actual interests. Indeed, I was interested in very little but survival. Still, Mother and I were tied so intimately together, two female souls treading water in the patriarchal world of Father Knows Best, that for those first ten or twelve years her dreams were my reality. I would have done anything to please her, if only I could have. Dutifully, and with the passion of a child desperately eager to please, I tried each set of lessons that came along. Her only concession to my *child* needs was to make sure I always had a dog, an SPCA *multi-cultural* specimen, to whom I whispered my fears.

The truth is, I was clumsy at everything — even walking Juno. (Mother named each of our dogs Juno, after a goddess who, you'll notice, outranked a mere muse considerably.) By the time I reached age twelve, mother had abandoned my ballet, tap, acting, piano, singing, swimming, figure skating and gymnastics lessons. She had also noticed that I could not skip rope; I could not pick up sticks or jacks; I could not make a yo-yo *yo* even once. I could not catch or throw a ball, and the last time she pitched to me, hoping to teach me to bat before the Church Picnic ball game, I'd stepped into the ball with such perfect timing that I got it squarely in the eye. The only thing I could do well was read, and even that accomplishment was somewhat tainted by my crossed eyes and pink-flesh-coloured glasses. Mother was devastated — who'd ever heard of a cross-eyed entertainer who merely sat and read?

What no one else knew, or for that matter had reason to suspect, was that, at age seven, I began a passionate love affair with the game of hockey. Not, you understand, that I had ever seen a game of hockey. Oh, I'd seen the boys with their black skates at the rink, strutting onto the ice with their sticks and gloves as we white-booted figure skaters delicately picked our way off. And I'd been terrorized by the bullies on the pond at the end of our street who always used their hockey sticks to clear the ice of *girr-ulls*, that horrid two syllable species to which I seemed to belong. But I had never actually seen the game played. Mother's interest in sports seemed limited to the Church picnic, and like the car we didn't have, a TV was far too expensive. No *Hockey Night in Canada* for us.

So my love affair with hockey began as an aural experience. It soon became a completely nationalistic one, as I buried myself and Juno under the bed covers and, with my transistor radio pressed to my ear, listened to the Edmonton Mercurys win gold at the 1952 Olympic Games.

"Icing," called the announcer. "That brings the puck back into the Mercurys' end for a face-off." Icing? What is icing? I wondered. And a face-off? What could that be? I was baffled by almost everything I heard, except of course, "Number 9 fakes a pass across the goal. He shoots, he scores. The Canadian team wins it all!" That I understood very well. The heroes of my country were winning at our most important game. This was clear from the announcer's excitement. I was ecstatic.

That first experience with hockey was enough to mark me for life. It was as if I had somehow imprinted on the game. Like my mother, I left home early, though unlike her, I managed to do this without pregnancy, and also unlike her, I went west, to Vancouver. There, at age sixteen, I rented a fifteenth-floor high rise apartment in the West End (oh sophistication), acquired a bed and a television set from the nearby furniture Rent-To-Own store, and set about becoming an adult. Of course, needing to recreate some of the atmosphere of home, I also equipped myself with a gawky Irish Setter-Golden Retriever cross I named Rocket — the perfect pet for a downtown high rise, don't you agree?

It was the job market that turned my serene passage to adulthood into a rocky road. After discovering to my horror that the *Vancouver Sun* did not think my tenure as Grade Ten editor of my high school newspaper provided impeccable credentials for a reporter's job, I lowered my occupational sights. For the next few years, I worked as a waitress, a jewellery store clerk, a telephone operator, a telephone magazine solicitor, a door-to-door magazine seller, a chamber maid, a mail sorter, an elevator operator — and at many more jobs I try to forget.

My real life was in my apartment. On Saturday and then Wednesday nights I watched *Hockey Night in Canada*. I was a Canadiens fan and wore a white *home* jersey with the number four, celebrating Jean Béliveau's mastery. Year after year I raised the Stanley Cup over my head with the Canadiens, and I learned to drink champagne without sneezing as I celebrated their triumphs. I even attempted to play goalie for an otherwise all-British women's field hockey team — just because they called their sport *hockey.*

In the early seventies, I travelled in Europe, a free spirit — or, more to the point, a penniless spirit — hitchhiking and youth-hostelling like so many in the post-war generation. But unlike many of my fellow travellers, who wanted nothing to do with their roots, I always had my shortwave radio with me. I abandoned even the most interesting of newly-met friends and newfound philosophies to listen to Radio Canada International broadcast its NHL games. That static-thick voice shouting "He shoots, he scores!" was all I needed to stay in touch with home.

Luckily for my long-term mental health, I was on the Stefan Batory ocean liner travelling from Copenhagen to Montreal, far from any news outlet, during the first three disastrous games of the 1972 Russia Canada hockey series. I heard about them through the unemotional medium of a newspaper at the Montreal docks. I'm not sure how I would have survived the pain of actually watching those games. Like most Canadians, I remember exactly where I was when Paul Henderson scored the last of his three game-winning goals to clinch that series. I was in a bar, linked through a frantic outpouring of patriotic energy with dozens of people I didn't know personally, but whose hearts I knew intimately.

As I tried to resettle in Canada, my luck held: good luck with hockey, bad luck with jobs. I worked my way across the country, waitressing here, doing a bit of typing there, cleaning toilets in some of the dirtiest buildings of the country. I learned to typeset in Saskatoon and thought I was starting a real career until the owner left for Columbia with all his liquid assets, leaving me with a stack of unfinished projects, unpaid bills and unanswerable questions. It took a week of fast talking to explain that I knew nothing about the business.

Next, I spent six weeks in a to-be-nameless northern Alberta town, reporting for the *Moose Droppings Times*. "This is it at last!" I thought. I really *was* meant to be a writer and star reporter; the *Vancouver Sun* had been wrong. Alas, the editor/publisher of the *Times* made the mayor and local police so angry with his editorials that they set us up on a drug bust. No amount of fast talking helped this time. The newspaper went down and five of us went up, which is how I found myself near Edmonton, doing time in the Fort Saskatchewan Women's Prison with its god-forsaken bright pink cells. It was the same year Gretzky and the Edmonton Oilers joined the NHL.

Now I don't recommend breaking the law as a way of moving across the country, but the bus ride to "the Fort" was free and so were the up-grading classes that earned me my Grade Twelve during the months of hard time. Besides, I learned enough about law and crime while I was inside to prepare me for the bit of PI work I do now.

But it was hockey that saved my sanity again. At the Fort, we watched *Hockey Night in Canada* without fail. And when I arrived at last in the city of Edmonton, it was just in time to see *The Great One* in his first NHL playoffs. I spent the full forty-two dollars I'd earned from cleaning prison floors on one ticket in the blues to see Gretzky's game against the Flyers. He scored a natural hat trick and I fell head-over-hockey-stick in love.

For the next eight years, life was wonderful. With my newly enhanced education, I got a job as a cocktail waitress in a sports bar, made bucketloads of money, and bought my first pure bred, registered Golden Retriever. The Great Golden, I called him — GG for short. The Oilers of-ten came into the bar after their home games, and once they started win-ning the cup, they'd bring it in for us to hold. They'd even let us sneak a drink from it. Gretzky was just as nice in person as he appeared on the big-screen TV and he gave me one of his sticks, with his autograph. And, for eight years, I resisted the temptation to tell off my boss, just so I wouldn't lose the job and miss the guys coming in.

But don't mistake me. I wasn't just another Gretzky groupie; I was an expert. I consumed everything I could find about hockey. I read *Hockey News*; I bought Gretzky hockey cards; I read every book there was to read about hockey. I empathized with Rick Salutin as he struggled to make his play about *Les Canadiens* reflect everything there was to be said about relations between Quebec and the rest of Canada. I laughed and cried with Roch Carrier as he prayed for his abhorred Maple Leaf hockey sweater to be eaten by moths. I listened to Peter Gzowski rhap-sodize about the Canadian identity and reminisce about missing a goal on a perfect pass from Gretzky while he scrimmaged with the Oilers. Imagine — one of us mere mortals had received a pass from Gretzky. I applauded Ken Brown as he gained fame with his one-man play *Life after Hockey*. I knew everything about hockey.

And then, in 1988, Peter Pocklington traded Gretzky. It was a national disaster. In fact, it was the first disaster of free trade. In the name of free enterprise, we sold away a national treasure in order — so we were told — to improve American interest in *our* game. I was stunned; I quit my job and left town within the week. Who could face life in Edmonton without the Great One? The *Welcome to Edmonton, City of Champions* sign was not removed from the highway, but that was mere bravado. Edmonton's reign as the premiere city in the nation was over.

The Great Golden and I moved to Victoria, the least wintry of Canadian cities. I took up gardening — gardening all winter, that is. GG adored our daily trips to the ocean with his tennis balls. As the years passed, I gradually stopped catching every NHL game on TV. At first, I only missed the games in the fall; then I began to watch only the playoffs, then only the finals. Even Gretzky's games with the L.A. Kings lost their allure.

And then, a new acquaintance of mine just happened to mention that she played hockey.

"Hockey?" I asked. "Field hockey you mean?"

"No, ice hockey," she replied. "I play for the Victoria Vixens, a women's recreational hockey team."

Now you may ask how I had made it to 1994 without ever hearing of women's ice hockey — except, of course, for reports on the National Team and Manon Rhéaume. The answer is: I have no idea. I can only assume that my mother's determination that I should be an *artiste* simply anesthetized my awareness of women's hockey. But the moment I heard of it, I was seized by an overwhelming passion to play. It was an inner throbbing through my blood, a kind of Canadian genetic imperative which I hadn't even imagined was there, so firmly had it been repressed in the depths of my *you're-a-girr-ull* psyche.

"Uh … How good do you have to be to play?" I asked casually. In truth, my friend had never struck me as an athletic sort, so I wondered if … could it be possible … could a less-than-brilliant athlete play?

"Oh, anybody can play," she said. "Lots of women come who've never played before."

That was July. The knowledge that I was forty-nine and hadn't skated since I was twelve had absolutely no effect. I left my friend, excusing my sudden departure with the news that my freelance dog-walking business was very busy, and I headed for the nearest Canadian Tire store. An eager young man spent an hour fitting me with beautiful black hockey skates just as if I were an NHL prospect buying custom-made blades. My career was on its way.

Alas, my local arena wasn't open until September, and I could hardly contain my impatience. The young skate salesperson had told me to soak my skates in water and then wear them around the house until they dried, to help break them in. I did that. In fact, I wore them around the house for at least an hour every day from then on, clunking about in my skate guards, on the theory that the more I wore them, the better they'd feel when I finally got on the ice. It couldn't hurt, could it? And I watched my Gretzky video and TSN game replays as often as possible.

September finally arrived. My friend, whom I continued to badger with questions about her hockey team, informed me late one Saturday night that the team's first practice would occur the next day, at ten-thirty a.m. (the Vixens have great ice time). But I would have to have complete gear if I wanted to play. She suggested, gently, that I might come and watch the first practice, just to see how people were playing. No chance!

Early the next morning, back I went to Canadian Tire. This time I was in a hurry. The store didn't open until nine a.m. on Sundays, and I would need time to change. It took the clerk only thirty minutes to outfit me with shin pads, socks, garters, sock tape, pants, suspenders, elbow pads, shoulder pads, neck guard, hockey shirt, gloves, helmet with visor, stick, black-and-white stick tape and — much to my surprise — something known as a *jill strap*. Amazing what you don't know until you're almost fifty.

I rushed to the rink, and watching casually out of the corner of my eye, donned my new apparel in the same order as the other women. My friend introduced me to a few of the "old timers," but their names slipped out of my brain as quickly as they had gone in. I wanted to focus on the hockey and on controlling the butterflies icing the puck in my stomach.

At last, I was ready. Like the other players, I donned my helmet, pulled down my visor, pulled on one glove, picked up my stick, stuck the other glove under my arm, and headed out the door and down the corridor to the ice. A hurricane of recognition swept over me. This was exactly how the Oilers always looked walking out of the dressing room. How often had I seen the slightly bow-legged walk, produced by skates and padding? I was walking the same way. How often had I seen those gloves tucked under the arm, stick held front and centre with the other hand? I was holding my stick and glove the same way! Suddenly, I could hear the announcer: "Yes, we can see that Messier — no, that's Mariner — has got her game face on." I narrowed my eyes and focussed hard on the upcoming practice.

And then we hit the ice. Did I mention that I hadn't skated for thirty-seven years? And that I'd never before held a hockey stick except at the bar when Gretzky was signing it? "Hit the ice" describes exactly what I did. For the next hour and a half, while others skated, passed and scored, I hit the ice with my elbows, my knees, my head, my posterior, my shoulders. Every piece of my protective gear was challenged to perform. To my alarm and others' astonishment, when I tried a classic slap shot, I missed the puck and threw my stick and myself into a three-hundred-and-sixty-degree somersault through the air. By the end of the practice, my arms and legs were already turning black and blue. I loved every minute of it.

I could hear the play-by-play with each faltering glide down the ice. "And there goes Mariner, down the left wing, crossing over behind her centre. There she goes to the net. The puck is centred, Mariner shoots and oooohhhh — she just missed, the net that is, and crashed heavily to the boards. Look at that Mariner, she's up on her feet and fighting for the puck again. She's up, she's down, she's up, she's down ... " The coach nicknamed me "Crash" in the dressing room, but said nothing about sending me to the minors. My rookie season was launched.

That first practice taught me two things. First, I loved playing the game of hockey, *our* game, more than anything in my life except playing with dogs. And second, I desperately needed skating lessons. I could hear Howie Meeker complaining about these upstart players who tried to learn to score before they learned to skate. I phoned the local arena and signed up for beginners' lessons two days later. And there I was, dressed in full hockey gear. The next oldest player was ten, and short for his age. I was overwhelmed with a rush of tenderness for these tiny helmeted companions of mine, all of us struggling to become *real* Canadians — hockey players. We practised stroking, sculling, C-cuts, one-o'clock stops, hockey stops, backward sculls, cross-overs — and we fell at every other step. Yet we felt that each cut of each blade carried us deeper into history, farther into the line of Canadians who yearned and learned to play hockey.

The wonderful thing about the Victoria Vixens — and about most recreational teams — is that they encourage everyone to play, and put their weakest players on lines with their strongest, for balance. There was no sitting on the bench just because others are more skilled. Within two weeks, I was called for my first game. By then, I could do a hockey stop — to the left only — and occasionally I could receive the puck and pass it on without throwing myself off balance.

On Game Day, I watched my Gretzky video for inspiration, then headed to the pizza parlour for a pre-game meal of spaghetti — a little carbohydrate loading never hurt any athlete, I told myself, pleased with my extensive knowledge of training procedures. Then I paced and tried not to become too nervous. I got to the dressing room an hour and a half early to make sure I'd have lots of time to change.

And then the moment came. "What number sweater do you want?" asked our Captain.

I looked at the row of red and black Vixen shirts and almost panicked with the emotion of picking my number. Then I remembered that when Marty McSorley joined the Oilers, he had chosen number 33 because he figured he was about one third as good a player as Number 99. McSorley was the quintessential Canadian hero, I thought — not quite a star, perhaps, but an incredibly hard worker who would do anything to keep playing his favourite game. I was so nervous my voice had all but disappeared: "Number 33," I croaked. "I'll wear number 33."

Then we headed out to the ice. I could hear the Hockey Night in Canada theme playing in my head. I adjusted my game face. I warmed up with the others. Each time I stepped on the ice I could hear my personal play-by-play announcer broadcasting the moves. I couldn't always make it to where that voice said I should be, but I knew, in the very depths of my Canuck soul, exactly what this rhythmic ballet up and down the ice was about. Since I could rarely trap a pass, and even more rarely return a good pass, I parked myself in front of the opposing goalie, hoping to screen my linemates' shots. They were both natural athletes, brilliant in their skating and passing. They pointed out that their ages put together didn't add up to mine, and they patted me on the back and said "good shift" and "good positioning" each time I pulled my aged — and rapidly aging — body back to the bench. It was magnificent.

It's been a year since that first game, and I am into my *sophomore* season. I would like to report that my childhood clumsiness has fallen away and that I have blossomed into a brilliant left winger. Alas, that is not quite true. I have, however, played many periods of hockey in many arenas in towns I'd never before visited; I have driven with teammates through blizzards and darkness to play at midnight in small logging towns and smaller fishing villages — all the time imagining a kind of mystical bond with hundreds of similar teams driving through similar blizzards to games in similar small-town arenas. I have practised my hockey stop with the other ten-year-olds in my skating class until I can now stop in both directions. I have patrolled my wing, learned the *St. Louis* passing drill, and stayed after practice to work on my shot — just like the stars. My Rookie Card will show that this season I scored one goal, had three assists, and earned a two-minute penalty for tripping.

Of course, women's hockey is a bit different than either the NHL or the Olympic hockey we see on TV. It's not so much that ours is a *non-checking* game — the line between a simple shove away from the front of an opponent's goal and an actual body check is deceptively fine. But there are other differences: Don Cherry would undoubtedly cringe to see players stop to ask if a fallen opponent is okay *before* taking the opportunity to score; in most leagues, it would be unusual for teams to trade goalies in mid-game because one team is scoring too often on a novice; and a timekeeper at one of our recent games blushed crimson and averted his eyes when our first-line centre took time out in the penalty box to breastfeed her six-week-old son.

But, at the heart of things, this game of stick and puck and ice and heart is the same. This year, I have listened to Peter Gzowski and Roch Carrier and Ken Brown with a remarkable, new feeling of completeness. No longer am I merely a fan, cheering from the sidelines for the great Canadian game and the great Canadian players. I am one of "us": a hockey player, and therefore (I can't help feeling) a Canadian, fully-fledged at last.

On a Saturday night this year, I turned fifty. Exactly fifty years from my birth, almost to the minute, I stepped onto the ice for yet another game in another small arena — my own hockey night in Canada. But it was slightly different this time: instead of my old $7.50 Russian-made stick from Canadian Tire, I carried an *Easton*, Gretzky-advertised, aluminum stick. It was my birthday present from my mother and she was in the stands — one of the fifteen fans who attended that night. Despite my low scoring and my nickname *Crash*, I've finally become her star.

FANS AND PHILOSOPHERS

Goalie

❖ RUDY THAUBERGER

Nothing pleases him. Win or lose, he comes home angry, dragging his equipment bag up the driveway, sullen eyes staring down, seeing nothing, refusing to see. He throws the bag against the door. You hear him, fumbling with his keys, his hands sore, swollen and cold. He drops the keys. He kicks the door. You open it and he enters, glaring, not at you, not at the keys, but at everything, the bag, the walls, the house, the air, the sky.

His clothes are heavy with sweat. There are spots of blood on his jersey and on his pads. He moves past you, wordless, pulling his equipment inside, into the laundry room and then into the garage. You listen to him, tearing the equipment from the bag, throwing it. You hear the thump of heavy leather, the clatter of plastic, the heavy whisper of damp cloth. He leaves and you enter. The equipment is everywhere, scattered, draped over chairs, hung on hooks, thrown on the floor.

You imagine him on the ice: compact, alert, impossibly agile and quick. Then you stare at the equipment: helmet and throat protector, hockey pants, jersey, chest and arm protectors, athletic supporter, knee pads and leg pads, blocker, catching glove and skates. In the centre of the floor are three sticks, scattered, their broad blades chipped and worn. The clutter is deliberate, perhaps even necessary. His room is the same, pure chaos, clothes and magazines everywhere, spilling out of dresser drawers, into the closet. He says he knows where everything is. You imagine him on the ice, focussed, intense, single-minded. You understand the need for clutter.

When he isn't playing, he hates the equipment. It's heavy and awkward and bulky. It smells. He avoids it, scorns it. It disgusts him. Before a game, he gathers it together on the floor and stares at it. He lays each piece out carefully, obsessively, growling and snarling at anyone who comes too close. His mother calls him a gladiator, a bullfighter. But you know the truth, that gathering the equipment is a ritual of hatred, that every piece represents, to him, a particular variety of pain.

There are black marks scattered on the white plastic of his skates. He treats them like scars, reminders of pain. His glove hand is always swollen. His chest, his knees and his biceps are always bruised. After a hard game, he can barely move. "Do you enjoy it?" you ask, "Do you enjoy the game at least? Do you like playing?" He shrugs. "I love it," he says.

Without the game, he's miserable. He spends his summers restless and morose, skating every morning, lifting weights at night. He juggles absentmindedly; tennis balls, coins, apples, tossing them behind his back and under his leg, see-sawing two in one hand as he talks on the phone, bouncing them off walls and knees and feet. He plays golf and tennis with great fervour, but you suspect, underneath, he is indifferent to these games.

As fall approaches, you begin to find him in the basement, cleaning his skates, oiling his glove, taping his sticks. His hands move with precision and care. You sit with him and talk. He tells you stories. This save. That goal. Funny stories. He laughs. The funniest stories are about failure: the goal scored from centre ice, the goal scored on him by his own defenceman, the goal scored through a shattered stick. There is always a moral, the same moral every time. "You try your best and you lose."

He starts wearing the leg pads in September. Every evening, he wanders the house in them, wearing them with shorts and a T-shirt. He hops in them, does leg lifts and jumping jacks. He takes them off and sits on them, folding them into a squat pile to limber them up. He starts to shoot a tennis ball against the fence with his stick.

As practices begin, he comes home overwhelmed by despair. His skill is an illusion, a lie, a magic trick. Nothing you say reassures him. You're his father. Your praise is empty, invalid.

The injuries begin. Bruises. Sprains. His body betrays him. Too slow. Too clumsy. His ankles are weak, buckling under him. His muscles cramp. His nose bleeds. A nerve in his chest begins to knot and fray. No one understands. They believe he's invulnerable, the fans, his teammates. They stare at him blankly while he lies on the ice, white-blind, paralyzed, as his knee or his toe or his hand or his chest or his throat burns.

To be a goalie, you realize, is to be an adult too soon, to have too soon an intimate understanding of the inevitability of pain and failure. In the back yard, next to the garage, is an old garbage can filled with broken hockey sticks. The blades have shattered. The shafts are cracked. He keeps them all, adding a new one every two weeks. You imagine him, at the end of the season, burning them, purging his failure with a bonfire. But that doesn't happen. At the end of the season, he forgets them and you throw them away.

You watch him play. You sit in the stands with his mother, freezing, in an arena filled with echoes. He comes out without his helmet and stick, skating slowly around the rink. Others move around him deftly. He stares past them, disconnected, barely awake. They talk to him, call his name, hit his pads lightly with their sticks. He nods, smiles. You know he's had at least four cups of coffee. You've seen him, drinking, prowling the house frantically.

As the warm-up drills begin, he gets into the goal casually. Pucks fly over the ice, crashing into the boards, cluttering the net. He skates into the goal, pulling on his glove and blocker. He raps the posts with his stick. No one seems to notice, even when he starts deflecting shots. They come around to him slowly, firing easy shots at his pads. He scoops the pucks out of the net with his stick. He seems bored.

You shiver as you sit, watching him. You hardly speak. He ignores you. You think of the cost of his equipment. Sticks, forty dollars. Glove, one hundred and twenty. Leg pads, thirteen hundred dollars. The pads have patches. The glove is soft, the leather eaten away by his sweat.

The game begins, casually, without ceremony. The scoreboard lights up. The ice is cleared of pucks. Whistles blow. After the stillness of the face-off, you hardly notice the change, until you see him in goal, crouched over, staring.

You remember him in the back yard, six years old, standing in a ragged net wearing a parka and a baseball glove, holding an ordinary hockey stick, sawed off at the top. The puck is a tennis ball. The ice is cement. He falls down every time you shoot, ignoring the ball, trying to look like the goalies on TV. You score, even when you don't want to. He's too busy play-acting. He smiles, laughs, shouts.

You buy him a mask. He paints it. Yellow and black. Blue and white. Red and blue. It changes every month, as his heroes change. You make him a blocker out of cardboard and leg pads out of foam rubber. His mother makes him a chest protector. You play in the back yard, every evening, taking shot after shot, all winter.

It's hard to recall when you realize he's good. You come to a point where he starts to surprise you, snatching the ball out of the air with his glove, kicking it away with his shoe. You watch him one Saturday, playing with his friends. He humiliates them, stopping everything. They shout and curse. He comes in, frozen, tired and spellbound. "Did you see?" he says.

He learns to skate, moving off of the street and onto the ice. The pain begins. A shot to the shoulder paralyzes his arm for ten minutes. You buy him pads, protectors, thinking it will stop the pain. He begins to lose. Game after game. Fast reflexes are no longer enough. He is suddenly alone, separate from you. Miserable. Nothing you say helps. Keep trying. Stop. Concentrate. Hold your stick blade flat on the ice.

He begins to practise. He begins to realize that he is alone. You can't help him. His mother can't help him. That part of his life detaches from you, becoming independent, free. You fool yourself, going to his games, cheering, believing you're being supportive, refusing to understand that here, in the rink, you're irrelevant. When you're happy for him, he's angry. When you're sad for him, he's indifferent. He begins to collect trophies.

You watch the game, fascinated. You try to see it through his eyes. You watch him. His head moves rhythmically. His stick sweeps the ice and chops at it. When the shots come, he stands frozen in a crouch. Position is everything, he tells you. He moves, the movement so swift it seems to strike you physically. How does he do it? How? You don't see the puck, only his movement. Save or goal, it's all the same.

You try to see the game through his eyes, aware of everything, constantly alert. It's not enough to follow the puck. The position of the puck is old news. The game. You try to understand the game. You fail.

He seems unearthly, moving to cut down the angle, chopping the puck with his stick. Nothing is wasted. You can almost feel his mind at work, watching, calculating. Where does it come from, you wonder, this strange mind? You try to move with him, watching his eyes through his cage, and his hands. You remember the way he watches games on television, cross-legged, hands fluttering, eyes seeing everything.

Suddenly you succeed, or you think you do. Suddenly, you see the game, not as a series of events, but as a state, with every moment in time potentially a goal. Potentiality. Probability. These are words you think of afterwards. As you watch, there is only the game, pressing against you, soft now, then sharp, then rough, biting, shocking, burning, dull, cold. No players. Only forces, feelings, the white ice, the cold, the echo, all joined. A shot crashes into his helmet. He falls to his knees. You cry out.

He stands slowly, shaking his head, hacking at the ice furiously with his stick. They scored. You never noticed. Seeing the game is not enough. Feeling it is not enough. He wants more, to understand completely, to control. You look out at the ice. The game is chaos again.

He comes home, angry, limping up the driveway, victorious. You watch him, dragging his bag, sticks in his hand, leg pads over his shoulder. You wonder when it happened, when he became this sullen, driven young man. You hear whispers about scouts, rumours. Everyone adores him, adores his skill. But when you see his stiff, swollen hands, when he walks slowly into the kitchen in the mornings, every movement agony, you want to ask him why. Why does he do it? Why does he go on?

But you don't ask. Because you think you know the answer. You imagine him, looking at you and saying quietly, "What choice do I have? What else have I ever wanted to do?"

an excerpt from the novel *Two Solitudes*

❖   HUGH MacLENNAN

Leaning on her elbow beside him, Heather bent and looked close at his face. His eyes were closed and his lips slightly parted. She wanted to touch his hair and find out how it felt, particularly where it was a shade lighter and softer on the top of his head. Already faint lines showed at the corners of his eyes. It was strange to have him so quiet now, after all the talking he had done in her studio. She guessed it was more natural for him to be silent than otherwise. All his strength seemed to be held in leash. There was a scar on his left thigh, another on his chest; when he rolled over onto his stomach another appeared on the lower part of his back. She traced it with her finger.

"How did you get that?"

"Hockey."

"All of them?"

"Yes."

"It's a good thing you stopped playing."

"That's not why I stopped."

"Why did you?"

"It took too much out of me." He rolled over onto his back again. "After every game I was like a limp rag. And before every game I'd have to tighten myself up. You're useless unless you start nervous."

"You love hockey, don't you, Paul?"

"I used to." He shaded his eyes with his hands, his face wrinkling from the low-hanging sun. "Some winters I felt as if I lived in the Forum. I knew every scratch on the paint along the boards. There was one long gash near the south penalty box I used to touch before every game, and remember how it was made."

"How was it?"

"Eddie Shore kicked his skate into it once when he was sore."

"Were you superstitious?"

He looked at her from under nearly closed eyelids. "I was about hockey."

She touched the scar on his chest and then took her finger away quickly. "How did you happen to do it — play hockey like that, I mean?"

"Because I needed the money."

"No — I mean, why hockey and not something else?"

He thought a moment. "I guess it was the first professional game I ever saw. I was sixteen. Joliat, Morenz and Boucher were playing. After that I was willing to slave eight hours a day training just on the chance of being half as good as they were." He reached up and stroked her hair. "But now I'm an old man, and at the best I was never even a quarter as good."

"Now you're very, very serious."

"I know. Much too much so."

She grinned down at him, liking the rhythm of his moving fingers on her head, warm with the sense of him. Some men who seemed gentle enough were clumsy with their hands, but Paul whose body looked hard, was tender even through his finger-tips.

"I wonder if you'd like Daffy now," she said. "She's a natural blonde."

"What makes you think I like blondes?"

"She's tall and willowy, and she has skin like honey in the sun." When he made no reply she added, "And her figure is luscious. It looks as if it would melt in a man's arms."

"It must be a full-time job, being Daffy."

Heather laughed. "And she has a perfectly dreadful husband. I'm rather sorry for him, but not very much. Daphne says he rapes her."

"Is that possible?"

"Don't be horrid!"

"I meant, is it a physically possible thing to do? I've often wondered."

He sat up and they crouched on the sand looking at each other, the moment poised between them like a bubble, and then he jumped up and ran into the water, charging it so hard he tripped and went down with a splash. Heather watched him stroking out to deep water. He dove once and came up blowing, cruised a little, then crawled back and ran up the beach and dropped down on the warm earth beside her. She sat and looked at the rise and fall of his chest.

"I wish I knew more about hockey," she said. "Mother's never thought it quite proper for me to go to the Forum. Alan used to take me sometimes. I've never seen anything more beautiful; not a single ugly movement on the ice."

"Morenz, Joliat, Gagnon, Jackson, Smith — the whole lot of them are about the best artists this country ever turned out."

"Hooley Smith sent a man into the boards almost on top of me once. Without thinking what I was doing I booed him for it."

"That shows you didn't appreciate him. He did it beautifully and you never noticed."

She got up and walked to the car and he watched her as she returned with the sandwiches and beer. She put her bottles at the edge of the water, making them secure with small stones. Then she came back and stood over him. "Did you get into fights and get penalties?"

"Not if I could help it."

"I wish I'd seen you play."

"Too late now. My hockey days are definitely over."

an excerpt from the novel *The Loved and The Lost*

❖   MORLEY CALLAGHAN

At the Forum the sustained roaring echoing along the streets compelled Catherine to take his arm and go plunging into the cavernous corridors and up the flights of stairs, half running with the other late stragglers. The fact that he had been late and had come offering apologies had made her feel important to him. All week she had been wanting him to ask her to forgive him for some breach in their intimacy which she couldn't define; now she liked the way they were rushing up the stairs together. A fine blue homespun woollen scarf embroidered in pink and yellow trailed over the shoulder of her beaver coat. "Hey, not so fast! I'm out of breath," she gasped.

"Where were you this afternoon, Jim?" she asked, reaching for his hand at the turn.

"Well," he said, hesitating, "what time?"

"About four o'clock, when I phoned." They began to ascend the second flight of stairs.

"Oh, I must have been downstairs having a drink," he lied.

That it should be necessary to lie shocked him and made him realize how false his relationship with her had become. And soon she would learn of his relationship with Peggy. Wolgast had walked in on him; it meant that word about him and Peggy had probably already got around, and soon Catherine would hear of it. Everybody would know about it. It was happening too soon. He and Peggy were not yet ready; they couldn't as yet be truly together. They would be dragged into the open while everyone was against them. If word did get around to the Carvers and they rejected him and he lost his job, well, he could take it. If it had to happen — to hell with them — let it happen. He had made his choice. It would be all right if he had Peggy. As yet, though, he didn't have her.

Maybe he would never be able to count on her love. If that were so and he lost the Carvers and his job, and with his university post gone too, he would be left with nothing. His life would be ruined. It frightened him, and his head began to sweat.

Their seats opposite the Ranger blue line were in the centre of the section, and they had a little luck; as they started along the row, mumbling apologies, the Canadiens threatened the Ranger goal, everybody stood up and they got to their seats between a stout florid French Canadian in a brown overcoat who was eating a bag of peanuts and a short French Canadian priest with a pale bony face. The roaring came like waves rising, falling, breaking and always in motion. "Oh, that Richard!" Catherine screamed, pounding McAlpine's shoulder. "Who says he isn't the best right winger in the business? Look at him go!" Then the play shifted to the Canadien end, the lines were changed and the roaring subsided, with the background of gigantic humming always there. Behind them, three rows up, a fight broke out. A fair-haired boy in a leather jacket started swinging wildly at a prosperous-looking middle-aged man in a hard hat. They couldn't reach each other and flailed the air. So the fair boy grabbed the brim of the prosperous citizen's hard hat and jerked it down over his eyes. Everybody laughed.

McAlpine remained standing, apparently waiting for the fight to break out again, but really gazing at the rows of grinning, exuberant faces. They would all be with Malone. They would all agree that Wolgast, too, no matter what he was, had really spoken for them.

They were fairly prosperous people, for the very poor didn't have the money to go to hockey games. Some of the men wore fur caps and coonskin coats; others, pink-faced and freshly shaven, wore hard hats; but most of them had on snap-brimmed fedoras. The women in their fur coats huddled happily together with their men, row on row, the rich men looking like rich men, and doctors and lawyers with their wives, and the merchants and the salaried workers and the prosperous union men. They came from all the districts around the mountain; they came from wealthy Westmount and solid respectable French Outremont and from the Jewish shops along St. Catherine, and of course a few Negroes from St. Antoine would be in the cheap seats. There they were, citizens of the second biggest French-speaking city in the world, their faces rising row on row, French faces, American faces, Canadian faces, Jewish faces, all yelling in a grand chorus; they had found a way of sitting together, yelling together, living together, too, and though Milton Rogers could shrug and say, "Our society stinks," even he had his place in this House of All Nations, such as the one they had in Paris, and liked it. And Wolgast! Wolgast, their bouncer, would whisper as he grabbed Peggy to throw her out, "You goddamned amateur. Don't give me that tenderness and goodness routine. Our cheapest whores have lots of that stuff to throw around too."

"Look! Look!" Catherine screamed, tugging at his arm. The sea of faces rose around him, and it was rising around Peggy too; the waves washed over both of them.

"Hey, you in the hat! Sit down, you bum," somebody shouted at him. "Sit down or go home!"

"Jim, Jim," Catherine said. "What's the matter with you?"

"Hit him on the head! Sit down! You're a better door than a window!"

"Hey, you! Get out of the way!"

"For heaven's sake, Jim," Catherine called, grabbing at his arm. As he sat down she screamed, "Oh, look, look, look!"

A beautiful passing play had been set in motion by the Canadien goalie. Blocking a shot, he passed the puck to a defence man on the right who sent a long pass across the ice to a forward who raced up into position, circled and feinted his check out of position, then shot another long pass forward across the ice to a wing coming up fast from behind the blue line. The wing trapped it neatly, swerved in on the defence, shifted to the right, then back-handed a pass to the trailing Canadien centre coming in fast on the defence, now split wide open. He faked his shot to the lower right corner; the goalie sprawled for it, did the splits, and the centre calmly lifted the puck over his prone body.

"They score! They score!" Catherine cried ecstatically. "Oh, it was beautiful, Jim, wasn't it? What a pretty pattern! It's just like the ballet, isn't it?"

In the din his answer couldn't be heard. The florid man with the bag of peanuts sitting beside McAlpine, leaping to his feet, emptied the bag on McAlpine's coat, then slapped him on the back and hugged him, and the French Canadian priest, both hands raised in rapture, burst into eloquent French. Everybody was filled with a fine laughing happiness. But McAlpine, staring at the ice in a dream, thought, "Yes, Catherine's right. A beautiful pattern. Anything that breaks up the pattern is bad. And Peggy breaks up the pattern."

The siren sounded, and they crowded out into the crush of people seeking hot dogs and coffee. Soon they were all jammed together, shoulder to shoulder, swaying back and forth, unable to get near the coffee counter. Catherine saw two of her Junior League friends and she called to them. McAlpine found himself thrust chest to chest against the thin bony-faced French Canadian priest who had been sitting near him. The priest, who came only up to his shoulder, wore his hat square on the top of his head. His elbow was digging hard into McAlpine's ribs.

"Nice game," he said politely with a slight accent.

"Not bad."

"But the way the game is played these days, I don't like it. No?"

"It's skate, skate, skate," McAlpine agreed. "A long pass, and skate into position."

"Like watching moves on a checkerboard. No?"

"That's true," McAlpine said. The priest had a homely, intelligent face. Surely he was the one man who at least would have a professional interest in an amateur like Peggy. It would be good to talk to him and get his professional understanding and not feel so completely alone. But no! In the end he would line up with his flock and Wolgast. "When I was a kid they had those beautiful short passing combination plays. It used to look wonderful."

"It's a different game today," the priest agreed. "It's still all combination. But some of them can't hold on to the puck."

"That Richard can at least do that."

"From the blue line in. Yes."

"With great drive," McAlpine said. He was certain the priest would be against them too. Sure! Get her into a confessional with him: "I confess to the Almighty God and to thee, father. I confess to having no sense of discrimination. I confess to not keeping my love for the right ones. I confess to bringing out the worst in people and turning one man against another. Why do I bring no peace to anybody, father?" ... "My dear child, it's complicated. You must not be a nuisance. Guard yourself against the opinion that those who stand for law and order are always at war with those who stand for — well, this uncontrolled tenderness and goodness of yours. Examine it carefully, my dear child, in the light of the greater harmony. St. Augustine would say — "

"It's the coldest night of the year," the priest said vaguely, feeling he no longer had McAlpine's interest.

"How cold can it get around here?" McAlpine asked. And then the siren sounded, ending the intermission, and Catherine, who had been pushed four feet away from him, called, "This way Jim," and they went back to their seats.

In the corner to the left of the Canadiens goal a Ranger forward was blocked out and held against the boards by a Canadien defenceman, who cleared the puck up the ice. The Ranger forward, skating past the defenceman, turned and slashed at him, breaking the stick across his shoulder. The official didn't see it. The play was at the other end of the ice. The defenceman who had been slashed spun around crazily on his skates, dropped to his knees, and circled around holding his neck. The crowd screamed. The other Canadien defenceman, dropping his stick and gloves, charged at the Ranger forward and started swinging. The Ranger forward backed away, his stick up, trying to protect himself. The official, stopping the play, made frantic motions at the fist-swinging defenceman, waving him off the ice. Another Ranger forward came out of nowhere and dived at the defenceman and tackled him; then all the players converged on one another, each one picking an opponent in the widening huddle, fists swinging, gloves and sticks littering the ice. Some of the players fenced with their sticks. The crowd howled in glee. The referee finally separated the players and handed out penalties. He gave a major penalty to the Canadien defenceman who had first dropped his stick to attack the Ranger forward who had really precipitated the brawl; he gave a minor to the Ranger who had dived at this defenceman and tackled him. And the forward who had broken his stick over the defenceman's shoulder, the instigator, the real culprit, was permitted to escape. He skated around lazily, an indifferent innocent.

"What about him?" the priest asked Catherine as he pointed at the Ranger. "Yes, what about him? Look at the fake innocent," Catherine cried. She thrust out her arm accusingly. Ten thousand others stood up, pointed and screamed indignantly, "Hey, what about him? Why don't you give *him* a penalty?" The Ranger skated nonchalantly to the bench to get a new stick. His air of innocence was infuriating, yet the referee, the blind fool, was deceived by it. The players on the Canadian bench , all standing up, slapped their sticks on the boards, screamed at the referee, and pointed. The referee, his hands on his hips, went right on ignoring the angry booing. He proposed to face off the puck.

"Boo-boo-boo!" Catherine yelled, her handsome face twisted, her eyes glazed with indignation. "He's letting him go scot-free. The one who started the whole thing."

The stout French Canadian, who had been standing up shouting imprecations in bewilderingly rapid French, suddenly broke into English. Twelve thousand people were also screaming, but by shifting to English he imagined he would get the referee to listen to him. His jaw trembled, his eyes rolled back in their sockets, he was ready to weep; then his face became red and swollen, and he cried out passionately, "Blind man! Idiot! All night you are a blind man! A thief, a cheat! You're despicable — go on back home, go out and die! I spit on you!" He cupped his hands around his mouth and let out a gigantic moan.

The ice was now a small white space at the bottom of a great black pit where sacrificial figures writhed, and on the vast slopes of the pit a maniacal white-faced mob shrieked at the one with the innocent air who had broken the rules, and the one who tolerated the offence. It was a yapping frenzied roaring. Short and choppy above the sound of horns, whistles, and bells, the stout French Canadian pounded McAlpine's shoulder; he jumped up on his own seat, he reached down and tore off his rubbers and hurled them at the ice. A shower of rubber came from all sections of the arena and littered the ice as the players ducked and backed away. Hats sailed in wide arcs above the ice and floated down.

"They've all gone crazy," McAlpine muttered to Catherine. "Just a crazy howling mob." Their fury shocked him. Only a few moments ago he had imagined himself and Peggy facing the hostility of these people. Aside from the rule book, that player was guilty, he thought. I'm sure Peggy's innocent. That's the difference.

Someone in the row behind grabbed at McAlpine's hat and sent it sailing over the ice. His hands went up to his bare head and he whirled around belligerently.

"Jim, Jim, what's the matter with you?" Catherine cried, and she laughed.

"What's the matter with *me?*" he asked indignantly.

"Nobody's got anything against you, Jim. The way you're going on you'd think you were rooting for the visiting team. Aren't you with us?"

"What? Why do you say that?":

"Why quarrel with the home crowd?"

"I'm not," he muttered. "It was my hat. What am I going to do for a hat?"

"Oh, what's a hat at a time like this? Maybe you can get it afterwards. Ah, look," she cried, pointing to the referee, who was skating toward the Ranger bench to have a conversation with the coach. "Now we'll see." The coach beckoned to the fugitive, who came over to the bench, and the referee, tapping him on the shoulder, raising his arm dramatically, pointed to the penalty bench. But only a two-minute penalty, mind you! Oh, the fantastic ineptitude of the authorities! The pitiful mockery of justice! But everybody was pacified, and the boys with the snow ploughs came out to clean the debris from the ice.

The game was played out with the Canadiens keeping their lead and winning by two goals. McAlpine made little jokes about recovering his hat. On the way out he agreed with Catherine he would have no chance of finding the hat and he might as well forget about it. They had the good luck to get a taxi at the stand across the street.

In the taxi, with the excitement of the game all gone, they were really facing each other for the first time since McAlpine had acknowledged to himself the falseness of their relationship. Now he accepted with relief the fact that he might soon be revealed to her in a fantastic light. Well, to hell with them all!

50-50 Draw

❖   DON McKAY

Every pause pauses in its own style. This guy is standing in the entryway, not far enough in to see the ice surface, brought up short by the scritching of blades on ice. It is one of those sudden slowings when inertia throws the load forward, and he is suddenly aware of its weight. Nothing, but nothing could have dragged him back here, are you kidding, this thing is so degenerate they're selling the degeneracy, pretty soon they'll have hockey cards replicating famous contracts and endorsements, they'll induct lawyers into the hall of fame. Nothing. So, here he is. He is here because of some ancient wish; he is here because he once wrote love poems, if you can believe this, using hockey images; he is here because his grown-up children, who live in Halifax and cheer for the Citadels, have been egging him on. He is abject and deserves everything he gets. Twenty years ago he would actually harangue his children on the sweet anguish of an artform not quite breaking out, while decent parents were taking their kids to Sunday School or at least discussing the world's great religions. He played a full season of basement hockey with his son, including Stanley Cup playoffs (original six) which was won, unfortunately, by the Boston Bruins. He talked aesthetics, ritual and myth, the almost offside pass, delay delay on the two-on-one, the unexpected perfect move, the shot that imitates the wingbeat rather than the hammer. See? His daughter reading through it, game after game, Judy Blume to J.D. Salinger, lifting her head mildly (o, did someone score?) as the crowd, including her nuclear family, went wild.

And this intimate scritching now, like the noise of an old phonograph needle that sits, humbly, this side of the melody it unlocks, a fierce delicate carving that makes everything fluid, an etching of feathers. It is the noise of a class learning to write using straight pens and inkwells. He decides maybe he should get a coffee before he finds his seat, but it is already too late: he will be in for everything.

During this bout of fandom he will come to understand the minions of gravity: the hook, the hold, the glove in the face, the clutch-each-other-in-the-dance-of-everything-that-holds-you-down-or-fucks-you-up; he will understand "nagging injury," he will know "can't buy a goal." Often he will embarrass his seat-mates with hoarse critical shouts — Having a nice *sleep*, charron?, Heartbreak Hotel, goalie. If he should buy a 50-50 draw ticket between the first and second periods of the game against Moncton on January 23, he will miss winning $902 by only two digits. Meanwhile he will buy Fredericton Canadiens keychains, lighters, sweatshirts, even a cookbook with recipes (mostly barbecue) supplied by the players, and send them to his children in order to punish them. It is already too late. In his nightmares the organist attempts "Claire de lune."

He will be here for the Kentucky Fried Chicken Pepsi Poster Feature and the Ford Escort Shootout, week after week for the industrial-strength organ filling every niche with noise. He will be here when the plexiglass shatters, turning into a soft rain which falls into the laps of the first row. The team mascot, a life-sized stuffed animal, will perform tricks on an ATV between each period, and one game, two months from now, will toss a cheerful puck, into the stands which cuts an inattentive elderly person over the eye. Still later, when the mascot falls off the Ford Escort, the human being inside will himself sustain a concussion.

The Zamboni will oval the ice 913 times. There will be 206 sudden sags in tension when a goalie takes a hummingbird out of the air, and everyone drifts, his coil relaxing to curl and counter curl, slowly eddying to the faceoff circle or the bench. There will be another style of pause when a defenceman waits with the puck behind the net while the wingers wind up, circling then criss-crossing, and the defenceman holds their strands in his head as, once on a porch in August, someone might have braided her sister's hair. Between games he will hold in his own head the feel of the thoughtful soft pass delivered in the middle of the rush, like the erotic gift of vulnerability.

an excerpt from the novel *Coming Down from Wa*

❖   AUDREY THOMAS

All three were quite drunk by eight o'clock. William waved to them as they went down the corridor to the cinema (it turned out they would all be on the same plane as far as Paris) and then went to find the manager.

Who said it was impossible, Monsieur.

Who said perhaps it could be arranged *demain matin* but in fact the facility was closed to get ready for a competition.

William's mother had given him a bit of emergency money after he told her about the oranges. This was an emergency — sort of. Anyway, it was something he wanted to do. Money changed hands. Perhaps it could be arranged after all. The manager snapped his fingers, once, twice.

Which is how, while Bernard and Narcisse danced with wolves up above, William sat lacing on some grey skates — 700 CFA for rental fee — down at the *patinoire*. They had opened the doors and turned the lights on just for him.

He handed his jacket and his camera to the man who had brought him down and then he stood up and pushed away from the bench. "When I get going, when I'm ready, I'll yell 'Now' and you press this button, okay?" The man looked puzzled. What was button in French?

"*C'est automatique*," William said, "*pressez ici*." The man nodded but still looked dubious.

The rink was full size and he had it all to himself. He skated slowly to the far end and then turned and shut his eyes. Hockey Night in Africa!

Rinks were usually so cold that your face hurt when you skated but not here, not in the Montreal Forum. Here the air was so hot his throat burned and he broke into a sweat just thinking about taking a slapshot. Stanley Cup banners hung far above his head and the numbers of the immortals, No. 9, No. 4. Would they put his number up when he'd played his last game?

Like the banners, the fans seemed to hang down in sheets from the ceiling. Screaming and yelling, they crowded over the boards and glass watching his every move. He felt the weight of their constant scrutiny, but shrugged it off. Pushing all distractions aside, he began to skate.

Hearing his name echoing around the building he raised his stick to the crowd and then a few short powerful strides took him to centre. The national anthems dragged; minutes seemed like hours. He thought only of scoring goals, saw his shots as they hit the net, saw the red light blaze behind the glass. He shoots! He scores!

And later, with the game tied and under a minute left to play, Scotty Bowman looks down the bench and thinks about who he should play for the most crucial shift in such an important game. He taps William on the shoulder.

"Here's your big chance. Show me what you've got."

Opposite William is the hulking frame of Gordie Howe. "Are you lost, rookie?" he says. "You don't belong out here with us real men. Do you even shave yet?" William ignores him and concentrates only on the puck as it falls from the hand of the referee. It slides into his corner and he springs after it, warding off Howe's slashing stick with an outstretched arm. With the puck nicely cradled on his stick he swings around from behind the net. A clear lane appears ahead and he races for open ice. Nothing can stop him; he fakes to the outside, cuts back to the middle, only the goalie left to beat. The fans go wild. Mac! Mac! Mac! Mac! He can hear Chantal screaming above the rest.

Pulling the puck around the flailing stick of the goalie he launches a backhand shot just underneath the crossbar and into the net.

Mac — Mac — Mac — Mac!

"Now!" he yells as he opens his eyes and gives a last burst of speed. The workman presses the button.

"Thank you," said William, laughing and sweating. "*Merci.*"

"Please," said the workman, "*d'où venez-vous?*"

"Canada."

"Ah. Canada. Guy Lafleur. *Un beau pays.*"

Suddenly there was a loud crashing and banging at the door and in came Bernard and Narcisse, still drunk.

"We didn't care for the movie," Bernard said, "so we had a little nip and have come to dance with you."

"I was just leaving." William pointed to the skate in his hand.

"Oh no no no no *no.* You must have a little twirl with us. I have been telling Narcisse about *le centre Rockefeller*; he has never been on skates so now is a good time to try."

"How did you know I was here?"

"Bernard knows everything."

The man who had accompanied William to the skating rink was shaking his head.

"*C'est fermé.*"

Bernard unzipped his moneybelt. "Ten minutes?"

The man looked at him doubtfully.

"Ten minutes and we'll be out. Cross my heart and hope to die, stick a needle in my eye. Just go get us some skates, will you? *Vite! Vite!*"

William looked at Bernard and then at Narcisse, who was shivering in his thin silk shirt.

"You're drunk Bernard. You might hurt yourself. Narcisse too."

"Oh hush, don't be such an old woman. Help the boy on with his skates. He'll warm up once we get going."

William stood there, undecided. Then he shrugged. If Bernard broke his head, too bad. *Carpe diem.* He began to see the humour in it and he bent over Narcisse, lacing his skates up tight, then holding him up as they stepped out onto the ice.

Bernard was there before them, took a couple of running steps on the points of his skates and then, much to William's surprise, began to skate in a most elegant manner, cutting and turning and gliding, doing perfect figure eights.

"Surprise, surprise," he called, as he whizzed past the astonished William. "I am the belle of Rockefeller Centre, the belle the belle the belle of Rocke fell er fell er fell. We'll have our friend out there strutting his stuff in no time at all."

Narcisse was clinging desperately to William, too terrified to move.

"Come," Bernard said, swooping down on them. "You take one arm, I'll take the other and we'll go slowly, slowly, yes, that's it, that's wonderful darling, we'll get you a nice warm outfit when we hit New York."

And so, as Bernard described the beauties of Rockefeller Centre at Christmas to the very wobbly Narcisse, the three of them skated in a (more or less) straight line to the end of the rink and back.

Bernard began to hum the Skater's Waltz: "Da da da dum, da da da dum. Oh!" he said, "I haven't been so happy in a month of Sundays."

At that moment Narcisse's feet shot out from under him and he sat down hard.

"You are the slippery boy!" Bernard said, as they hauled him to his feet.

"Out!" shouted the man with the keys. "*Fini. Allez-y!*" He flicked the light switch on and off impatiently.

"Okay, okay," William said. Then, "Wait a minute. *Un moment.*" He sped over to his camera. "*Encore une photographie.* Please."

He set the camera and then skated back to Bernard and Narcisse. Both were laughing madly.

"All right," William said, "let's go. When I shout 'Now!' please put on your best smiles."

"La la la la," sang Bernard at the top of his voice, "la la la la. Dum dum de Dum Dum de Dum Dum Dum." Then, very low, "I'm dying William; my last Rockefeller Centre Christmas tree."

"Oh Bernard."

"Just kidding," he said. "Anyway, it wouldn't matter, would it? Seize the day. Shout now, will you please."

"Now!" shouted William and the man pressed the button. Whirr. Click.

"Thank you," said Bernard. "Will you send me a print? Fairly soon?"

They unlaced their skates and the man turned out the lights behind them.

"A nightcap?" suggested Bernard.

"Why not?" said William.

"Shall we have it here at the very very grand or shall we repair to the barely grand?"

"The Grand, I think. I'm almost broke."

"Excellent choice."

They stumbled out of the Hotel Ivoire and into the hot night.

"Get us a taxi, my good man," said Bernard to the uniformed door-man. "A taxi to the Grand Hotel."

"Cheer up, William," he said, laying his hand on William's shoulder. "Everybody dies sometime and hasn't Africa been *fun*?"

Righteous Speedboat

❖   MARK ANTHONY JARMAN

For no animal admires another animal.
                    — Blaise Pascal (1623-1662)

Even now the vibrating screen maims the very molecules of my eyes but how I have to gaze. How many bent berserkers, how many peckerwood imposters will they call to the silver microphone before they call to me, here with my nigh on ruined vision? No finish at the net and hands of stone but I can read a play, backcheck like a madman and I move malevolently inside a snarling wind. Pins go down. That ought to be worth *something*, a few paydays, a winning smile from the bankteller. Tampa could take me down there with their palmetto bugs. Need be I'll go to the moon, I'll skate on Mars.

Maybe a scrounging team will grab me in a late round. Scrounging is okay, late round is okay. I could help a club in the Colonial League, work my way up. Just give me a contract. Or else I'm toast. I'm over-age, I can't go back to my junior team. I burnt a few bridges there, pissed off the scunt-eyed coach. I caught an elbow in the nose and saw visions of gasping lightning while the guy with said elbow slid away like a pulse to score the winning goal, to bury it topshelf. All season who had the best plus-minus on the club? *Moi.* I repeat: I had the best plus-minus on the team. Yet in front of everyone the coach really reamed me out. Up and down, went to town. He had no need to do that, to humiliate me.

Elbowed nose still throbbing, I moved in close to the coach, paused to get him wondering, feinted, then I gave his nose a shot; I clocked the coach. Nothing really. They want you to hit everyone else; *Him*, they say in Spokane, and you know what they mean. Bing bang bong. Do it to *them* though, touch *them* and it's the end of the fucking world. They tell the reporters you're "difficult," you're a cancer on the team. Control freak wimps. Blue-legged fops. Pukely ticket-punchers. I say this much is obvious: the "difficult" players are the real action, living it, lean as whippets; they throb, eat at the air like engines.

I call my agent long-distance and he allows, *This is he.*

Doesn't look good, he says. Our noisy years are moments, he says.

I call my mother and she sighs, "You had so much potential."

I'd call my friend from Salmon Arm but Ryan's lost his head. The bloody trail across the gravel road I still dream of, and the green radiator water burning my hair. Ryan's head rolling.

Once upon a time this was a happening bar but now it's a loser bar. The bar has no view at all, a pocked pallid concrete bunker, which is good. Night for day, no trees and no sky. You pay extra for trees and sky, the darkening harbour. You need no view. You need to hear your name echoing in that distant subsidized convention centre; those two sweet words in that room of tasteful blurred suits. Your name.

I like loser bars. They're quiet and I can think.

I think there is always some injustice. We depend on tales of injustice. At the small curved bar an intense young man is telling a dark-eyed woman his specific story of injustice. He's well dressed: black custom cut pants and a beautiful shirt that is white and tapered. Gel gleams evenly in his hair. I decide his name is Laszlo. Someone looks after Laszlo's cuticles. Laszlo smokes. He collects things: plenitude, kudos, ivory elephants. The young woman is listening yet she is clearly fidgety, restless. Her dark eyes move in a sad poised face. I watch her dark eyes shiver. Her lipstick is almost black. She shows her teeth in a sad brief smile and it is everything. You learn everything. I can't stand the idea that it's all random.

Here's a guy, Laszlo says leaning right at her, real good guy, he says. Here's a guy, I don't know, so-called best friend.

Laszlo lowers his voice but I can still hear him. He's too close to her.

This is a guy that. Feed him breakfast. Pick him up, take him to work. Give him a job and uh, *float* him. And uh, my mom has his cheque, some deductions of course, he looks at it, something's wrong, he says.

The young woman asks Laszlo a question.

Yeah, my mum, she had it. And he stole! He stole from us! Laszlo cuts the air with flat hand. I went by the next day. This is not the agreed … What is this — this, this holding company? None of your business. Well, I said. I was ready to kill —

The dark-eyed woman breaks into his story.

Sorry, she says, I *really* have to run. Give me a call, she says. Gotta go!

Oh, he says. A-O-KAY! he says brightly. Laszlo tries to get funnier after the serious story. He needs a fast transition. He picks up her key ring, a tiny flashlight hooked on it, and he sings into the tiny flashlight as if it's a microphone: I DID IT MY WAY! he belts out.

My Funny Valentine, he croons softly, eyebrows up like Elvis Costello.

They both try to laugh but still she takes her keys back, plunging them deep within her Peruvian satchel.

The young woman leaves briskly, outside to oaks up like oars in a spooky sky, and Laszlo glances around, ill at ease now, alone, no longer singing. Now he has to adjust himself, recast the last moments, her exit. His status has changed here. He peers around at the subterranean concrete tomb as if for the first time, at the monotonous hockey draft unscrolling on the monster TV screen. It's a crap shoot. Some of us are wanted in the first or second round. Some players wait all day and no one calls. I'm not flying down east for nothing, for crocodile tears in the arena seats and maybe your parents phoning your hotel room, telling you there's next year, or you could play in Italy or Blackpool. Everyone will lie to you at some point. They decide they know best. Some are allowed dignity; others scramble. I will scramble if necessary. I'm not 6'5" but I'll run my cranium into the Zamboni if that's what they desire. They can croon my name, tap me on the shoulder, and I'll get it done. Only connect. Call my name. I'm shallow. I want to hear my muddled name run through a silver microphone, to shake hands with a million people I don't know.

Laszlo shows the red-haired bartender something from his wallet. A sunlit photo, waterfront property, a speedboat docked. The speedboat has a blue canopy and a blue racing stripe.

Looksee, he says. Is that a nice place or is that a nice place? Just up island. Hey, tell you what. You want to go there, let me know. I'm driving up there practically every week. All the goddamn time.

He carries a photo of property in his wallet. Now: would I be any different? I'd probably carry a photo too.

Laszlo scribbles a note left-handed, passes it over. The bartender does not read the note. I order a Greyhound, bite from the small onion I always carry in my coat. I'd like some chowder or chili, some good cornbread or sweet potato. Carbohydrate loading just in case I get picked.

Laszlo points with his sterling silver pen at the bartender's red hair.

You must be Irish, eh?

No, says the red-haired bartender, looking irritated.

Our place up island: we've got ten acres, two hundred grand. Bay goes in like this — we own from this peak to here. Goes back, big trees. Ten acres.

Laszlo keeps smoking. He opens his wallet again. He likes to open his wallet. The ferry system, this is how ... The schedule. Thursday. No, hold that. Tuesday.

Right. You know why Tuesday?

He lights another smoke. Dull Clapton plays: post-heroin Clapton, post-lobotomy Clapton. I'm truly sorry his little kid fell out of the highrise but I don't like the tape. I like Art Bergman's new single: *create a monster, something something, we got a contract, contract, who's using who?* Art Bergman, crown prince of detox. The hockey draft is still on the screen. My draft. I'm so close to a contract, to treasure. Mr. Eric Clapton sells a billion boring records and no one wants me. The bartender doesn't ask why Tuesday.

On TV men in suits argue and wave clean hands en route to the silver microphone; they must speak their pick, announce who will skate, who will consider a million seven, who will buy a sleek growling speedboat. Something is wrong though; men in suits argue like they're chewing a mouthful of bees. They act as if they don't know their pick.

I'm available! I shoot out mental telepathy messages from this edge of the country. Me! I have a head on my shoulders.

The erudite GM bends over; he seeks the ear of the frowning coach. The GM straightens, walks to talk with the worried head scout, then puts glasses on the end of his nose, peers over some papers. A weird delay of some kind, a plot complication at the meat market. Just past the media tables I can see the cackling old owner who was jailed for fraud and mob connections, for taking the Fifth, for taking the assets, for chortling. Well, no one figured he was a choirboy.

They'll take a d-man, says one customer.

No, they need a centre. Definitely a centre, says another.

A GM at the mike finally mouths the name of the anointed, the chosen. A goalie!

Takes a goalie! They have goalies in the system. They have goalies coming out the yin yang. Trade bait, but who? Trade the young guy? The backup goalie? Trade the older goalie the former cokehead?

They screwed up, someone in the bar says. They screwed up. He says this four times in a row.

They've been tricked. They traded up to get the franchise bruiser they wanted; they made a deal, and all parties agreed to square dance, to give and take. They agreed what bodies would be available when they got to the microphone but at the last second another team, a team without scruples, traded draft choices and future considerations, snatching the franchise bruiser out from under their red noses. Stole from them. Their *property*. We've been snookered, states the GM, we've been submarined. The GM's Byzantine maneuvers and agreements are useless. I traded up for nothing, he thinks, all that trouble for another goalie. The troubled scout tears the bruiser's name off their jersey, his sweater waiting at their table. How sure they were. They don't have my name on a jersey. They have different tables for each team, like it's the United Nations, like it's the fate of the free world. Then there are prickly-pear and sea lions, sooty terns and albatrosses and California sea lions dripping in the sun on the colour TV. Another highly illogical car commercial that seems to be selling something other than cars. What exactly is it they are hawking? Nature? Oceanfront? Does it work? Does it actually sell cars?

Insects crash at the screen, hearkening tragically into their multi-hued harbour. They want to eat the TV light, the only game in town. I keep studying the draft but Laszlo studies two women who seat themselves at the bar. The first woman keeps her sunglasses on inside. She is taller than me. I see her and think *stature, presence*. Her friend is shorter, with lighter hair and the small peaceful face of a follower.

The woman in the dark glasses inhales hugely, exhales: Well, we broke up. Went pretty well considering.

Woman #2: No sobbing?

Woman #1: A little. (She pauses.) Him. Not me.

Woman #2: Let's go prowling!

Woman #1: No thanks.

Woman #2: Oh yeah. You're in THAT phase. Wait two weeks and you'll be crawling the walls.

Woman #1: No. I don't think so.

I realize she has someone lusty waiting, someone already drafted, but she hasn't told her friend. She broke it off with one guy to move to another. She possesses a five year plan. Woman #2 complains, My roommates are doing it all the time and I have to sit and listen. I mean I can't help but hear it. I can't afford my own place. And he has to end up with *her*. I had such a crush on him. It was supposed to be *me*. I had hopes. Now I'm going nuts. Why do I have such bad luck with guys I like?

They sip their drink specials.

Woman #1 says, This older guy took me to an Icelandic film festival. The movies were like, what the fuck!?

AHA! An older guy is chosen.

For me the charm of hockey was always its lack of charm. It wasn't hip. My agent says he'll call me back. He's busy with his "real" clients. I walk to the washroom and see a nickel gleaming at the bottom of the porcelain urinal. I do not pick it up. I look out at my nation. I have no nation. Okay — I have a wormwood nation.

Laszlo is talking to the two women: We'll take my Dad's speedboat across. If you don't have tackle we can get you some. Waterfront. On the water. Everyone said we paid too much. Local yokels laughing. Day later, twenty-thousand dollars more. Who's laughing now? Very rare find. Very rare. Nice beach. Arbutus and oak. Beautiful property. We'll get some people. We'll go up there. Road trip! Road trip!

Well now isn't waterfront always on the water? Woman #2 wonders.

What's the catch? I wonder. Why does Laszlo have to cajole people to go to this Shangri La? Doesn't it come stocked with beautiful people? The way they stock a fish farm? A fat farm?

I realize Laszlo is talking to a different bartender. Bartender #2.

Bob Hope, Laszlo exclaims. Bob Hope's been there. We'd just fumigated so he wasn't too happy. Log cabin, some bugs. Ants I guess. Cedar. Wouldn't think so. Puzzling. That loser shirt, Laszlo says laughing at the bartender.

Hey sport. Hey pal. This is my brother's shirt. My brother who died in an accident. A *fatal* accident.

Oh. Sorry.

Laszlo lights another smoke, looks around. On TV a GM slides right by a team's table, a team he used to coach. He jumped ship. He doesn't look and they don't look at him. He found the loophole he needed to break his contract, to dance with another party, a party other than the one that 'brung' him.

Bob Hope's a card. Bob Hope says, Any chance of anything here? Something other than pinochle and ovaltine? Nyuck. Know what I mean? Country girls, nice country girls.

He wanted some action. Horny old bugger. We caught a cod. Engine broke down, going slow, get a blueback, keeper, three pounder, eat salmon that night. But I'd rather catch one big one. One big chinook, a tyee, a king. Bob Hope bitching at me all day in that irritating voice. I'm looking for this ledge, I'm looking for this ledge with a depth finder. Jigged, buzz bombed, mooched, nothing. Tried a new lure, a silver one I found in Dad's tacklebox.

(Now it's Bartender #3 half-listening, a guy in a muscle shirt. I think the bartenders must take shifts with Laszlo, then go hide back in the cooler.)

ZING! GOT IT! Laszlo mimics a fishing rod and a sudden strike on the line. ZING! He doesn't finish the fishing story. He smokes non-stop. I have another Greyhound. Maybe they don't draft players who punch their coaches. Maybe there's a secret agreement, rules they don't tell you about. I'm bitter (wormwood, wormwood). I'm starting to feel like saussurite, like schist, like stone.

A stoned voice bellows in the direction of the jukebox: "PLAY SOMETHING ... BY SOMEBODY ... WHO KILLED THEMSELVES!

This desire to be fucked up, and think it something special, something to be attained.

That's rich. Ask my friend Ryan if he's happy now.

All my friends are lawyers, Laszlo says. And the women are incredible! They work so hard they don't have time to meet anyone else. You want to meet great women hang out with lawyers.

Yeah. Like I really want to hang out with lawyers, Bartender #3 growls.

On TV the GM in the suit is helping the young hockey player pull on his new team sweater. It's too intimate. There is some awkward tugging at clothes, then embarrassed smiles and camera flashes for the sports cards.

Who's this clown they pick? Who's this sack of hammers?

Some Swede faggot. A *foreigner.*

You on a team? Laszlo asks the muscled bartender.

Used to be. Same old used to be.

Now I recognize Bartender #3: a fantastically shifty forward with Tri-Cities. He had moves like a humpback salmon, and Pittsburgh was after him until he was submarined, blew out both knees big time. Good old Tom What's his name. They said he'd never walk again. Huge writhing scars each side of his knees. Twins. A suicide pass. Skate into the middle and CRANG!, you flip over with a quicksilver crunching, then they carry you off, a sudden screeching pauper. Wheelbarrows of cash will alter anyone, but he's been changed by the cash he never got, by what could have been that draft year. He could have been the one under the blinding television lights, the one getting offered a million seven. Instead. Well instead he watches with me. Now Tom What's his name is a major drunk with rehab muscles. I'm not as shifty but at least my knees are okay. My knees are not too shabby. I cast a shadow, I get my back up, show up for every game. Buffalo could take me. The Jets. There's that windy corner. The Sharks. This sounds like West Side Story.

I'm going to drive up there to the property tomorrow. Come on along. Pick up my cousin and bullshit. Deli grub, some Heineken. Greenies. You like Heineken? No? The airport and take the speedboat across.

Laszlo has told three different bartenders about the speedboat.

Laszlo asks, How does that bear joke go again? Let's see. Bartender tells the bear he can't serve him because he's on drugs. This part I can never remember. Drugs. What drugs. You help me yeah. Oh, the *barbiturate*. The bar-bitch-you-ate! Ya ya. Ha ha. That's a good one.

The two women do not share Laszlo's love of the bear joke.

We're lucky you know, Laszlo says to the women, that place up island. Played our cards right. Cheap locals can go jump in a lake. If they knew anything they'd be somewhere else, right? Road goes around pretty little bay. Speedboat. No waiting. Catch a big one. No tackle we'll take care of you. Little general store not far. Good beef jerky. If we don't have it you don't need it. That's what they say on their sign. They don't have it you don't need it. That's their hick philosophy, their London School of Economics approach to local yokel marketing. Road goes around nice little bay. See the smooth golden stones at the bottom. A beautiful place. We own it. It's ours.

Lizard King Jim Morrison says Hello. Jim Morrison says he loves me. Jim Morrison says he wants to know my name. The jukebox decides what to play. And the big screen shows the famous footage: Big surly Eric Lindros refuses the sweater. He stares off, dark mad eyes and curly hair. A thick neck, a bull. He'll never sign with this team. Maybe they called his name but that doesn't mean they own him, that doesn't mean he's their *property*. He refuses their blue uniform, their lovely stone city, their scheming owner. In this hexed process, this amateur hour crapshoot, here's what I wish to know, to *divine*: who has the real power and who is the victim? That's what I have to learn, even though I already know the truth.

Wait until Lindros is on the ice, the young man says to Bartender #4. He'll pay then.

Someone'll stick him good. Get his bad knee.

I say nothing. They shouldn't talk like that. I've seen too many torn up knees. Hurt!? Are you fucking kidding? Un-fucking-believable. Anterior cruciate; that's the worst. It digs into my stomach just thinking of ruined knees.

Just how many bartenders are back there? Do they have a bartender *pool*? There are more bartenders than customers.

Everyone thinks Lindros is a greedy arrogant asshole but meanwhile the team's owner is mulling over juicy offers of seventy-five million U.S. dollars for the franchise. The Quebec owner will sell in the night; the owner will hustle the team out of Canada with a tearful press conference. The owner will cry all the way to the bank. Who's the greedy asshole then? What did our pal Peter Pocklington get for selling Gretzky to Los Angeles, for selling a person, a *human being*? Twenty million dollars? (For he is an honourable man.) And how much money does Peter the meatpacker owe the Alberta government right now? He's in so deep they can't touch his house of cards, his dead pigs and stuffed sausages and offal, his slit-throat palace over the river valley. So the players are greedy? The players are arrogant? Give me a break. Get real.

No one gives me a break. No one gets real. Instead they draft a dead guy. In fact they draft Ryan, my friend from Salmon Arm. His last night on earth we were riding in what journalists would later refer to as the death car. I was passed out in the backseat. Ryan was in the passenger seat. Then I woke up in the ditch, in the rhubarb where the world was utterly different. Green water was pouring out of the upside down radiator, burning me. The power pole was in three pieces, its line sparking. Ryan's head rolled across the gravel road, his brain still sending messages, questions, trying to find out what's wrong. I took off my wet shirt and hid my friend's head. I was afraid to pick it up so I just covered it with my shirt. What would you do? The car looked like modern sculpture, the driver still curled inside it like a foetus. Not a scratch on me, though my teeth were chattering and my hair was steaming. My friend's head: pebbles and dust stuck on it. And this brain of mine. Then some kind of gleaming milk truck came by and the driver said Jesus.

And the big club must not know he's dead. If Ryan was alive he'd laugh. Here they are throwing away a pick on him before they'll draft me.

I have watched the drunken screen for hours, eating the past, wrapping my head in it, and my eyes complain at the images, at the labour; my eyes are shifting right out of focus. Can't they make a big screen that doesn't kill you?

I am one of God's creatures but no one is taking me. Not the Lightning in Tampa, not the Panthers. Not the Jets. Not the San Jose Sharks. They're taking hundreds of snipers, killers, muckers, headcases, piranhas, pretenders. They call out polyglot Latvian names at the silver microphone. They don't care about my plus-minus, they don't care about my Grade Eight blues records or sensitive feelings or that I move like silt and stick like glue. What about the San Diego Gulls or Las Vegas and the Russian guy named Radek Bonk? This is a great name for a player. Bonk! Pass me the puck! Hit him Bonk. Bonk him! Marty McSorley was going to sign with Las Vegas, play in the desert. I'd play in the desert. I can't go back to the fucking last place Cougars. I know I'm *this* close to making it but the

Cougars have dragged me down, they've buried me, made me invisible. In a seething minute you are made to pay for your geography, for being in the snake-bit boonies; the centre doesn't hold for *you*.

I'll have to try my luck as a free agent. Some good players aren't picked but they make it later as a walk on. They force the issue, bull their way in the door. Courtnall, Joey Mullen, Dino Cicarelli, Adam Oates, and that guy on the Habs. It happens. Brett Hull wasn't taken until the 117th pick, and Fleury was 166th this year. Nemchinov didn't go to New York until the 224th pick overall in 1990. Now he has a Stanley Cup ring. Every Cup team has its free agents, its "difficult" players. They made it, crawled out of the ooze. You hear their names: a mantra repeated. There's a free-agent camp somewhere in the States; the scouts look you over, look inside your head, see what you've got.

Courtnall has it made in the shade now, big money, owns restaurants and a spiffy log cabin on a cliff over the crashing ocean. Douglas fir and ferns and fishing boats in the harbour where the whales come in to rub. A view. This is Geoff, not Russ. Russ was drafted first round and he married a movie starlet; Russ Courtnall has no idea what it's like to be invisible, to wait all day and be slowly made crazy, to want to punch out a guy named Laszlo. I'm so close, so close to treasure. Is it a litmus test Russ? No. It's not a litmus test. Just look inside your rolling head, the head and source of all your son's distemper.

I wish the woman with dark eyes hadn't left. Why does one person seem different and necessary? I chose to interpret the angle of her neck, slurred messages the speed of blood inside her unknown neck and uncertain smile, her teeth and her lips with the darkest darkest lipstick. I watched the draft while I watched her eyes move, her brain shift into an uncertain smile, and I knew she was leaving just then to become a bus window or a blur in the rain in the raw city of colours, just as I knew I would not be drafted, as I knew they would take a dead man before they would take a player who clocked a coach.

On the Cougars Geoff punched anyone who touched his little brother Russ. I bet now both brothers bomb around in righteous speedboats, ocean their blue and white freeway while a pretty woman from Hollywood naps down in the V-berth. She is waiting for you and you are waiting for her. You are waiting to catch a big one. You stand wide-legged at the wheel and gaze at the sky over arbutus trees and your hair slides back in the salt breeze. You think your head is attached to your shoulders.

Expensive sunglasses protect your eyes, zinc your fair skin, for you cast a shadow, you are the paragon of animals, you have connected the dots. Frantic lawyers and children clamour for your signature, your autograph; children and lawyers shout out your name in the sonic echoing arenas, in Inglewood, in Florida, in United Centre, in General Motors Place.

There is money moving out there, green as absinthe, green as anti-freeze, and everyone has a chance at it. Take this from this, if this be otherwise.

That's the *system*. You think they are going to change it just for you?

The Drubbing of Nesterenko

❖ HANFORD WOODS

Anyone who saw the fight between John Ferguson and Eric Nesterenko in the 1964-65 Stanley Cup finals will never forget it. I was not at the game but watched it alone on television. Ferguson was always a great fighter, a crude hockey player to whom it was most important not to lose a fight. He took his fighting role seriously, he sincerely believed it was a basic ingredient in the Montreal Canadiens' winning formula. Canadiens' fans, players, coaches agreed with his conviction, forgetting that before his time and without similar brawling talents the team won five consecutive Stanley Cups. Ferguson undoubtedly did contribute something to a number of the winning years; he was also a guilty party to a few of the losing seasons. He was hardness itself, a face of rock-solid bone, a body of ungainly, awkward muscle. He had no style: he remains to this day the one hockey player who could lose a puck when no-one had challenged him for it. He would pick up a free puck, lose it in his skates, and, like a dog chasing its tail, whirl furiously, vainly seeking it. A craftsman would approach the outer limits of this berserk creature and deftly retrieve the puck from its wildly thrashing parts. His disastrous encounters with the game's technical side never embarrassed Fergy. He laboured on, mounting rushes, firing aimless passes to the four corners of the rink. He was often exasperated by his linemates' inability to adapt to the rhythm of his game. But his frustration never lasted long. He knew that soon a fight would beckon. He need not go to any subtle provocative lengths: any minor clash or incursion upon whatever he considered to be his territory provided ample pretext. With stick and arms raised he barged into an opponent and thus the battle was on. Nonetheless he was somewhat indirect. He never looked his opponent in the eye to see whether or not he wanted to fight. Which was to Fergy's advantage: it assured him of a

244

head start. He dropped his stick and was punching with a quickness incredible in one so clumsy. He hit automatically, as though working out on a speed bag. With his left hand holding the enemy jersey he threw overhand rights into the captive face. The psychological victory was a consequence of the headbashing. He entered each fight with an absolute confidence in his ability to win it, though he rarely mixed with the other good fighters in the league — Howe, Kurtenbach, Horton. He seemed a completely mindless brute, though after the fight, something like a vain exultation rose to his sturdy, coarse face. Then he became almost self-conscious. He continued to disregard his opponent, but he was always a little embarrassed while skating to the penalty box, his head bowed under the storm of adulation and abuse his bouts occasioned. Before he entered the penalty box he would straighten his sweater, adjust his elbow and shoulder pads and look up at the clock. They were nervous rituals: his sweater did not need straightening, the clock had nothing to tell him. The wide berth his fights created made him uncomfortable.

I thought I hated him more than any other Canadien player. I swore it would give me pleasure to see him injured. On one of his typically headstrong rushes, he tried to leap through the Toronto defencemen Bobby Baun and Carl Brewer, was stopped cold, and thrown on his back. He rose slowly and skated off the ice, stunned. He was really hurt, so it could not have been his head that struck the ice (the sports fan's idea of a joke). His spine had taken the knock. The mere thought of injury, let alone the sight of it, will usually cause empathetic tremors to vibrate through my frame. But it gave me pleasure to watch Ferguson's spasmodic, dazed efforts to leave the ice. I was not alarmed at this nor did I feel remorse. I was disappointed when he returned to the game.

My desire to see him injured was the reflex of my physical fear. Standing behind the second-level blue seats, Fergy within earshot, I bounced clever insults off his impenetrable skull during lulls in the game. My words never gave me the pleasure I hoped for: my voice cracked, uncertain in its delivery. I feared lest he should hear me, imagined him climbing into the stands and beating me to a pulp. I understood that wit was not his strong suit, could only rile him and lead to a painful physical assault.

Eric Nesterenko was my favourite hockey player, an eccentric choice. He still plays with the same weaknesses in his game, but none of his old peculiar effectiveness. It is not that he is no longer my favourite player: as I grow older I make less of such things. Nesterenko is very much a shadow of his former self, a memory of a player, so I tend not to think of him, or when I do, think of him as he was. It even embarrasses me that I used always to have a favourite player and that at one time Nesterenko wore this mantle. I want him to retire, to spare us the humiliation that comes of an over-the-hill veteran's unwillingness to recognize his decline. With Nesterenko I have given up hope.

At one time, though, he was the apple of my eye. He could never shoot well, skated aimlessly, had the unready habit of trailing his stick behind him in one hand and without exception never played well with any other individual or as a member of a line. The flaws in his game were always more apparent than the virtues but the flaws were merely apparent, the virtues solid and true. He had some beautiful moves, long parabolic skating strides, smooth and lazy shifts that were deceptive. He was a strong penalty killer, his roaming style adapted to breaking up rushes before they started. He was an especially great penalty killer when his team was two men short. Swooping in upon the puck carrier, harassing him with his long, gangling reach, retreating to intercept passes, ragging the puck for a few seconds before shovelling it deep into the opposition zone, he was able to reduce the most disciplined power-play to a rabble. He had a way of turning a game around. While the rest of the players on the ice became feverish, ineffective, Nesterenko alone would remain calm, surging between attack and defence, creating the chances for his heavy-shooting teammates. His is a minor legend of uncelebrated works, at a shy remove from the boys reeling off their vainglorious barroom tales. Unfortunately, this is not the time to dwell upon the legend, its pale, delicate flowers: they are of the past. The blows with which Ferguson hammered Nesterenko to his knees are not of the past. Although only Nesterenko can awaken in the dark to the nightmare they rain down, in my own way I, too, can summon them. They taught me an unheeded lesson: to observe the most timid limits, they are a fate to be avoided at all costs. Ferguson's fists, immune from the Law, brutally smash me (swoon), the image of me as a beautiful creature belonging to a world of play and therefore a world lawlessly divine. It was as though, on that occasion, a fear that I should be violated had materialized, when my deepest instinct was always to remain untouched, to use the world but to produce a perfect narcissistic liberty.

A hockey player is an innocent who believes that it is important to win, who will risk a lot of himself in many different ways to reach that end. People who find hockey brutal are unnecessarily squeamish; like the players, for the purpose of argument, they forget that hockey is only a game, a stylized activity, a grossly distorted, incomplete miniature of life with all sorts of illusory goals and rewards attached to it. Hockey fights, even the worst of them, are burlesques. A player has to lose his head before anything real takes place, and what then happens has nothing to do with hockey. A man gets up each day and drives to work, in the evening he drives home. This is a pleasant charade, more or less like a hockey game. Reality is only admitted into this world when, crossing an intersection, his car is rammed by the reckless fool who has run a red light. Even then, it's rare if anything serious happens. The principals climb from their cars, the one angry at the other, the other angry with himself, they exchange insurance cards, wait for the police to arrive, worry over their cars. Two players clash for the puck in hockey, one tries to gain an advantage by holding the other's stick, the latter retaliates with an elbow in the neck, the former drops his stick and gloves, the latter follows suit, they begin a foolish bout of punching, shoving and grabbing. The object is to pull your opponent's sweater over his head and administer a good drubbing and publicly humiliate the resultant mummy. The linesmen intervene, generally before the end has accomplished itself in its full glory. The fight becomes a clownish wrestling match. The players, finally separated, menace and growl, unable to get at one another. They don't really want to, the thing has blown over, but they must blindly follow rituals. By performing in this tedious denouement they console themselves that their pride is intact. So in this world turned vain and idle, is honour maintained.

The Nesterenko-Ferguson fight violates these patterns. No contact preceded Ferguson's machine-gun punching, at least I saw none. Of course, the fight on these pages is not the fight as it was, but is the one that, implanted within me, has long lain buried in the sacred soil that nourishes all repressed events. And the original event is not so much the seed as the manure to some yet more ancient, timeless seed. I breathe this rich odour of decay.

I can still hear the voice of Danny Gallivan … *now Jarrett with the puck in the Chicago end, plays it along the boards toward the centre. Ferguson and Nesterenko race after it, they contest it along the boards … now Ferguson has dropped his gloves, Ferguson is going after Nesterenko, they're going at it … Ferguson pummels Nesterenko with a series of right hooks, Nesterenko is on his knees, he's not fighting back, he's cut, he's bleeding badly … linesman Pavlitch is struggling to pull Ferguson off Nesterenko, they can't get him off …*

I was mesmerized, my heart swollen with outrage, impotence, terror. Nesterenko had a reputation for sharp elbows, a tendency to clutch and grab: he was the type of player likely to irritate Ferguson. But Ferguson's attack was not in response to any real or imagined aggression, it was entirely primitive and brutal. Ferguson was always impatient, could not bide his time or hold himself back, could never envision victory as something to be wooed and tempted through time. Instead, with his every bullish move, he crashed headlong toward the goal, a beast in its fury. His opponents were at a disadvantage: they had long since mastered this fury and could not counter it with one, equally murderous, of their own. So Nesterenko, a player who often dreamed of other things as he played, who might infringe the rules in the same absent-minded way he might obey them, hardly thought to engage in this battle for the puck. Despite his indifference, the engagement was bound to be settled in his favour because of its open nature. And Ferguson was either cursed or blessed with the bestial stupidity that forced him to see his incipient defeat and nothing else. He was unable to contrive a solution either to the immediate problem, loss of the puck, or any future problems, all of which took on the character of this one. He was enraged at Nesterenko, his abstraction, his unconcern at winning or losing. Ferguson had to win, now and always. Winning was life and losing death, and winning sanctified whatever means used. It seemed that Nesterenko was almost absent from the fight. Ferguson's fists hammered at him and continued to hammer at him after he was little more than butchered meat. Nesterenko slumped to his knees, his arms dangled at his sides, he was unconscious before he hit the ice. On the television his blood was the deepest black.

The outcome of the series was determined by the fight. Nesterenko, his head wrapped in a towel, was helped from the ice although he returned to the game later on. He skated from the clinic at the south end of the Forum to the Chicago players' bench, skated through the swaggering contempt of the Canadiens on the ice. Ferguson was one of them, impatiently circling, his anger unappeasable, and those on the bench were malevolently alert to the signal defeat of his broken posture. He skated through the resignation of his teammates who, with eyes lowered, were already fixing him as the scapegoat of the defeat inevitably settling upon them and then he dragged himself listlessly through the gate and took his seat on the bench. He knew of no way to explain to Ferguson his feelings, to clarify his fear. In the eyes of the world he was guilty and must bear the marks of his guilt: a swollen lip, an ugly cut over his left eye that would soon discolour hideously. I could not turn off the set. The score mounted in Montreal's favour, 6-0, a total wipe-out. I was drained of all strength, did not care to defend myself from the din of the celebrating Montreal crowd. I didn't sleep at all that night, tossing from side to side, struggling to banish the dim image, the ugly line of Nesterenko's blood, not red but dark like the plague. I read the Montreal papers the next day with an avid loathing and my shame dogged me. I imagined the newsprint smearing my fingers was Nesterenko's blood, dirty and reviled, ignobly displayed. The columnists probed the wound mercilessly and brought down their verdict: Nesterenko had been guilty of some indefeasible incursion into Fergy's domain, he should never have been there, Fergy had acted within his rights. The writers drew strength for the pronouncement from the act's utter inexplicability. Talk on the streets was only of the fight, the fans vaunted Fergy's prowess as their own. The entire city revelled in their mean, stupid triumph but to denounce them would have been to confess my own inability to defend myself. Let all weak men die and abuse be heaped on their bones.

A couple of games later, when Montreal had won the series and the two teams were shaking hands, I knew that Ferguson extended his hand to Nesterenko as though no one were there, as though the man he had beaten up had ceased to exist. Nesterenko must have ventured a timid glance at Ferguson, pondering momentarily whether to smash his stick over his head. He would have smiled slightly, weakly possessed of a desire to take Ferguson aside, hoping to entice him from his brutal purposes so that he (Nesterenko) might feel safe again. Nesterenko probably wondered if he were permanently embittered, if he could ever shake off his feelings of cowardice. For his part, as time passed, Ferguson grew more solid and stupid, especially after the Montreal team captain, Jean Béliveau, paid specific tribute to the work of his hammering fists. But Ferguson was merely the blind instrument of destruction. He reaped no rewards from his outburst other than a share in the winning team's glory and the knowledge that his anger continued to rule. Rather it was Béliveau, smooth, gilded idol of all Montreal, who was looked upon as the heart of the team, the architect of victory: his the glory. But Béliveau was no longer the gifted player he had once been and, in acknowledging Ferguson, was deferring deceitfully to the true, crude sources of victory. He spoke the truth that it might be void. Béliveau's words were law, they stamped Ferguson's act with the legitimate seal of power and success. And it was Béliveau whom I detested, Béliveau, the unholy marriage of French toadying to English condescension. Ferguson could never be the torchbearer for the myth of the flying Frenchmen, the myth of the unvanquishable blood-red Habitant jersey. And this lie perpetuated that myth: that the win was the consequence of superior skills rather than of an aberrant rush into brute force. While the entire city fortified itself on the team's win, smugly eating their poisoned fruit, I silently drank my cup of gall, unconsoled for being the solitary guardian of these bitter truths. I would have gladly traded places with the winners, would have preferred any ill-gotten victory to this defeat. I must suffer Nesterenko's fate in my imagination, would willingly have rewound that reel from my history. I had failed to learn anything. I was still floating listlessly through an undefined haze of antagonisms toward the city of Montreal.

So it was, some four years later, that the Boston Bruins skated out against the Montreal Canadiens in the opening game of their series. I wanted to forget I had my day in court to face. I cursed my stupidity, hung on, vainly regretted my action. I could neither forgive myself nor accept the ever so slight change I seemed to have willed into my life. I was angry. The city, its streets and buildings, and my father with his slightly fumbling prepossession, fed my anger. I made no attempt to purge myself. Instead, I focussed my fires on the Canadiens. Through the Bruins I was sure to have my revenge and my anger would expel itself in a vindictive, triumphant outburst.

I do not know how my father and I wound up standing at the game together. We had never done so before. Since my arrest I had been nursing my grievances secretly. All was outward calm. I had reformed, was modest and deferential, had stepped humbly back into the family portrait, servant to its fragile harmonies. I must have suggested we go to the game together, urging that we learn to live with our conflicting loyalties and tolerate, no, appreciate even, each other's point of view. The game would strengthen our resolve to live at peace. I was, supposedly, going to the game in a fresh spirit but really my heart was seething and I was anticipating the Canadiens' and my father's fall.

We had tickets for standing behind the grey seats at the north end, North Circle standing. In order to get a good place you had to arrive early. Usually I stand a level lower, behind the blue, but it's more crowded, the jockeying for places next to the rail more fierce. No need to expose my father to the inevitable squabbling and pushing of blue standing. Besides, the blue has places only along the sides and with grey standing we could stand at the end and command the back and forth streaming, which is the game's primary attraction to my way of thinking. Still, my father would have to undergo initiation into the basic ritual of standing at a hockey game.

The game was scheduled for eight o'clock, the turnstiles would open at seven sharp. We arrived at the Forum about six-thirty and hurried into the nearly vacant lobby. I was preoccupied with the prospect of not finding a place next to the rail. Anyone who arrived later than ourselves and took up a position near the entrance, indifferent to the lines already formed, I regarded as a thief after our merited rations, one capable of stealing the last crumbs from starving mouths. Until seven we must wait. Meanwhile the lobby filled, the shouts of the vendors bounced off the walls, the noise from the throng rose in anticipation. Each time the glass doors to the street opened, we were hit by a blast of cold air: a crowd becomes a bigger crowd by accretions.

About quarter to seven, the girls came out to sell programs:

"Programme de la Soiree, Hockey Line-up Program": flute-like voices sing their wares. The girls are beautiful, their flimsy red jackets and bell-bottom black slacks a bold challenge to the Montreal winter, fashion's poor response to the slashing cold. The girls' accents are one in their French sing-song; they exist specifically for the consumption of the wealthy season-ticket holders: on the one hand the English wishing to forget the army of proletarians at their backs flinging about their incomprehensible joual, on the other a certain middle-class segment of the French uneasy over their origins, pleased to have these artfully fashioned melodious instruments to titillate their ears.

I bought a program, flipped through it, digesting its meagre information, one eye on the articles, the other on the hordes of line jumpers bent on keeping us from a spot next the rail. Players arrived periodically, some self-conscious in their street clothes, others swaggering through the crowd, others already intent on the game ahead. None acknowledged the remarks tossed their way, but all the same we knew they were public property. About five to seven the ticket takers began lugging the turnstiles into place, removing the iron grilles separating the crowd from the stairway to the upper levels. The ticket takers leaned against the turnstiles, chatted among themselves. Their position on the inside invested their predictions with an utterly unmerited authority. The excitement was building. Prior to the actual opening of the turnstiles, the ticket takers always tear the tickets of the first three or four people in line who can then be let through the moment the signal is given to lessen just that little bit of the initial crush. At seven o'clock, as on every other Saturday night for the last six months — save one, the week the ice show was in town and the Canadiens banished to a foreign arena — the head usher came to the stairway landing, calmly took in the nervous milling throng and called out, "Okay, open 'em up!" Then the crowd's reflexive forward surge, no lines, a dozen or so abreast, the fans had somehow to funnel their way into three entrances. Despite the aggravating slowness of the ticket takers (old men whose hands trembled as they tore the tickets), despite the alarming efficiency of everyone else at slithering, pushing, sliding his way beyond us (though I did manage to cut off that small monkey-like greaseball: I was damned if I was going to let him past), despite the unbearable pressure of the frantic mob behind us, despite the heart-sinking moment when I believed I'd lost my ticket, so tightly was I clutching it, despite all the risks to life and limb undertaken in just this way every Saturday evening, I was finally pressed into the turnstile, my ticket torn in half, the stub returned, as simultaneously my thigh drove the turnstile arm forward and down. Miraculously I found myself on the inside of the Montreal Forum.

But the race had only begun. I had all those stairs to climb. I never thought to take the escalator where I might be trapped behind people content with its sluggardly pace. I raced past the souvenir vendors and the lame and the old climbing as best they could, rose ever higher, no less than four turnings in the course of my ascension, arrived at the mouth of the circle standing, flashed my stub at the indifferent usher, the one behind him moved to block my path, insisted on verifying the ticket, satisfied himself, moved aside and then at last I was free to see where I was, to notice for the first time that I was once again ludicrously early and had the choice of every standing place in the building. Yet I ran on, from the south end to the north, laid claim to the spot directly behind the net, tore off my jacket and threw it over the rail, thereby claiming the spot beside me for my father who, slower than I, bewildered by my mad flight and disappearance, was just now emerging at the south end. Slowly he turned through a half circle, seemed to catch sight of me, and began to walk, half run in my direction.

My father slowed down, then quickened his stride again, covering the last few steps in a characteristic shambling trot. All those stairs must have been a strain but he managed a smile. What had induced him to participate in this rite? We now had an hour to kill before game time. He removed his coat and laid it on the rail next to mine. We took in the scene before us, the empty seats, the standing level rapidly filling. He looked at his watch: Fifty-seven minutes to go. Our eyes met, we had nothing to say. We turned toward the rink. I wanted to tell him this was the moment I liked best, the ice surface smooth, clean and pure, the lines freshly painted, the goals a graphic illusion rising out of the ice. But before I could form these impressions into words, an ice cream vendor was upon us and my father wanted to know if I wanted an ice cream. I didn't but I jumped at the offer: if father and son were to go to the hockey game together, then it was the father's prerogative to cram the youngster full of the goodies he imagined him craving. I thanked him, thanked the vendor also. We ate our ice cream in silence and I dutifully licked the wrapper clean.

We did not broach the subject of the game, for neither of us could be trusted not to use it as a weapon against the other. It was a blank, joyless wait interrupted for me only by brief internal attacks of anxiety: my impending trial. And yet I had nothing to fear. The result was a forgone conclusion and that result could leave me neither more nor less free than I already was.

At 7:27 the Bruins skated out for the warmup, followed some two minutes later by the Canadiens. My father watched the Canadiens directly below us. They were already super-charged, flying as they would fly once the game began. My gaze drifted to the far end where the Bruins circled lazily, taking it easy in these last minutes before the storm. My father's heart was set on Ralph Backstrom, his favourite player, admired for his pinwheel motions, his tireless skating. And I had Orr. I smiled at the comparison.

I suggested we try to guess which Canadien would be the last to leave the ice when the warmup ended. I knew that Terry Harper, possessed of some superstition in this matter, made a ritual of staying out longer than all his teammates. My father was decisive: "J.C. Tremblay." Should I astonish him? I pretended to deliberate, then: I'll take Ralph Backstrom." The siren sounded and the players flew around the rink for the last time. Almost as one J.C. Tremblay and Ralph Backstrom dropped from the pack, passed from the ice into the dressing-room. We enjoyed our reversal. I bought us each a bag of peanuts which we consumed mechanically, mindlessly, even happily. The countdown continued.

By game time I was damp with sweat, my limbs were shaking, my teeth chattering. My father was stamping impatiently, first one foot then the other, grinding his teeth. A great current of sound swelled and swept through the building at the Canadiens' appearance. The Bruins were on the ice moments later, my wild savage shouts and pounding hands drowning out the boos. I heard nothing of the national anthem, saw nothing of my father. The red of the red line was the blood pumping through the veins behind my eyes. The ice sheet, with the players and officials standing at attention upon it, had taken its dazzling place inside my head, about to explode. The puck was dropped and the game was on.

Boston had conceived a brutal plan. While the Canadiens' fast skaters whirled through the opening shift, the Bruins patiently crouched, waited their chance to pounce upon them. First it was Cashman, a hatchet man who caught Cournoyer a hard check against the boards, then dropped his gloves and levelled the smaller man with a fast series of punches. As Cashman beat up Cournoyer, Derek Sanderson, a mod thug, waded into another small opponent, Dick Duff; victories for the Bruins. The crowd roared and screamed for justice and retribution, my father was silent, frowning, his pleasure spoiled by this resort to violence. I said nothing, my gloating not entirely free of shame.

The crude stratagem had worked. The Canadiens were intimidated, the Bruins had a free hand to go about their business like true professionals. As the game wore on the Canadiens contrived no serious attacking threats. And when, midway through the third period, Derek Anderson waltzed around the Canadiens' defence and scored a shorthanded goal, Boston led 2-0. The game was as good as won. But by then my pleasure was beginning to wane. Up to a point I had enjoyed my father's performance. I had been called upon to say nothing while his frustration, screwed-up ever tighter, expressed itself, at first in clickings of the tongue against the palate. Then it became suppressed cries of "Jesus Murphy!" and finally it errupted into shouts of bitterness toward his favourites. He tried, unsuccessfully, to temper his wrath, give it a speculative character: "Tremblay, you goat! What's wrong with that crowd anyway?" I explained to him in my mildest manner that they were not making the mistakes on purpose, that Boston was doing a good job of containing the Canadiens. And I pointed out, truthfully I thought, that the Bruins had Orr who had dominated the game as only he could and who in himself was the difference. My father would not listen to reason, only stammered more angrily. Another Tremblay pass went astray, my father turned to me, grabbed my arm. "Did you see that? Did you see that?" I could only shrug; he was becoming a wildman, creating a scene. My poor father turned away from me, snorted in disgust, convinced — of what? That there was a conspiracy afoot whose cruel end was to put the maximum strain on his already aggravated emotions. He calmed down a little and at the next break in the action I looked to see how he was doing. Leaning against the railing for support, his head was sunk into his arms, his eyes shut. He had been standing for over three hours and he looked so old and tired that Boston might have inflicted a bushel of goals upon him without lifting him out of his weariness. He spat on the concrete, slowly drew himself up, focussed on the arena where he expected, demanded, so much pleasure and received, instead, so much torment.

Fifty-five minutes of hockey had swept by. Two periods and the space of two intermissions, the third period winding to a close; it was a long and taxing evening for my father but a fleeting one for myself. My animosity toward the Canadiens had all but disappeared. I was even mildly sympathetic to their frantic labours though unwilling to indulge their need to win, which was becoming the more hysterical as the prospect of defeat became the more likely. Defeat was a just reproof, would make them better, more thoughtful men.

And as Ferguson charged down the ice alone, hugging the left-wing boards, his head down, I smiled a superior parental smile. I was alongside Dallas Smith who was perfectly positioned to block any direct move Fergy might make for the goal. He had skated himself into a bad angle, could do nothing but swipe angrily at the puck which was on its end and about to bounce free. Smith moved to block the shot with a poke-check but it skipped by his stick, fluttered weakly in the air, what little momentum it had rapidly diminishing, its death throes a malicious parody of Fergy's efforts. It bounced to about ten feet from Cheevers. And Cheevers, conscientious to the last, playing them, weak and strong alike, with the same nervous care, fell to his knees to block it with his body. The puck took another harmless skip and Cheevers readied to gather it in. Warily, he followed it bouncing directly before him, then, impossible, finding an opening where surely there was none, it skittered through his pads and concluded its ugly little dance into the net. The Forum erupted in the predictable roar, my father's bellows joined to it. He unleashed a gleeful wallop across my spine. I jerked about, eyes blazing in anger. My father was already sheepish, aware that moments before he was fretting and fuming, more or less intent on depriving me of the pleasure I might have taken in my triumph. But he had tasted blood and had a prophet's certainty that the night would yet be his. He reined himself in and as the cheering died, tossed a pitying accolade in Cheevers' direction. "Really, it's a shame, wasn't so much a mistake as just one of those things, Cheevers deserved his shutout, he's played such a strong game. Fifty-five minutes of total domination and only two goals to show for it, then that asshole Ferguson scores on a fucking freak shot!" My father would pursue the matter no further. He had seen this sort of intemperance before. Admittedly, his own words might have unwittingly added fuel. Perhaps he should have said nothing. I apologized sulkily and he trotted out something to the effect that he could understand, though of course it was only a game.

The game was delayed while the rink attendant swept up the debris thrown in celebration of the goal. I had convinced myself that it was a terribly unjust goal and that my father should understand and at least share the truth of that conviction. But we had always seen these matters differently, even when aligned.

The first Grey Cup football game I ever saw, I watched with my father on a neighbour's television. In those days the west was always the underdog, the east an almost routine winner. I was born in the west so my loyalty lay there. I had lived all my seven years in the east but had already developed a notion of my exile, even believing in a second birth and a second life so that I might relive those same years in the west. My father too supported the western challenger, the Winnipeg Blue Bombers. The pain of losing had not yet become insupportable to him and besides, everyone else in the room was cheering for the Hamilton Tiger Cats so he felt that I needed some aid and comfort. So Winnipeg played beautifully, gave promise of winning, but were behind by a touchdown with the game almost over. They mounted a last stirring drive, Indian Jack Jacobs moving them downfield on his golden passing arm. With time for just one more play, the ball on the Hamilton three-yard line, Jacobs dropped back to pass, floated the ball into the flat for his favourite receiver, Tom Casey. But Lou Kusserow, Hamilton defensive back, had anticipated the play, and the moment the ball arrived he hit Casey a jarring tackle. The ball popped in the air and fell to the ground. Incomplete. Rejoicing all around me; for me an instant of bewilderment and then as I understood what had happened, I wept unchecked. As we got up to leave, my father insisted I dry my eyes, thank our host. I performed this duty as best I could but was unable to shake the sobs from my voice. Our host, an old man who took things easily, smiled, tousled my hair, suggested I wait till next year, it'd be my turn then. I wasn't interested in next year. As the door closed behind us, I burst into tears again, repeating over and over, "Is that ever dirty!" My father suggested we take a walk together and took me by the hand. I made a fist with my free hand, rubbed at the tears that continued to flow. What was dirty he wanted to know. That Winnipeg lost, that ... that ... that the referee hadn't called interference on the last play. "Did you see interference?" my father asked. Yes, I had. This falsehood assuaged my feelings some and eventually it would be as though Winnipeg had not lost. Rather, malign action had stolen the game. My father began to explain that while you might not agree with the referees you still had to abide by their decisions, that they were usually better placed than you were to make the calls. Obviously I could not adjust my sights to this view, my bitterness rose within me as strong as ever, it was still *dirty*. No, my father was sure it wasn't dirty, he could understand how unhappy I was, but dirty it wasn't. To say it was dirty was to miss the point. And he would illustrate that point. He could recall a disappointment of his as great as my own.

He was playing in a championship basketball game. His team were the underdogs but had carried their favoured opponents to the series limit. Slowly, painstakingly, he described the last game, his team's glorious, climactic fight, countering their opponents' height advantage with excellent outside shooting, free-wheeling playmaking and a tight, tenacious defence. Gradually, the bitter taste dissolved. I listened, rapt, forgetful of the moral of the story, certain my father's team was going to come through with the miraculous upset, my father himself the architect of victory. And, sure enough, with but two seconds remaining, his team down by two points, my father was fouled in the act of shooting. Yes, he would make the shots, would send his team on to a smashing overtime win. He stepped to the line, composed, sure of himself. *Swish*. He makes the first shot, I knew he would. He steps back, takes a deep breath, receives the ball from the referee, bounces it once, bounces it twice, eyes the basket, crouches ever so slightly, balances the ball between his shooting hand, the left hand, and the cup formed by the palm of his right hand, rocks backward lightly, pumps once, pumps twice, his arm flicks forward to its full extension, his hand releases the ball, it flies from his fingertips, arches toward the net. *Swish*! The game is tied; I dance a little jig of joy. But the referee is shaking his head, his arms signaling no score, my father's left foot is on the foul line. As suddenly as it shone through, my joy was clouded over, I was myself again, angry, bitter, cheated. I ventured to put words to this new catastrophe: "Is that ever dirty!" My father, his artistry all for naught, displeased with this embittered obstinacy, took up the hand he had released in telling his story and dragged home his doubly aggrieved, unregenerate son.

The game resumed, the Canadiens going at it every man for himself, the little method in their play abandoned to the wings of a mad, disorderly flight. At such times in the Forum, the deep roar characteristic of a crowd of about eighteen thousand persons, mostly men, disappears, transformed into shrill, bird-like screams. For some reason it rarely fails to unnerve either me or my team. But Boston could survive, Boston had Orr to take charge of the game, see his team through this crisis, restore them to themselves; for their nerves had overcome them, the discipline had gone from their game.

But Orr, though he had not panicked, seemed confused, unwilling to accept the reversal in Boston's fortunes. He wanted to continue playing the game he was playing that had bewitched Montreal. I sensed that Orr was too young not to regret what could not be undone. He too was disturbed by the injustice of Fergy's goal, the image of that goal was eating away at all of us. Orr's preoccupation grew fatally; he was playing himself out of his own game and not the hands of the Canadiens. He lost confidence in his teammates, who without confidence in themselves, were in a hurry to shift the entire burden to his shoulders. Orr, who by drawing a teammate within his orbit could raise that player's game, was failing to distribute his skills. But what was most astonishing to see was Orr himself playing ineffectively, even badly.

Time seemed to be in Boston's favour, but time was not going to let the Bruins off the hook. And despite the senseless character of Montreal's game, players colliding with one another and themselves, two and three teammates chasing the same puck, wild shots careening into corners of the rink, it was evident the Canadiens were not about to make any self-defeating mistakes. It would be left to Boston to do that.

With less than a minute to play, Vachon, the Montreal goalie, raced off the ice and was replaced by a sixth attacker. The Canadiens were pressing deep in the Bruins' end with only one defenceman, J.C. Tremblay, back at the blue line. The puck, perilously close to the net, squirted free to Bruin winger, Ken Hodge, halfway between his goal and the blue line. In this situation he has two good alternatives before him. He can play the puck into the centre ice area, where even if Tremblay gets to it first the Canadiens will be faced with the difficult task of regrouping outside the Boston zone before reorganizing their attack. Or he can choose to carry the puck; if Tremblay is foolhardy enough to meet him inside the blue line the odds are overwhelmingly in favour of Hodge getting by him and having a clear path to the empty goal. If Tremblay retreats in the hope that a teammate will get back to help out, Hodge still has a good scoring chance. Even if he doesn't score, Boston retains possession of the puck and precious seconds and territory are gained. But Hodge had long since ceased to deliberate. The puck no sooner reached his stick than it left it, heedlessly swept down the ice behind the Montreal goal. Icing. All that Montreal needed. From the ensuing face-off Béliveau knocked the puck into the Boston goal mouth where Serge Savard, the sixth attacker, deflected it past Cheevers. The Orr check that sprawled Savard into the net was too late and only made Savard the more heroic. The programs rained down from the stands again, the Canadiens' players streamed over the boards to join the winding circle of joy. Cheevers skated from his goal to the Boston bench. And Orr, who was down on both knees, after raising himself to one skate, suddenly hurled his stick against the glass behind the Boston goal. His anger was that much greater that it fell unbroken to the ice.

The period ended, another intermission to be waited out before the Canadiens would deliver the overtime death blow. I told my father to hold my place while I took a walk. I did not ask if there was anything I could get him, and when I turned my back on him, it was with the consciousness that I could hurt him only by hurting myself. And the pain that was strangling me had so obscured my vision that I failed to see that my father was so tired he had not noticed me leave his side. His immediate rejuvenation would be borne on the stick that fired the winning goal. Our mutually inflicted wounds could only be healed face to face, not as we were, side by side. I wanted to turn back, fight my way to my father, tear out my morbid thoughts as I moved along with the crowd. I had lost my reasons for coming to the game and the purposes for which I'd hoped to misuse it. I stood in line for a hotdog, the air heavy with cigarette smoke, the odour of grease, the stench of spilt beer. I did not want a hotdog, I seemed to have lost my will, was carried in the sluggish tide of the surrounding crowd. Everyone was more cheerful than I, their lively chatter contrasting with the fetid mouths from which it issued. They would gorge themselves in this intermission, belch contentedly, give up what little alertness remained to them. On this evening they were certain they could look to their team to satisfy their needs. I felt I owed it to the Bruins to be the best prepared person in the building. I pulled out of the hotdog line, pushed my way to the fringes of the crowd, stopped short: I knew that the outcome was not entirely beyond my determination but I had assumed I need only give voice to the Bruins' cause, pray exceedingly hard or lend them my sharp eyes. But that was not enough. I was baffled, something else was required and at this time, whatever it was, I lacked it. I made my way back to my father, slowly, in a vacant stroll killing what remained of the intermission. The best I could do was to give up my hopes but they never left me. My father, a wiser fan than I, his back to the railing, was sitting cross-legged on his coat on the concrete floor. He must have forgotten he had spat on that very spot.

He looked up and smiled a dog-tired smile. I extended my hand and helped him to his feet. He replaced his coat on the railing, drew himself up, rubbed his hands vigorously: "Now we'll get 'em!" We were both possessed of the same truth; we had arrived at it from opposite directions. But I could not suffer resignedly what I knew must happen, I must continue to hope against hope. I was intent upon the Bruins as they took the ice, my eyes at the ends of their stalks: absolute concentration might override the fear and trembling. I was this unchanging bundle of intense concentration through the twenty or thirty seconds the overtime lasted. Each mistake the Bruins made, bringing them nearer the end, did not call for the usual curse or gasp but merely caused me to blink. The Bruins lost the face-off. Blink. The Canadiens shot the puck into the Bruins' zone, Orr lost it as he carried back to mid-ice. Blink. The Canadiens brought up the puck and from a position of about twenty feet out, whipped it past Orr, who had gone to his knees to block the shot, past Cheevers on the stick side and into the net that billowed with its force, I did not blink, but stared ever harder, certain the game was not over, that all these acts were reversible, that my father's cries of triumph would cease ringing in my ears.

an excerpt from the novel

The Hockey Fan Came Riding

❖   BIRK SPROXTON

The Beginning is Language
1.   The word fan is short for fanatic.
2.   My mother quit going to the rink when she learned that hockey
     can be heard as well as seen.
3.   The word puck is not in the Bible.

Riding The Pine
Riding the pine means collecting slivers in your ass while you sit on the
bench. We had a guy on our team who got drunk because he was riding
the pine and who rode the pine because he was always drunk. We dressed
him for every game though, like a turkey for thanksgiving, just because
he was so ugly. I forget what position he played on the ice, but we called
him our tight end.

Blood and Guts
The hockey fan likes blood and guts, especially the enemy's guts and
blood. But you can't always tell who the enemy is. One time I got
highsticked in the chops and fell to the ice in a heap. Our trainer came
running out and when he saw I wasn't bleeding, he gave me a little shot
in the nose trying to draw some blood so the other guy would get five
minutes.

    Once I crashed into the boards with another guy and we started
slugging at each other. A woman behind the screen said, Beat the snot

outa that creep and I could tell she liked my style. I guess we would have killed each other, but the referee got in the way — stuck his finger in my eye and his thumb up my nose, which wasn't too bad considering it was supposed to be a fight, except that he was the brother-in-law of the guy that I was trying to kill and was trying to kill me.

Song of the Stay-At-Home Defenceman

The last time I tried to score I got knocked ass over tea kettle at the blue line and they broke in on a two on one and tied the game. The coach yelled at me, screamed so hard he got a hernia. I got sent down for two weeks.

Those guys don't send you to the minors, they send you to the mines. You have to work, underground, in the miner leagues. You come out looking like a mole, you get squinty eyes and dirty pores and dirty gauchies, your eyes grow about two inches wider from squinting in the shadows. And hot. You get closer to hell and it heats up. Yup it heats up as you go down.

You have to be there, you can't hot dog around, streak with the wingers, deke everybody out of their underwear, scoring all the time. You just have to suck it up and hang in. Protect things. Stay home and look after the crease. Take the banging and whacking, lay a few good whacks yourself.

Other guys get the fun. You've got responsibilities. Keep them out of the slot, out of the crease. That's what you're there for. Keep it clean in front.

The Hockey Fan Makes A Point About Style

He begins in the third person and then shifts into second: "The Oilers are piling up in front of the net to set up a screen or make a deflection and you have to be tough in there. Why not talk a little to the goalie and try to throw him off his game, maybe cause a breakdown in concentration?"

You are the second person of course, and I am the first, and those guys over there are third, but when you stand here beside me and we point to those guys we can sight along the same finger and see sort of the same things, so why stick you in the middle of our sights, still within spearing range? That's how people get hurt.

First Blood, 1950

Unused to the new zippered style, the hockey fan catches himself, up, short, draws blood, seeks help howling from his giggling sister (two hands are not enough). He maketh a storm; he prayeth devoutly for buttons; he contemplate the religious conversion.

The Hockey Fan Hits Middle Age

I was right pissed off when I found she had put my skates in a garage sale. We don't even have a garage. Those skates had no blade left so I suppose they got thrown out, like garbage, as if they were worthless. I liked those skates. Pro's and Tacks, the best you could buy in Bell's Hardware in 1960. The boots were short — you had to sew your own tendon guards — and made of leather, not that rubber and plastic crap they try to pass off for skate boots now. And the blades were steel, too. Just steel — not clear plastic, or blue plastic, or white plastic. All steel. And none of them wimpy rubber nibs on the tip of the heel. Made good weapons those skates. I got one in the head once but I've never seen the scar since I quit wearing a brush cut. Have long thick hair now and long slender eyelashes. And a pair of skates made of nylon, each with a little rubber tip on the heel of the blade.

The Pastoral Tradition

Do you remember when the kids on defence stood back close to the goalie, lifting their sticks into the air and tilting heads back to catch snowflakes on their tongues?

At the other end kids flock around the puck.

Hockey Is A Transition Game

My father used to tell stories about how poor he was. "So poor," he said, "we were so poor we didn't have hockey sticks. Used bent willow branches and horse apples for a puck and snot string for laces. We were so poor we ate turnips all the time. At Christmas we got cranberry sauce with our turnips and Mother cut off the bottoms of our pockets so we'd have something to play with."

Now, for my sons, things have changed. They travel everywhere. Now they don't go to the pond; they go across the pond. Last year they played in Finland, Sweden and the Soviet Union.

The Hockey Fan Takes Shelter

One of our games was in a bomb shelter, ten storeys down into Finnish bedrock. A cavern big enough for two ice surfaces, Olympic size, but no bleachers for the fans. Spooky, the ceiling coated with some kind of waterproof stuff, a sparkley white colour: ghost sheets woven with tinsel.

Vending machines guard the stairs and you can see the closed circuit television trained on the stairwell. The coffee has run out. Our opponents are from Rockford, Illinois, west of Chicago. They don't like us and we don't like them. Mark borrows my mitts; he has left his in the hotel. Where I stand, the ice sneaks out under the boards but I stay there anyway, like a dummy until the chill works its way up and down from brain to cock to toe. My feet are cold. My hands are cold. Whoever said the centre of the earth was hot? (Warmest place in the shelter is the men's room, but you can stand around only so long, hands like parentheses cuddling your jewels, before someone thinks you're weird.)

The Hockey Fan Goes Cruising

The cruise ship (Stockholm to Helsinki) snuggled into the pier at the bottom of a long runway. Down and down and down the chute we slumped, sheep-like, lugging huge wool coats and bags and bags and bags, each lugging three bags full of hockey sweaters and skates, toques and shirts (plastic bread bags), Canadian Club and V.O. (not to mention Johnny Walker Black Label) down and down the chute we carried the bags, dancing to our rooms, we danced through dinner, the ship shivering and shifting its way through pack ice, we dance, light on our feet, side-step the heavy check of tables and posts, we dance through dinner, humming the old tunes, dance on the floor, laughing I put my hand on her bottom (we're dancing), and she lifts her knee just inside my thighs and nuzzles up, gently, and whispers, do you like male sopranos, she did, she said it, just like that and a mean thing it was too considering I had risked a ribbing good hernia hauling those bags on board. And she said that to me. Look at her, she's still smiling.

Hockey Night in Leningrad

Tonight the boys play outdoors. We bundle up and hustle past the grinning snowman in the foyer, line up for the buses, trying to remember which one smells of diesel fumes and which one is okay. I wear my Leningrad overshoes: one sock, one bread bag, another sock, another bread bag. Warmest my feet have been since we landed in Helsinki two weeks ago. The night is frosty and festive; steamed-up windows filter city lights.

This game is the hockey highlight of the tour (tomorrow we go to the ballet, Friday to the circus). We know they will pull all sorts of crooked tricks to beat us. The favourite scenario has it that each period they will ice a different and more experienced team than the last, saving their national team for the third. This is serious. In Finland the home crowd had a special chant especially for our fans. "Go Canada Go," the Canucks shouted. "Go Canada Go Home," the Finns shouted, as if we were Americans or something. And if the Finns didn't like us, and they're supposed to be on our side, imagine what these guys will do. Shave off whiskers, hunch down into their boots to look like thirteen-year-old kids, stick Tretiak into goal, anything to wipe out the rotten capitalist Canadians.

At the sports centre the flags are straight out, the temperature is minus twenty Celsius. A crowd has gathered and they gawk politely as we are directed into the hall to get warm. We are eighteen hockey players, and thirty mothers and fathers and sisters and grandmothers and friends. We share the warm hall with a few hockey officials, trade some pins and buttons.

Outside in the wind people are packed four or five deep around the rink. There must be three hundred here, shouting, stomping, breaths fogging the soft fluffy snow. This is a community sports centre, sponsored by Aeroflot, big letters painted on the boards. Red and white and orange, we weave into a dark field of fur hats and warm coats. I stamp my feet.

"Fred."

A tug at my sleeve. I have to turn my whole body, my hood is up and I can't see past the fur.

"Fred. You want a drink?" A young man in his twenties. He's talking to me.

"Yes," I say, "Vodka?"

"No," he says, "vino."

We walk to his two companions, one of whom has a bottle tucked under his coat. He hands me a tumbler, pours it full. We lift glasses in salute. The wine is warm and good.

The second man lights a cigarette. I offer my pack.

"American, Salem Menthol," says the first man and takes one, proud of his English.

"My sons," I say pointing to Mark and Denis, who stand together behind the screen. Denis still wears the top half of his goal equipment; he has just finished his turn in goal (we're now leading eight to nothing) and he has been quick to get off his skates and back out into the cold. He looks incredibly puff-bellied and skinny-legged, his orange hockey sweater trimmed with blue, a Canadian flag on his sleeve. He looks like a strange exotic bird who landed here by mistake. Mark too an odd creature in red jacket with white sleeves, huge leather mitts, a purple-coloured camera bag on his belly, and a grey Russian fur hat, a coup made earlier on the street near the Winter Palace. Together the boys define motley.

As we light cigarettes, a hand pokes in front of me. I am being offered coins. I shake my head. My friend Fred say, "Nyet, nyet, no beesiness here." We smoke and thank each other as the crowd noise picks up. The Russians attack our goal, but leave themselves open on defence and we break away only to be foiled by their goaltender. An exciting moment. I turn to my comrades but they have disappeared and my feet are getting cold.

In the hall a man gives us postcard pictures of the city. He explains by gesturing with his palms down that the gifts are from the boys on the hockey team. In return he accepts bubble gum. We are invited into our team's dressing room. Two tables standing end to end are spread with pastries and rolls. A giant silver urn of tea shines buddha-like in the corner.

Outside in the wind the goals add up. The Russian boys finally score. The crowd cheers. The wine bottle is gone.

My belly is warm.

The Return of Aurel Joliat

❖   DAVID GOWDEY

With thanks to Bob McKeowan/Michael Boland's "Les Canadiens."

The winter I lived in Ottawa was a long one. The snow that began to fall in October stayed on the ground through April and into the middle of May. I was compiling records on the gold rush at the Public Archives, clipping articles, sifting old photographs, giving them labels and order. As I worked the contours of the past began to form, and a separate vein of memory became apparent. Perhaps it would be mined by another researcher, or perhaps it would remain undiscovered.

I was in the habit in those days of skating to work along the Rideau Canal. The natural ice of the canal was cleared before dawn by city workers with shovels and pushcart ice machines, and each morning thousands like me would escape the commute by skating. It was a fine way to begin a day, though when it snowed heavily overnight, which was often, the skate was impossible until well after nine.

For me, working more or less on my own time, the days after a snowfall were best. I would start out under a blue sky, street shoes in a pack on my back, the clean air speeding into my system, blowing away the cobwebs. I would take the most circuitous route, gliding alongside the other stragglers, the unemployed, college students, school-kids taking the morning off, housewives running errands.

On days when the ice was slow, if I'd started early I'd head over to a stretch on Carlton Street which offered a wealth of cheap amusements. For thirty cents I lingered over a third coffee in Passalalpi's, and for the price of a morning paper I could read a sheaf of magazines in Stan's Bytown Variety. A dollar-fifty bought a full treatment shave at Twitchell's Barber Pole — 3 Barbers 3 — and for two dollars Twitchell would throw in a trim, allowing me another precious half hour before the decisions about the past began.

More often than I would have thought, I found myself at Twitchell's. The third partner had evidently departed: his chair remained vacant at the end of the room while the other two, Twitchell and Lamontagne, dealt with the flow of customers. Twitchell had a brushcut and dark horn-rimmed glasses, while Lamontagne's hair was longer and sleek. Lamontagne favoured a wide assortment of red, blue and green tinted liquids on the counter in front of his chair. I only once saw a bottle ever put to use — a green one, used as a preshave — but they gave his area a more festive flavour than Twitchell's, and a haircut from him seemed somehow less drastic. Twitchell shunned the bottles completely, content to use only a small tin of talcum powder, and then only when asked.

The small rituals of the place drew men back week after week at ages when the need for constant hair attention had long since disappeared. We basked in the luxury of our heads being touched, of the talk of sports and Canadian politicians, in the smell of the alcohol-laden lotions and the heat of the steaming towels.

It was on one of these morning that I first met Aurel Joliat. I didn't know it at the time but the small man with thin legs in the corner of the room had been one of hockey's greatest stars in the 1920s. He had played Gehrig to Morenz's Ruth with the first great Canadiens teams, flitting past the cheerful roughnecks of the ten team NHL. Joliat hadn't been as fast as Morenz, but he was tricky and very agile, with a great ability to accelerate while turning. The two had raced through the league together, changing the face of the game.

That morning Joliat sat forward in his chair, his elbows on his knees. He looked like a horse trainer, or a dog handler, someone who'd spent much of his life around animals. He spoke about the racetrack, a horse he'd had running — I first had the impression that he owned it himself. Joliat had been there when I arrived. He waved his hand without looking at me, motioning me to go ahead of him so that he could continue to talk. He spoke half in French, half in English, for the benefit of both the barbers, who each spoke only a little of the other's language.

I had my trim, listened, contemplated the bottled colours and Joliat's reflection in the mirror. Finally he checked the weather outside, said his goodbyes, put on his coat and left. Lamontagne made sure that I knew who he was.

"He wasn't a scorer like Morenz?" I asked.

"He was great himself without Morenz — but he missed him when he was gone." Morenz of course had died, in the legend from a broken heart, ten days after a severely fractured leg had ended his hockey career. His body had lain in state at centre ice of the Forum — the arena, packed to capacity, observed an eerie total silence as twenty thousand people paid their respects, waiting together soundlessly for a last chance to experience Morenz's spell. Joliat had played another year before retiring.

"He would look around him for someone to pass to," said Twitchell, "but no one could keep up with him."

After that morning I started to notice Joliat skating on the canal. Lamontagne told me that he was there every morning, but somehow I'd always missed him before. He was certainly conspicuous enough, an eighty-year-old man with a hockey stick, pushing a puck in front of him, sometimes in a red Canadiens sweater and always with the cap he'd worn on the ice throughout his career. Once I brought a stick along with me and skated quite near him, hanging back a little — I'm sure he knew I was there but he wasn't yet ready to pass.

The next day I was out on the ice early, skating by myself in a driving wind, shooting a puck and sprinting after it. Joliat, skates over his shoulders, stood on the shore for a long time, smoking a cigarette. Finally he put his skates on and joined me, waving his stick for the puck. We spoke little, passing back and forth, until the puck disappeared in a deep snowdrift and we called it quits for the day.

As we sat together drawing the snow from our blades he mentioned that he'd soon have to get into shape. He was going back to Montreal into the Forum for a salute to the Canadiens that month. The game would be televised across the country. The Rocket would be there, Harvey, Blake, Dickie Moore, all the stars still left from the most dominant teams in sports history. It would be the largest tribute to the team ever mounted, and they wanted him to be last on the ice.

I was committed to staying in Ottawa that Saturday — I wished it could have been otherwise. As it was I had to break away early, racing to a tavern along icy roads to catch the beginning of the game. The bar was crowded but a seat opened up and gratefully I squeezed myself in. Dick Irvin and Danny Gallivan were still filling time — "this historic event" — and although Molson's no longer owned the team I ordered a Molson's Canadian.

My heart sped up, my breathing grew quick — it was like a playoff game against the Flyers. The Canadiens of old were introduced and at the bar we all applauded. The names and faces meant the same thing to all of us — the tribal legend was being told once again.

Finally the camera focussed on the corner doors at the end of the ice.

Claude Mouton on the P.A. gave the introduction in two languages, and in the passageway appeared Joliat. Wearing his cap he came bounding down the ramp, growing visible to more and more of the crowd who greeted him with a roar.

He leapt down onto the ice and made several strides across the face-off circle. The ovation continued to grow. He was carrying a puck in his glove and began to throw it, but suddenly found himself too close to the boards — he tried to swerve away, lost his balance and tumbled.

It seemed as if the voice of the crowd had knocked him over. People laughed and cheered, then cheered again, as he shook off the Buffalo player who helped him to his feet and broke away pushing the puck across the blue line, his eyes pointed straight ahead. "They made 'em tough when they made this man," said Danny Gallivan.

My throat tightened as the cheering for him surged, the crowd larger than any he had ever played before, and he seemed to swell with pride crossing centre ice. He began to focus intently on the goalie, Gump Worsley, at the far end. He swept near the red carpet where the old-timers stood, Moore, Richard, Béliveau, nearer, too near, skidded against it, tried to run across to keep his balance, lost it, tumbled again onto his shoulder, somersaulted over on the ice.

This time no one helped him up, but it looked like Doug Harvey might have said something to him, and after a moment of pain he broke into a grin. He set his cap straight, picked up the puck and again he set off, this time more cautiously, with Harvey trailing behind.

He looked like he might lose possession for a moment but he recovered on his turn and cut across the goalmouth — Worsley went down and he swept it into the net.

The crowd laughed and cheered for a final time. He tore off his cap and waved to them, both arms flung into the air. Again he neared the fateful carpet, but Harvey and Toe Blake grabbed him under the arms. He stood there once more in the centre of the Forum, where Howie Morenz had lain in state forty-five years before, where he'd taken face-offs and held the Stanley Cup, and the cheering rained down, the Canadiens surrounded him, Larry Robinson tapped him on the shin-pads with his stick.

I don't remember if the Canadiens won. I played pick-up hockey after the game, and later we went back to the bar. Everyone talked about other things. The days and nights passed and my work went quickly, but I didn't see Joliat all week.

The next Saturday Canadiens were away, so we got the Toronto game instead. They lost. That night, we were at the rink early, and the other goalie didn't show — we skated, passed the puck too often, didn't shoot until we had to. The game was listless, maybe from watching the Leafs. We all went home early from the bar. I tried to stay up to do some work, but the energy level never reached critical mass and I ended up falling asleep.

But I woke up suddenly in the middle of the night. The snow shifted outside and I walked to the window, gradually clearing my eyes. From the dark room I looked out onto the canal, and in the distance I noticed a skater approaching, down the miles of open ice.

He was pushing a puck in front of him, and I saw as he drew nearer that he was wearing a cap. It was Joliat. Tonight there was nothing in his way, no boards, no players, no carpet. He drove towards me, labouring a little, clouds of breath vanishing over his shoulder. He was skating as fast as he could. The wind rushed in, roaring in his ears like a crowd, and he swept down the ice past me going full tilt, the way he had always desired.

ACKNOWLEDGEMENTS

"The Hockey Sweater" reprinted with permission of Stoddart Publishing Company Limited; "Saturday Evenings in the Church of Hockey Night in Canada" reprinted with kind permission of the author, Judith Fitzgerald; "I'm Dreaming of Rocket Richard" reprinted with permission of General Publishing Company Limited; Excerpt from *The Divine Ryans* by Wayne Johnston used by permission of McClelland & Stewart Inc., The Canadian Publishers; "The Hockey Game" by Wes Fineday reprinted by permission of Fifth House Publishers; Excerpt from *Saxophone Winter* © 1988 by Robert Harlow, reprinted with permission of Douglas and McIntyre Limited; "Hockey Night in Canada" from the book *Hockey Night in Canada* © 1987 by Diane Schoemperlen, reprinted with permission of Quarry Press Limited; Excerpt from *The Age of Longing* by Richard B.Wright, © 1995 by Richard Wright, published by HarperCollins Publishing Limited and reprinted by permission of HarperCollins Publishing Limited; Excerpt from *The Bus Ride* © 1974 by Don Gutteridge, reprinted with kind permission of the author; "The Sportive Centre of Saint Vincent de Paul" reprinted with kind permission of the author, Hugh Hood; Excerpt from *The Last Season* © 1983 by Roy MacGregor, reprinted with permission of Macmillan of Canada; "Truth" from *The Fencepost Chronicles* by W.P. Kinsella © 1986 by W.P. Kinsella, reprinted with permission from The Colbert Agency; Excerpt from *King Leary* © 1987 by Paul Quarrington, reprinted with permission of Doubleday Canada Limited; Excerpt from *Peckertracks* by Stan Dragland © 1978 by Stan Dragland, reprinted by permission of Coach House Press Limited; "My Career with the Leafs" from the book *My Career with the Leafs* © 1982 by Brian Fawcett, reprinted with permission of Talon Books Limited; "Wives" reprinted from *Night Driving* © 1987 by Peter Behrens, reprinted with permission of Macmillan of Canada; Excerpt from *Two Solitudes* by Hugh MacLennan © 1945, reprinted by permission of Macmillan of Canada; Excerpt from *The Loved and the Lost* by Morley Callaghan © 1951, reprinted with permission of Macmillan of Canada; "50-50 Draw" from *Apparatus* by Don McKay, used by permission of McClelland & Stewart, Inc., The Canadian Publishers; Excerpt from *Coming Down from Wa* by Audrey Thomas © 1995 by Audrey Thomas, reprinted by permission of Penguin Books Canada Limited.

BRIGHT LIGHTS FROM POLESTAR

Polestar Book Publishers takes pride in creating books that enrich our understanding of the world and introduce discriminating readers to exciting writers. These independant voices illuminate our history, stretch the imagination and engage our sympathies. Here are some of our best-selling sports titles.

BEHIND THE MASK:
THE IAN YOUNG GOALTENDING METHOD
Ian Young & Christopher Gudgeon
Drills, practice techniques, equipment considerations and more are part of this unique goaltending guide.
$18.95 CAN / $14.95 US

BEYOND THE MASK: THE IAN YOUNG
GOALTENDING METHOD, BOOK TWO
Ian Young & Christopher Gudgeon
Book Two of this effective goaltending series focuses on intermediate goalies and their coaches.
$18.95 CAN / $14.95 US

CELEBRATING EXCELLENCE:
CANADIAN WOMEN ATHLETES
Wendy Long
A collection of biographical essays and photos that showcases more than 200 athletes who have achieved excellence.
$29.95 CAN / $24.95 US

COUNTRY ON ICE
Doug Beardsley
The evocative story of Canada's compelling attraction to hockey.
$9.95 CAN / $8.95 US

GET THE EDGE:
AUDREY BAKEWELL'S POWER SKATING
Audrey Bakewell
Skating specialist Audrey Bakewell provides basic and advanced drills for power skating, a skill fundamental to the game of hockey.
$18.95 CAN / $16.95 US

HOCKEY'S YOUNG SUPERSTARS
Eric Dwyer
Profiles and action photos of Bure, Jagr, Lindros, Mogilny, Sakic, Modano and others.
$9.95 CAN / $8.95 US

LORDS OF THE RINK
Ian Young & Terry Walker
Here is every goaltenders handbook, including physical and psychological techniques, and many game-action photos. The final book in the Ian Young goaltending trilogy.
$18.95 CAN / $14.95 US

THRU THE SMOKY END BOARDS:
CANADIAN POETRY ABOUT SPORTS AND GAMES
Kevin Brooks & Sean Brooks, editors
The glory of sport is celebrated in this anthology of poems from more than 70 poets.
$16.95 CAN / $14.95 US

TOO MANY MEN ON THE ICE:
WOMEN'S HOCKEY IN NORTH AMERICA
Joanna Avery & Julie Stevens
An examination of all levels of women's hockey in Canada and the United States, including in-depth profiles of prominent players.
$19.95 CAN / $16.95 US

Polestar titles are available from your local bookseller. For a copy of our catalogue, contact:

Polestar Book Publishers, publicity office
103-1014 Homer Street
Vancouver, British Columbia
Canada   V6B 2W9
http://mypage.direct.ca/p/polestar